CW00597012

Praise for *Very Bad People*

'More usually found in the pages of thrillers, these stories are frighteningly true. Corruption is one of the greatest enemies of democracy, to win the fight we need champions like Global Witness.'

 – George Soros

'Very few activists have the ability to turn the object of their attentions into a quivering mess. Global Witness are fearless.'

 – Gordon Roddick, campaigner and co-founder of The Body Shop

'This book is inspirational. It shows how young people with sufficient passion and intelligence have the capacity to go after some of the most powerful governments and corporations, and shame, humiliate and just push governments to suppost important reforms that can make this a more decent world.'

 – Frank Vogle, co-founder of Transparency International

'The story told in this book of three youthful idealists who go from eating cold baked beans in a draughty London flat to the Thai-Cambodian border where they posed as traders in illegally felled timber is simply riveting. Don't miss it.'

 – Misha Glenny, author of *McMafia*

'*Very Bad People* reads like a John Le Carré novel but is, in fact, the very real story of [Alley's] adventures in this thrilling and terrifying world.'

 – *The Big Issue*

'Alley has produced a clear-eyed account of a world poisoned by dark money, and a welcome reminder than resistance is possible. As it turns out, his book is even more timely than he could have hoped.'
   – *Irish Times*

'*Very Bad People* would be a hugely enjoyable thriller if it wasn't all true...'
   – Isabella Tree, author of *Wildling*

'Part true-crime tale, part investigative procedural, this is the account of the brilliant superheroes of Global Witness, whose superpower is the truth.'
   – Edward Zwick, director of *Blood Diamond*

'Warlords, crooks, oil tycoons and dictators. A shocking, important and page-turning book that gives a unique insight into a hidden world of criminality.'
   – Jeff Skoll, founder and chairman, Participant Media,
   Skoll Foundation

Author of *Very Bad People*

Patrick Alley

Terrible Humans

The world's most corrupt
super-villains – and the fight to
bring them down

monoray

First published in Great Britain in 2024 by Monoray, an imprint of
Octopus Publishing Group Ltd
Carmelite House
50 Victoria Embankment
London EC4Y 0DZ

www.octopusbooks.co.uk
An Hachette UK Company
www.hachette.co.uk

Distributed in the US by
Hachette Book Group
1290 Avenue of the Americas
4th and 5th Floors
New York, NY 10104

Distributed in Canada by
Canadian Manda Group
664 Annette St.
Toronto, Ontario, Canada M6S 2C8

ISBN 978-1-80096-238-5 (Hardback)
ISBN 978-1-80096-198-2 (Trade paperback)

A CIP catalogue record for this book is available from the British Library.

Printed and bound in the UK

Typeset in 11.5/18pt Heldane Text by Jouve (UK), Milton Keynes

10 9 8 7 6 5 4 3 2 1

This FSC® label means that materials used
for the product have been responsibly sourced.

This monoray book was crafted and published by Jake Lingwood, Mala Sanghera-Warren,
Alex Stetter, Monica Hope, Mel Four, David Eldridge, Lucy Carter and Nic Jones.

Extract from *Complicity* by Iain Banks, Copyright © Iain Banks 1993, reproduced with
permission of Little, Brown Book Group Ltd through PLSclear.

To all those people around the world who stand up to the Terrible Humans that this book is about, and to the memory of Jess Search, friend, filmmaker and 'Lucky Fucker' who made a difference.

AUTHOR'S NOTE

It would not have been possible to write this book without the courage and dedication of the people who bring to light the actions of terrible humans. These are their stories.

CONTENTS

'We have chosen to put profits before people, money before morality, dividends before decency, fanaticism before fairness, and our own trivial comforts before the unspeakable agonies of others.'

Iain Banks, *Complicity*

PREAMBLE

In my first book, *Very Bad People*, I wrote about how, in the early 1990s, my friends Charmian Gooch and Simon Taylor and I met while working for a tiny environmental group and had a hare-brained idea. Downing lagers in the bar of the Betsey Trotwood pub in London's then very ungentrified district of Clerkenwell, we were pondering whether the civil war in Cambodia, big news at the time, would ever end.

The Khmer Rouge regime had been responsible for killing millions of people in the greatest genocide since the Nazi Holocaust. Kicked out of power, they became a fugitive but deadly, dedicated and well-trained rebel army occupying the dense rainforests of western and northern Cambodia. There they waged a brutal civil war against the newly elected democratic government and collaborated with its corrupt leaders to rob the country dry.

We had read press reports that the Khmer Rouge was trading rainforest timber with Thailand. We guessed that this trade must be generating funds for its war effort. Maybe if that trade was closed down, we thought, the money supply would be cut off and the war brought to an end. 'Why doesn't someone do that?' we asked ourselves. And then, 'Why don't we?'

Like all the best ideas, there were countless reasons why not. We had no experience, no money, no organization and, frankly, no fucking clue, so we decided to do it. We created an investigative organization and called it Global Witness. It took us 18 months to scrape together some money but then, armed with secret cameras, some US Vietnam War-era maps and tummies full of butterflies, we set off for the borderlands of Thailand's Wild East, posing as European timber buyers to try to infiltrate the Thai logging Mafia.

That was the birth of Global Witness. From that first hair-raising investigation, Global Witness went on to expose the issue of blood diamonds to the world, spawning a Hollywood movie in the process. Also, oddly for a bunch of idiots like us, we got nominated for the 2003 Nobel Peace Prize. We went on to identify how warlords like Liberia's Charles Taylor were funding their bloody adventures and cut those funds; we pried into the boardrooms of multinational companies and exposed the corruption carried out by some of the biggest criminals on Earth (whom we named the Pinstripe Army); and we followed the gargantuan sums of money stolen from their countries by oligarchs and tracked it to their luxury mansions in London, New York and the other playgrounds of the super-rich. In so doing we became unwitting pioneers of the global anti-corruption movement. No one was more surprised than we were.

This book will tell you what happened next.

On 23 August 2023, a privately owned Embraer Legacy jet en route from Moscow to St Petersburg fell out of the sky. Local people told reporters they had heard a distinct boom, and one man in his garden in Kuzhenkino, north of Moscow, was quick enough to grab his smartphone. The blurry video footage he took, eerily silent, shows what looks like the wingless fuselage of the plane descending horizontally, almost gracefully for a few moments, before it flips into a steep dive with white smoke pouring from it. The plane goes out of shot as it disappears behind a slatted wooden garden fence and a few more seconds pass before a dense plume of grey smoke billows into the sky.

The crash brought a sudden end to the careers of Yevgeny Prigozhin and the top lieutenants of the Wagner Group, the notorious Russian mercenary army whose brutality had become a watchword in a series of wars across Africa, the Middle East and Ukraine. Perhaps mourned by their families and diehard fanatics, those passengers won't be much missed by those who have suffered at their hands or those of Russia's president, Vladimir Putin. It didn't take a rocket scientist to work out that following Prigozhin's challenge to Putin's power in an attempted coup a couple of months before, the ticking time bomb he was sitting on wasn't just metaphorical. It is quite likely exactly what killed him.

Four days earlier, a relaxed-looking Prigozhin, dressed in civilian clothes and a light, short-sleeved summer shirt, appearing less bullish than usual, looked into the camera as a couple of his smiling fans stood either side of him and took a selfie. He was in Bangui, the capital of the Central African Republic (CAR). This resource-rich but grindingly poor and battle-scarred country is arguably the jewel in Wagner's crown. Since 2017, it has become a de facto Russian colony and forward military base deep in the heart of Africa. In a pattern repeated across the continent, the mercenary group had been quick in taking over the country's rich diamond and gold mines in exchange for offering their muscle to the ruling clique. Their extreme violence against anyone who gets in their way is perhaps the most honest expression of modern-day Russian diplomacy in action.

Much of what we know about what goes on in CAR – this new Heart of Darkness – is in large part down to one of the courageous investigators I interviewed for this book. 'Leave No Trace' (see page 121) gives a terrifying insight into how a new Russian empire is being created across Africa. Such was the understanding I gained from my interviews with my source that when I heard that nearby Niger's democratically elected government was ousted by a military coup in July 2023, I was not at all surprised to learn that the crowds welcoming the new regime were waving Russian flags.

As with *Very Bad People*, *Terrible Humans* tells a few more stories from the Global Witness archives and the daring, innovative investigators that I am so happy to be able to work with. But I also wanted to write about some of my heroes in other organizations who work on different but equally crucial issues – things I would love to have done myself, but never had the time or the headspace.

I learned so much as I relived several Global Witness investigations through interviewing my colleagues who carried them out. They took me across continents to witness networks of secret companies being established to carry out massive and corrupt mining deals behind closed doors, and in the shadow of the Russian invasion of Ukraine they showed me how the money moves around, how the machines of war were powered and by who. I was a fly on the walls of the boardrooms of mega-corporations and taken into those dark corners where globally significant dodgy deals were hammered out in secret. And, through the eyes of our amazing investigators, I saw how some of the most vulnerable but important people on Earth hold firm against violence and malevolent political power.

Then I was taken into areas new to me as I made contact with old Global Witness friends who, over the years, had moved on to different organizations, pioneering new areas of work. And I talked with people I had never met before. As old friendships were rekindled and new ones forged, I became immersed in investigations into the dark corridors of organized crime and was taken to some of the wildest places on the planet.

The people I follow in this book are heroes – and the world needs more heroes; but you, the reader, are going to meet the villains too. As with *Very Bad People*, some of these crooks may seem to live in a world far away from your own, but nothing could be further from the truth. In this increasingly interconnected world, what some criminal does on the other side of the planet may well affect you. And of course, the crimes may not be on the other side of the world, but instead being carried out in some city boardroom or a shady accountant's office in a small town. Or maybe the criminal masterminds live just down the road from you.

Despite the extraordinary situations and circumstances I document in this book, these are, in the end, stories about ordinary people who took on villains worthy of a John le Carré novel. In addition to our heroes – journalists, cops and former cops, indigenous peoples and the investigators of Global Witness and sister organizations – the cast includes crooks, spies, the bosses of multinational companies, warlords, high-class sex workers, mercenaries and corrupt politicians. And whereas the stories can appear to be eight investigations into a disparate group of situations, they are all linked.

I am a child of the first Cold War, growing up with the ever-present threat of a nuclear apocalypse. The relief we all felt when the Soviet Union collapsed in the last decade of the previous century was palpable, and I entered adulthood with an enhanced sense of hope and peace. It was nice while it lasted. As the threats brought by climate change become a reality, the politics and mechanics of globalization has delayed necessary action by decades. As standards of living in the Global North have grown exponentially, they have done so at a direct cost to those in the Global South. And just when we really need collective effort to tackle the greatest threats humanity has ever faced, we are becoming increasingly divided – not just by wealth versus poverty, but also by disinformation versus the truth, which in turn fuels extreme political division. Into this mix, Putin's invasion of Ukraine has thrust us into Cold War II.

One could give up in despair, but I don't despair. I have hope because I know that the very good people I write about in this book exist and any one of them can change the world. If this book encourages just a few more people to emulate them, then it has been worth it.

1

FUELLING THE FIRE

CHERNIHIV, UKRAINE, 3 MARCH 2022

The car slowed down as it took the right turn off Liubets'ka Street, then accelerated again as it headed down Vulytsya Vyacheslava Chornovola Street. The road was, as usual now, empty of traffic. Just after the car passed the grey frontage of the Viko electrical store on its right, a series of massive explosions shook the intersection only 150m (500ft) ahead, blasting debris and plumes of smoke high into the clear sky. The car slammed to a halt and the dashcam footage showed that, wisely, the driver did a quick U-turn and headed back the way he had come.

The inhabitants of the 18-storey apartment building and the other blocks that surrounded the intersection weren't so lucky. 'It was like a windstorm as the whole basement filled up with dust,' a local doctor told a Human Rights Watch researcher by phone. 'Then there was an explosion. Several windows were blown out, and there was a lot of vibration. We have explosions every day, but this one was very powerful.'

According to Human Rights Watch, the doctor said that among the 35 injured people he treated that day, 'he remembered "one boy whose ankle was cut open and a girl who had a metal fragment from the munition in her face. A boy about 12 had metal shards in his brain and damage to the skull.'"

A resident of one of the blasted buildings, Olena Piatkina, was sheltering in her basement when the bombs struck. 'After the explosion, I looked left and saw light coming into the basement,' she told Human Rights Watch. 'I started crawling out through the rubble. I saw lots of fires outside. As I was getting out of the basement, a man handed me a baby that was covered in blood and asked me to help him get out another three children who were there in an apartment. There was one girl who had been hit in the head and was covered in blood. The children were all in shock and crying.'

At least 5 unguided FAB 500 high-explosive bombs had been dropped around that intersection that day by Russian SU-34 fighter bombers. The explosions that had ripped through the apartment buildings had killed at least 47 civilians and wounded 32 more. Through an interpreter the city's mayor, Vladyslav Atroshenko, told a reporter from US National Public Radio, 'People saw the aircraft flying at a very low altitude – something like 300, 400, 500 meters maximum. And there was not one cloud in the sky. The sun was shining brightly.'

Not far away, on the same day, two schools were hit, but fortunately they were closed and casualties were lighter. This was the new reality for the citizens of Ukraine. Just 10 days earlier, Vladimir Putin had launched his special military operation (SMO), his euphemism for the invasion of Ukraine. The city of Chernihiv, just 85km (55 miles) from the Russian border, was an early target, a key stepping stone on the Russian army's route to Kyiv. Russian forces began to lay siege to the city and subjected it to daily bombing raids and missile attacks, forcing the city's population of just under 300,000 people to live in their freezing basements, cut off from heat, light and water. An unimaginable scenario in what, just a few weeks before, had been a country at peace.

The citizens of Mariupol in the Donetsk region suffered the most. Around a thousand people, men, women and children – cold and scared – were sheltering in the stately Donetsk Academic Regional Drama Theatre as the Russians besieged their city. Their desperate situation as they crowded into the theatre's elegant auditorium and foyers, where they were fed and watered by the Red Cross, contrasted starkly with the plaster bas-reliefs that graced the inside of the theatre; symbols of culture, creativity and the memories of the peace that they had enjoyed until just over three weeks before. Outside, on the tarmac of the car park, one of the theatre staff had painted 'ДЕТИ' – 'children' – in Russian Cyrillic letters 4.5m (14.7ft) high.

It was what turned out to be a vain attempt to advertise to any passing planes that the theatre was not a military target. At around 10am on 16 March, an SU-34 jet released a bomb above the theatre. It crashed through the elegant dome and exploded in the auditorium. The Ukrainian government initially estimated that 300 people had been killed. A subsequent Associated Press investigation reckoned the figure was closer to 600, with hundreds more injured. At the time of writing, in September 2023, the word ДЕТИ is still there in front of the now devastated building. It would not only have been clearly visible to a military jet; a quick glance at Google Earth shows that you can see it from space.

Mariupol fell to Russian forces in May 2022. The Ukrainian government estimated 20,000 civilians died there while over 300,000 were forced to leave. The United Nations estimated that 90 per cent of the city's residential buildings had been damaged – many flattened.

Mariupol was just one of the many victims of this new blitzkrieg, as the Russian Air Force 'softened up' Ukrainian cities ahead of the convoys of Russian tanks and troops that rolled over the border, headed for Kyiv. Western companies who had invested in Russia rushed to come to terms with the new situation. Russia was the largest energy producer in the world and its single biggest export was crude oil, worth around US$123 billion per year, 60 per cent of which is sold to Europe, with another US$111 billion in export earnings brought in from petrol, gas and coal. The country is also the world's largest exporter of liquid natural gas (LNG), supplying 45 per cent of Europe's demand alone. It wasn't long before media attention began to focus on the role of Western fossil-fuel companies in the Russian economy.

Doubtless these companies had not wanted the war and weren't responsible for the Kremlin's actions, but some of them were a little too close to Putin's despotic regime for comfort. Following Russia's annexation of Crimea and backing of a separatist war in the Donbass in 2014, topped off by the shooting down of a Malaysian passenger jet, the country was hit by a wave of sanctions imposed by the EU, Canada and the US among others. These included an arms embargo and the targeting of Russian banks. The energy industry was hit as special permits would now be required to export some specialist equipment to Russia but, critically, the trading of oil and gas was not sanctioned.

This was good news for the then CEO of French oil giant TotalEnergies, Christophe de Margerie, who was evidently a fan of Vladimir Putin. At the St Petersburg International Economic Forum (SPIEF) that year he made clear his view of the recently imposed sanctions against Russia. 'Total has always been very clear: we don't think sanctions are improving anything[. . .]' he said. 'My message to Russia is simple – business as usual.'

That was certainly the mantra Total appeared to follow from that point on, and early indications following Russia's attempted invasion of Ukraine in 2022 suggested that Total didn't think this was a serious enough issue to warrant a change in policy.

With their hunger for Russian oil and gas, Total, together with other Western oil companies like Shell and BP, had been investing in Russia and providing state-of-the-art technology to it since the fall of the Soviet Union, despite the corruption and democratic decline under Putin. Without these companies, Russia could not have become the fossil-fuel superpower it now is, so they bear some responsibility for the situation. Now, like it or not, they were deeply involved.

As Putin's forces unleashed fire and death across Ukraine, the fresh wave of sanctions against Russia included asset freezes, targeted sanctions against key individuals – including Putin himself and a whole bunch of oligarchs – plus a swathe of economic sanctions. Russia's huge energy sector was a key target and new investments in it were banned. BP and Shell went further than the scope of these sanctions and within a week of the invasion announced they were giving up their stakes in two Russian state-owned oil companies, Rosneft and Gazprom. There was only one major European holdout: TotalEnergies.

In a statement issued on 1 March 2022, Total condemned the war, saying it would abide with 'the scope and strength of the sanctions put in place by Europe and will implement them regardless of the consequences'. The company generously stated that it would not inject capital into any new projects in Russia; but, given that to do so would have contravened these new sanctions, this was an empty pledge. Oddly, the company made no mention of its two existing and vast joint-venture projects with Russian companies: one with Yamal LNG and the other with Novatek, which prides itself on being the largest independent natural-gas producer in Russia. Perhaps they hoped no one would notice.

GLOBAL WITNESS OFFICE, LONDON, ENGLAND, SPRING 2022

At Global Witness we looked on in horror as a new Cold War began to emerge from the castellated walls of the Kremlin. With a 30-year history of investigating corruption and resource-funded wars and delving into the dark corridors of power, maybe there was something we at Global Witness could contribute. We had investigated corruption in the fossil-fuel industry for over two decades and, as the enormity of the climate crisis manifested itself, shifted to tackling the causes of it. It was an industry we knew pretty well. We knew that Russia was the world's largest energy producer and that the EU was its main energy market. It was clear to us that for Russia this was going to be a fossil-fuel-funded war.

We decided to put a special team together to work on Ukraine and the role of fossil fuels in the war. Headed by Sam Leon, who led our data-investigations unit, the team included his fellow data investigator Louis Goddard who, like Sam, was expert in picking up and pursuing evidential threads hidden in the labyrinths of megadata; veteran US-based Global Witness investigator Lela Stanley, drafted across from her work exposing environmental abuses and deforestation in Papua New Guinea; Jon Noronha-Gant, a veteran Global Witness investigator who had cut his teeth investigating illegal logging in Liberia before focusing on corruption in the fossil-fuel industry – an inexhaustible subject – and its role in fuelling climate change; and Mai Rosner, who had joined Global Witness a year before as a campaigner. 'It was a really interesting challenge,' Mai told me. 'I became the "Sanctions Lady" even though I had no law training and I didn't have any previous experience on sanctions.' She had discovered that at Global Witness you can get thrown into a topic, upskill in it and learn it completely.

It was going to be crucial that we got the message out there about what we were doing and the role of fossil fuels in funding the war, so the team was bolstered with one of our top comms advisers, Louis Wilson.

To build up momentum, the team embarked on a series of quickfire investigations highlighting the vast revenues Russia was earning from exporting its oil to Europe, the UK and the US. In turn, as the international price of oil skyrocketed due to the war, we worked with sister organizations like Greenpeace USA and Oil Change International to turn a spotlight onto the vastly increased profits oil companies were making on the back of the war and the consequent impact on the cost of living for ordinary people as they struggled to pay their heating bills. This was OK as a first foray, but we knew we needed to do more.

'We had piqued the public's interest,' Sam Leon said. 'But we felt there was a deeper story there.' To Sam it seemed fairly obvious. If you knew that Western companies were fundamental to enabling Russia to exploit its hydrocarbons, then surely elements of the Russian military must be partly dependent on that. 'The challenge for us was to test this hypothesis: that there must be Western-produced oil or gas finding its way into the supply chain for the Russian military,' he said.

Tanks and planes don't run on air, but it would be an impossible task to analyse all the flows of oil and gas in Russia to see which of them ended up in the military's fuel tanks. It wasn't until late July 2022 that Sam Leon and

Louis Goddard embarked on their research, and it wasn't long before they realized that they would effectively need to think backwards. They would have to start with a crime and reverse engineer it.

Eleven days after the bombing raid on Chernihiv, Greenpeace France and Les Amis de la Terre (Friends of the Earth, in France) wrote to Christophe de Margerie's successor as CEO of TotalEnergies, Patrick Pouyanné. Citing a 2017 French law, the two organizations pointed out that

> As a French legal entity, TotalEnergies and its directors may be held criminally liable for any offenses under the French criminal code, particularly complicity in war crimes and crimes against humanity.
>
> We hereby formally request that you [. . .] put an end without delay to your activities connected with the Russian oil and gas market to cease any business relationships that may contribute to the commission of serious violations of human rights.

TotalEnergies took umbrage.

> [. . .] It cannot be seriously considered that the military aggression of Ukraine by Russia could result from the activities of [. . .] companies with which TotalEnergies maintains commercial relations, nor that the Russian military operations in Ukraine would in any way be attached to this relationship.
>
> [. . .] The activities of Novatek and Yamal LNG, from which TotalEnergies buys LNG in the context of an established commercial relationship, are completely unrelated to the conduct of military operations by Russia in Ukraine.

Total may have thought this put the lid on the issue, but at Global Witness we were used to lifting up rocks to see what was squirming underneath. Was TotalEnergies telling the whole truth? Was it even possible to find out where the truth lay in the chaos of war? Research by team member Jon Noronha-Gant into joint-venture projects between Russian and Western energy companies had confirmed that Total was an ideal campaign target.

As Louis and Sam perused the website of Energy Intelligence, a subscription service aimed at people in the oil and gas industry, they got the germ of an idea. 'Energy Intelligence had done an interesting basic analysis showing the movements of jet fuel and diesel to the Russian oblasts [regions] bordering Ukraine,' Louis explained. He and Sam wondered whether the same methodology could be used to track not just these general movements, but also very specific flows. Could we track jet fuel to military airbases that were bombing Ukraine and if so, could we identify who owned the oil or gas fields that fuel came from?

First, Sam and Louis would need to examine the list of Western joint-venture oil and gas projects in Russia that Jon had put together, then identify Russian military airbases within easy striking distance of Ukraine. Then they would need to triangulate this information with the refineries that were producing the jet fuel. To be able to do all this they would need to take a crash course in jet-fuel production.

TotalEnergies had two joint-venture projects with Russian energy companies. One of these was the Termokarstovoye Gas and Condensate Field in Russia's Yamalo-Nenets Autonomous District in northern Siberia, an investment that Vladimir Putin had personally lauded in 2009 when drilling began. In fact, he and Total's Christophe de Margerie seemed to have been very close. Following de Margerie's death – his plane crashed into a snow plough at Moscow airport in October 2014 – Putin said: 'In

Christophe de Margerie, we lost a real friend of our country, whom we will remember with the greatest warmth.' He went on to award de Margerie a posthumous medal of honour.

Patrick Pouyanné continued his predecessor's legacy of brown-nosing Putin when he met him in November that year at the Russian resort of Sochi on the Black Sea. He rather immodestly said to Putin: 'You mentioned French–Russian relations too. Total is a private company, but it is also one of the biggest French companies and so in some respects could be said to represent the country. You can count on me to do what I can to influence relations between our countries. I will do all within my power.'

The following year, 2015, the Termokarstovoye field came online. It was operated by a company called Terneftegaz, a joint venture between TotalEnergies – which owned 49 per cent of it – and Russia's largest independent producer of natural gas, Novatek, which owned the remaining 51 per cent. In turn, Total owned 19.4 per cent of Novatek. One of Novatek's board members was Gennady Timchenko, a key Putin ally and, according to *Forbes* magazine in 2021, Russia's sixth-richest billionaire, worth some US$22 billion. It all looked very cosy. Until Russia invaded Ukraine. Timchenko was an early victim of the new sanctions and resigned from Novatek's board.

Remote and built to cope with the permafrost and the harsh Arctic weather that renders it inaccessible for eight months of the year, the Termokarstovoye gas field can daily produce 186,891m^3 (6.6 million ft^3) of natural gas and 20,000 barrels of what's known as 'unstable gas condensate' – a snappily named biproduct of the gas-extraction process and a crucial element of this story. This unstable condensate must first be stabilized, after which it becomes a raw material that, among other things, can be refined into kerosene: jet fuel.

Two pipelines emanate from Termokarstovoye. One carries gas destined for export to the Baltic port of Ust-Luga, not far from St Petersburg, where it is shipped across the world. The other pipeline snakes 200km (124 miles) across the tundra carrying the unstable gas condensate to the Novatek-owned Purovsky processing plant. Here it is stabilized and then transported to various refineries that can turn the now stabilized condensate into other products, including petrol, diesel and jet fuel. The next challenge for Louis and Sam was to find out which refineries.

To do this, they needed to be able to follow the movements of the unstable gas condensate from the gas fields to the refineries where it was processed into jet fuel. Then they needed to follow this fuel from the refineries to the final destinations – the military airbases that were used to bomb Ukraine. From the outside this seemed like an impossible task, but not if you knew where to look.

A key resource for Louis and Sam was Refinitiv, a subsidiary of the London Stock Exchange. Its database provides financial and economic data, including the trade in commodities. Louis began analysing Refinitiv's Russian rail-freight data, commercially available to anyone who pays a subscription – in this case, freight forwarders, shipping brokers and agents who want to keep track of their cargoes. And us. Refinitiv is live-updated and with it Louis began to track the movement of gas and jet fuel along the tracks of Russia's vast railway network. He needed to be careful – not all jet fuel was for military use and not all Russian Air Force bases were used to bomb Ukraine.

As Louis examined gas fields part-owned by Western interests, two refineries loomed large in the team's sights. Louis considered the massive refinery owned by Lukoil at Nizhny Novgorod on the Volga but discarded it. From the endless columns in the Refinitiv database, it was another railway station that stuck out: Kombinatskaya, a large rail hub located in the northeast of the city of Omsk in southwest Siberia, home of the Omsk Gazprom Neft refinery.

'We needed an attack to fit the flows,' Louis told me. There was no shortage of attacks as Putin's forces pummelled Ukraine on the ground and from the air with a Hitlerite intensity, but they needed a specific type of attack that fit the flow of fuel they were tracking. Louis began to search for links between specific airbases and planes from these bases that had inflicted atrocities on Ukraine. 'We were particularly interested in anything that had been described as a potential war crime by credible organizations,' Louis said.

The war provided an unforgiving deadline. The longer Russian oil or gas linked to Western companies flowed, the more Russian military attacks those companies were culpable for. The team hunted for investigations into war crimes carried out by groups we trusted and respected, and they didn't have to look too far. In early March, both Amnesty International and Human Rights Watch sent investigators to Chernihiv – Mariupol was off-limits to them as it was Russian occupied – to determine whether the bombing raids amounted to war crimes under international law. Both organizations were unequivocal. 'The Prosecutor of the International Criminal Court should investigate this airstrike as a war crime. Those responsible for such crimes must be brought to justice, and victims and their families must receive full reparation,' Amnesty International's Joanne Mariner told the press.

Following their own investigations, Human Rights Watch noted that, 'Four of these attacks, from the air and ground, were in clear violation of the laws of war. They included the bombing of an apartment complex that killed 47 civilians, an attack that killed at least 17 people in a bread line outside a supermarket, and two separate attacks, including one using widely banned cluster munitions, that damaged two hospitals.' Now we had our crime and although the architects of it were out of our reach, perhaps the enablers were not.

Louis and Sam again probed the columns of shipments in Refinitiv's spreadsheet and then, just maybe, they found what they were looking for. Some of the output of the Novatek-owned Purovsky processing plant was stabilized gas condensate and some of this was being transported by rail to the Gazprom Neft refinery at Omsk. Here it was refined into other products, including petrol, diesel and jet fuel and was shipped around the country from the refinery's local station, Kombinatskaya.

Sam and Louis sat back – they had ticked two of the boxes in their triangulation. If they could tick the third box and track the next stage of the journey to a military airfield, then maybe we were onto something.

Turning back to the Refinitiv spreadsheets, they delved into shipments between Kombinatskaya – ergo the Omsk refinery – and any rail stations close to Russian airbases that could have been involved in the attacks on Chernihiv and Mariupol. Here, a Russian pilot's bad luck became a piece of the investigation's good luck. Thirsty for more blood two days after the Chernihiv raid that killed forty-seven civilians, the SU-34 fighter bombers returned to attack again. One was shot down. The number '24' was clearly visible on its tailplane, which protruded from the chaos of the crash and the rubble of the buildings around it. Arda Mevlütoğlu, a Turkish military-aviation expert active on X (formerly Twitter), identified the plane as operating out of one of two SU-34 bases near the Ukrainian border: Voronezh Malshevo or Morozovsk, home of the 559th Bomber Aviation Regiment.

Again, Refinitiv came up with the goods. Between February and

July 2022, 40,000 tonnes of jet fuel had been shipped from Omsk to both Morozovsk and Voronezh, enough to refuel an SU-34 fighter bomber 3,000 times over. The first shipment had arrived two days before Putin launched his unprovoked attack on Ukraine. Louis and Sam also noted that until these recent shipments, the last delivery of jet fuel from Omsk to Morozovsk had been in 2017. Evidently the Russian Air Force was expecting a run on it.

Louis and Sam turned to satellite imagery to see if there were more clues there. Tasking a satellite to take a specific high-resolution photograph can be an expensive business, but since the invasion of Ukraine, Russian military airbases had become among the most photographed places on Earth, which was handy. Scouring the data library of satellite-imaging company Maxar Technologies, Louis found what he was looking for. One photo, taken on 31 July 2022, showed a line of seven rail tank wagons neatly parked in a siding off the main railway track on the north side of Morozovsk airbase, less than 500m (1,640ft) from the line of blue and grey SU-34 fighter bombers parked on the apron.

Louis and Sam knew from the data that Morozovsk train station had received several shipments of jet fuel during July, all transported in seven tank wagons. The last shipment from Omsk had arrived on 30 July, the day before the satellite photo had been taken. The task now was to join the dots.

Using Refinitiv, Louis and Sam found that 8 per cent of the unstable gas condensate processed by the Omsk refinery had derived from Novatek's Purovsky processing plant. In turn, we knew that unstable gas condensate from the TotalEnergies–Novatek joint-venture gas field at Termokarstovoye had been sent by pipeline to the Purovsky processing plant to be stabilized. The data showed that some of this now 'stabilized' condensate had been transported by rail from there to the Omsk refinery and that jet fuel had been shipped from Omsk refinery, again by rail, to Russian military airbases involved with bombing Ukraine. We had a chain of supply but we had a problem too, because Omsk also processed condensate from other gas fields, produced products other than jet fuel and had customers other than the Russian military. This posed a conundrum that the team nicknamed 'the black box'.

'The key issue is how you treat a facility that has multiple inputs and outputs,' Louis explained. 'We know that condensate from the Termokarstovoye gas field is going into the Purovsky processing plant, and we know that some processed condensate is coming out of that plant and being sold into the domestic market to produce jet fuel.'

Sam elaborated on the point. 'Can you say with 100 per cent certainty that molecules of condensate from the Termokarstovoye field were in the stabilized gas condensate going to Omsk and then refined into jet fuel? No, because you weren't inside the refinery at that time. What you can say is that there's a very high chance, because this is how the supply chain is set up.'

The key point was that it's highly unlikely that the end product didn't contain some of the condensate from Termokarstovoye, and there was no way that Total could prove that it didn't. Our investigation exposed the risk that Total's joint venture with Novatek was highly likely to be contributing directly to the Russian war effort. In a war, that's a risk they shouldn't take. 'Added to this, Total owned 20 per cent of Novatek so they de facto held a stake in the [Novatek-owned] Purovsky processing plant,' Sam told me. 'Regardless of what proportion of the condensate from Termokarstovoye ended up as military jet fuel, Total was tainted by it.'

The entire data investigation had taken Sam and Louis just a few days, but the biggest chunk of work was to come. We needed to get it out there and have the maximum possible impact. Louis Wilson, the comms brain of the team, began to write a briefing we could send to the press and was confronted with two headaches. One was the legal check that every Global Witness publication goes through, but that is even more tense than usual when you're about to spill the beans on a multibillion-dollar oil company. The other was that it would be August before the publication would be ready and August is always a terrible time of year to break a story. Especially this one. TotalEnergies being a French oil company, France was where the news needed to hit hardest if we were to achieve any campaign impact, and August is when the majority of French people go on holiday. 'We'd been told by numerous people in France, "Do not fucking attempt to do anything in France in August,"' Louis said. But he felt we had a really strong story and, in our experience, strong stories don't tend to store well. 'We decided to get it out there, not least because it was about a live military conflict.'

Louis contacted Julien Bouissou, a journalist with top French newspaper *Le Monde* and someone Louis had a lot of respect for. Like millions of his compatriots, Julien was on holiday, but he told Louis that he would take a look. Two days later, Louis received a WhatsApp from him. It congratulated him for what Julien said was an 'astonishing' investigation. 'That's when we realized we had a big story, a real story,' Louis told me. While Julien and fellow *Le Monde* journalist Emmanuel Grynszpan carried out their own investigation, including verifying our findings, we embarked on the all-important legal check.

We sent an 'opportunity to comment' (OTC)* letter to Total and didn't

---

* OTCs are part of best journalistic practice. They alert the subjects of an article or report to allegations the author or organization intends to make and provides an opportunity for them to comment on them.

get any response other than a holding message from a press officer saying something like, 'We'll get back to you.' 'They obviously didn't consider this a major threat to their business,' Louis Goddard told me. But when *Le Monde* wrote to them it all changed. 'They immediately panicked and sent back loads of stuff,' Louis remembered. 'They also shot themselves in the foot because *Le Monde* only went to them for comment very shortly before publication, whereas we went two weeks before, so they were scrambling to respond.'

We released our short briefing, 'French cash, Russian fuel, Ukrainian blood', on 24 August 2022. *Le Monde*'s front page the same day was headlined 'How TotalEnergies gas is used as fuel for Russian fighter planes in Ukraine'. The article confirmed Global Witness's findings and presented the further steps they'd taken. Much of our case rested on connecting the kerosene that fuelled the Russian fighter bombers that bombed Chernihiv with the unstable gas condensate produced by the Total–Novatek Termokarstovoye gas field, which had then been processed at the Purovsky processing plant. In this *Le Monde* had been thorough.

They had analysed images from the European Sentinel-2 satellite and had consulted NASA data as they examined the 200-km (124-mile) length of pipeline that transports the unstable condensate from the Termokarstovoye field to the Purovsky processing plant. You can't see gas passing through a pipeline but you can detect the presence of flares burning off excess gas into the atmosphere; these demonstrated that the pipeline was active during the period in question. *Le Monde* went on to report that a week after the tragic bombings at Mariupol, the TotalEnergies–Novatek joint venture had continued to supply the Omsk refinery, which in turn continued to ship jet fuel to the Morozovsk airbase.

Their article also quoted Amnesty International, who said, 'The

Russian aircraft most likely to have carried out the attack is a multirole combat aircraft of the SU-25, SU-30 or SU-34 type, which are deployed at neighbouring airfields.' The article firmly laid the blame on the Morozovsk airbase, where most of the bombing raids operated from. Various survivors from Mariupol confirmed to *Le Monde* that they had been bombed by SU-type planes.

Defending the indefensible is never easy and Total had spectacularly failed to rise to the task in their response to *Le Monde*'s own OTC. As Russian bombers continued to pound Ukraine, Total tried to turn it into a numbers game. They claimed that as the Termokarstovoye gas field was operated by Terneftegaz, which was 51 per cent owned by Novatek, Total played no role in 'condensate recovery decisions by Novatek'. Total appeared to think that their mere 49 per cent ownership of Terneftegaz let them off scot-free. They also forgot to mention that they owned 19.4 per cent of Novatek. Total is not renowned in the oil industry for being a shrinking violet, but the Russian invasion of Ukraine had evidently instilled a new delicacy in the company's top management.

Oleg Ustenko, a senior economic adviser to Ukraine's President Zelensky, was not so shy. He told *Le Monde*, 'We have been warning companies for months that by buying Putin's blood oil they are financing the murder of civilians, but TotalEnergies has taken a further step by fuelling war crimes.'

In the same edition, *Le Monde* devoted its editorial to the story: 'TotalEnergies in Russia: stop turning a blind eye'.

It is difficult to find a more strategic product than fuel in a war. More than anyone else, the leaders of the French oil giant TotalEnergies cannot ignore it. However, by owning a share of the Termokarstovoye deposit, from which a liquid hydrocarbon is extracted, which, transformed into kerosene, is used to refuel Russian fighter jets engaged in the war against Ukraine, they expose themselves to a terrible accusation: helping Moscow in its armed aggression which, for six months, has transformed part of Europe into a zone of death and desolation and threatens the integrity of a sovereign state [. . .]

TotalEnergies denies any wrongdoing: the gas condensate produced by Terneftegaz is not a fuel, and the refinery that ultimately produces kerosene does not belong to it. Moreover, the oil giant respects the decisions of the European Union, which include an embargo on Russian oil but not, in the immediate future, on gas [. . .]

Yet how could a large French company that claims to be a 'citizen' and to subscribe to UN human-rights commitments continue its deliveries of gas condensate that can be converted into kerosene after the outbreak of aggression against Ukraine on February 24? How can its managers maintain that they have nothing to do with the transformation of gas condensate, when they own 19 per cent of Novatek, which owns the plant where it operates? How can they claim that Novatek is not linked to the Russian state, when one of its main shareholders is an acquaintance of Vladimir Putin targeted by Western sanctions?

The reality is that TotalEnergies, the only Western oil major to maintain its activities in Russia, is playing with fire and trying to hide behind ignorance of the way the product it puts on the market is used [. . .]

The day after the *Le Monde* piece was published, a political row began to brew, with French transport minister Clément Beaune telling

France 2, 'This is an extremely serious matter [. . .] there needs to be a check on whether, willingly or not, there's been a bypass on sanctions or a diversion of the energy that a company, French or not, would produce.'

If the bosses of TotalEnergies had been enjoying their summer holidays they certainly weren't now – they were at the sharp end of an international scandal. 'I think Total realized that they had cocked up their initial response and that they needed to go a little bit further,' explained Louis Wilson, a master of understatement. 'But by then [. . .] the story had already travelled very far.'

One of the unintended consequences of our report's publication was that the all-important Refinitiv Russian rail-freight data promptly went offline. 'Refinitiv stopped working with a Russian subsidiary that provided the data feed, so it disappeared from the platform,' Louis Goddard told me. We didn't know whether this had anything to do with the story, but the timing was interesting.

Whatever the cause, it left the team with a problem. Although we had all the data for the publication, we would need to do follow-up investigations and keep the data updated. An old contact of Sam's came to the rescue. David Szakonyi, the founder of the Washington, DC-based Anti-Corruption Data Collective, better known as ACDC, was an assistant professor of political science at George Washington University in Washington and an expert on researching Russian corruption. With his knowledge, the team managed to regain access to the Russian rail-freight data flows via another source.

Friday 26 August was a beautiful summer day in London and the beginning of a long Bank Holiday weekend. After the past few weeks of frenetic activity, Sam, the two Louis and the rest of the team were looking forward to a well-earned rest. Louis Goddard had taken the Friday afternoon off and was at his sister's house when his phone pinged; a message had gone round the Signal group the team had been using during the investigation. Total had just issued a press release announcing the sale of their 49 per cent stake in Terneftegaz, the operator of the Termokarstovoye field, to their joint-venture partner Novatek. The result, it said, of an agreement reached just over a month previously, on 18 July.

Was this a consequence of our investigation? Logically it seems unlikely that such an agreement could have been arrived at in such a short time, but it was interesting that the announcement of the sale came two days after the launch of our report and *Le Monde*'s coverage. 'I was incredibly excited and happy when we got that message, a real vindication of the work we'd been doing,' Louis Goddard told me. 'We had been stressing out over the previous few days – the doubt that's put in your mind when a multinational oil company is coming back to you with all these statements. It was such a moment of relief and the feeling of impact.'

Sam felt much the same. 'It was one of those rare moments that happen every now and again, when there was a big impact in such a short timeframe. We had stirred the giant and they had felt the heat. We were elated,' he told me.

Total, clutching at some rather flimsy straws, continued to vehemently deny that its production of gas condensate from the Termokarstovoye field could be linked to supplies of jet fuel to the Russian military. On 9 September 2022, it issued 'TotalEnergies Right of Reply to *Le Monde*', which included a statement from its partner, Novatek:

All of the unstable condensate produced by our subsidiaries and joint ventures, including Terneftegaz, comes into our Purovsky condensate processing plant. The Purovsky Plant also stabilizes condensate from other Russian producers, whose share in the plant's load does not exceed 20 per cent. The entirety of stable condensate produced at the Purovsky Plant from the feedstock coming from Novatek's subsidiaries and affiliates, including Terneftegaz, is delivered to the Ust-Luga processing complex in the Leningrad Region. *The range of products derived from processing operations at the Ust-Luga Complex includes jet fuel (Jet A-1) that is exclusively exported outside Russia, and this jet fuel does not even have the required certification for marketing on the Russian market [. . .] Therefore the Termokarstovoye field condensate is not used to provide jet fuel to the Russian army, and this allegation is not supported by any serious factual evidence.* *

Could Novatek's word be trusted? Was 100 per cent of the condensate produced at Purovsky exported? Quite apart from the fact that Novatek was almost 20 per cent owned by Total, Louis Wilson was unimpressed for a different reason. 'So, they got Novatek to swear in a statement,' he said. 'But how much can you put by the word of a Russian oil company which frankly doesn't give a shit how it's perceived in the West, saying that all of that stuff gets separated at the plant and sent for export? We have no way of disproving that. But they haven't proven it either.'

Perhaps the truth lay in Novatek's 2021 annual report. Pages 10 and 11 included a schematic diagram that, in not-very-small print, seemed to

---

* Emphasis is mine.

contradict their own public statement. It showed that their Purovsky treatment plant did indeed sell 16 per cent of the gas stabilized condensate into the domestic market, which means it could have ended up in Russian fighter jets eventually. Their 2022 annual report showed that domestic sales of stabilized gas condensate continued.

On a sunny day in September 2022, Global Witness's so-called Sanctions Lady, Mai Rosner, and Louis Wilson were in Paris to ramp up the political pressure on Total. There they met Boris Vallaud, the leader of the Socialist Party in the French National Assembly. As he listened to Louis and Mai go into more detail, and specifically into the culpability of Total, the politician was evidently shocked.

'You often go into these meetings with politicians, and they're like, yeah, great, thanks for letting me know, please follow up in a few months,' Mai told me. 'But Boris Vallaud wanted to take action.' Vallaud told them that some energy-company bosses had already been summoned to the National Assembly to answer questions on the super-profits they were making and the possibility of windfall taxes; among them was Total's CEO Patrick Pouyanné. Vallaud suggested that he put a question directly to Pouyanné regarding their still-existing 19.4 per cent stake in Novatek.

After talking to Mai and Louis, Boris told them that he would also table an amendment at the National Assembly to tax any French company profits and dividends earned in Russia at 100 per cent, with those taxes to be committed to the green reconstruction of Ukraine. Vallaud was evidently a nice guy. Following the meeting he was keen to show Mai and Louis around the historic National Assembly building. There they were awed by the extraordinary library and magnificent domed assembly chamber with its white and gold pillars, frescoed roof and arena of tiered crimson-velvet benches where so many debates had occurred and where, in October, Boris was as good as his word and put his motion to the vote.

Mai told me, 'It was close: 157 against, and 149 in favour.' Although this was disappointing, the fact the vote had been put and was this close further attacked Total's already diminished standing as a good corporate citizen.

That same month, Louis Goddard exchanged his jeans and comfortable jumper for a blazer and slacks. He was off to a special occasion: the annual Energy Intelligence Forum, which was being held over three days at the Intercontinental Hotel in London's exclusive Park Lane. He had spotted that Patrick Pouyanné was speaking at what Louis described as a 'softball' Q&A with the host, which was mostly about Total and the big news of the day: the new Organization of the Petroleum Exporting Countries (OPEC) production cuts.

When Pouyanné had finished speaking, the floor was opened up for questions. Louis' hand shot up and he was picked first. The young campaigner was nervous; he was, after all, in a lion's den of the energy industry, ranging from senior executives of international oil companies through government ministers from the Gulf states to bank analysts and traders.

'I'd like to return to Russia briefly,' Louis began. 'We recently published an investigation looking at Total's business in Russia, particularly looking at its involvement with Novatek and links to the supply chain for military jet fuel in Russia. There's been a public disagreement on this and a controversy. At no point has Total disputed the allegation that gas condensate, processed at Novatek's facilities, ultimately is shipped to refineries producing Russian military jet fuel [. . .] Focusing on [its] stake in Novatek [. . .] do you think this is a sustainable position for Total in the long term? [. . .] I understand there are restrictions to do with the sanctions about selling Total's stake immediately, but do you think this is a sustainable long-term position for Total to be in?'

Pouyanné didn't take it well.

'Our position on Russia is very clear,' he said. 'There is no more investment in new projects. We will continue to ship LNG from Russia as long as there is no sanction from Europe on the gas because we contribute to the security of supply for Europe. If there are sanctions, immediately we stop all the operations. Regarding your report, I think we had many opportunities to state that is a wrong statement. There is not a single condensate from Termokarstovoye which went to any refinery in Russia and I repeat it today. And I'm sorry but you continue to diffuse this information which is a misstatement and I'm afraid we will have to take action now. Because we cannot accept to live in a society where anybody can say something's wrong and become a reality because you repeat it. It's wrong. Absolutely wrong. And you absolutely cannot find a single proof that there was a single condensate of Termokarstovoye going to any refinery in Russia.'

In short, he was furious.

'I think that's clear. Next question,' the moderators concluded to titters among the audience.

Louis left immediately after Pouyanné's answer. 'It was a fun experience, if slightly nerve-racking,' he later recalled.

Global Witness's report and the *Le Monde* piece had led to a media landslide in France and internationally and it wasn't over yet. Following Novatek's announcement in 2022 that the company's shareholders would be able to divvy up a whopping US$2.27 billion in dividends for the first half of 2022, boosted by soaring energy prices, two of Ukrainian president Volodymyr Zelensky's key advisers, Oleg Ustenko and Mykhailo

Podolyak, wrote to Patrick Pouyanné asking him about his intentions with Total's share, which would be a healthy US$440 million based on their 19.4 per cent stake in Novatek.

'This is blood money,' the advisers wrote. They suggested that TotalEnergies reject the dividend or redirect the money to Ukrainian war victims. 'As you well know,' they stated, 'these figures are inflated in large part because of profiteering at the expense of the Ukrainian people.'

TotalEnergies did not comment, but, according to the *Wall Street Journal*: 'In April, Mr. Pouyanné told analysts the French company was entitled to a dividend as a Novatek shareholder, adding that it was unclear whether sanctions would prevent his company from receiving the payment. "I don't know if we'll have access or we will keep the roubles somewhere in an account in Russia," he said.'

By 9 December, however, TotalEnergies had realized that the game was up. They announced that they would withdraw its two board directors from Novatek, that they would take a US$3.7 billion 'impairment' for the last quarter of 2022 and would no longer 'equity account' for their 19.4 per cent stake in Novatek.

Paraphrasing Winston Churchill, 'You can always rely on TotalEnergies to do the right thing, just as soon as they've exhausted all the alternatives.'

During that first year of war, over 7,000 Ukrainian civilians were killed and around 14 million displaced. Ukraine doesn't publish casualty lists of its armed forces but tens of thousands of troops must have been killed or injured. Ukraine was not the only victim; the war had made 2022 a brutal year all over the world. It had brought turmoil to the energy markets and forced up to 95 million people into extreme poverty. As the export of Ukrainian grain was threatened, food prices rose globally. Meanwhile, climate related floods, storms, heatwaves, droughts and fires wreaked havoc across the globe. In Pakistan alone, over 1,730 people died in catastrophic floods, while tens of millions were severely impacted, losing their homes, land and livelihoods.

But the fossil-fuel industry wasn't suffering. Global energy prices rocketed because of the war, while the costs of production remained constant. We thought we would take a look at how the fossil-fuel industry was faring.

Jon began poring over the financial statements of five of the most powerful Western oil majors: BP, Chevron, ExxonMobil, Shell and TotalEnergies. What he found, especially given the parlous global situation, was shocking. In 2022, these five companies alone made a profit of US$195 billion. This was 120 per cent more than they made during the previous year and the biggest profits they had made in their history. Of this vast sum, US$134 billion was 'excess' profit – meaning the share of the profit that was not due to any actions taken by the companies, but that was instead the result of external events, chief of which was the Russia–Ukraine war. Then Jon decided to see what these 'excess profits' could have bought.

Our press release, issued on 9 February 2023, sparked outrage. With its excess profits BP could have picked up Pakistan's $14.9 billion in flood damages and still have had $3.8 billion in excess profits left. Based on figures published by the think tank Bruegel, Chevron's $27 billion in excess profit could have covered the combined spending of the governments of Bulgaria, Croatia, Romania, Czechia, Latvia, Slovenia and Estonia to shield domestic and business consumers from soaring energy bills. TotalEnergies too was sitting pretty – its share of these excess profits was $22 billion, which, as we pointed out, was enough to cover the entire

$4.3 billion requested by the United Nations in 2022 to provide humanitarian relief to all Ukrainians in need, five times over.

So how does the fossil-fuel industry, described by the Organization for Economic Co-Operation and Development (OECD) as one of the most corrupt industries on Earth, that is mired in scandal after scandal, responsible for catastrophic incidents of pollution, that funds wars and is the single biggest cause of the climate crisis get away with it?

In 1992, representatives of 180 countries, including over 100 heads of state, attended the first international Earth Summit in Rio de Janeiro and, among other things, signed the United Nations Framework Convention on Climate Change (UNFCCC) into existence. In so doing they pledged to drastically reduce global carbon emissions to prevent runaway climate change. Since the original summit, the UNFCCC has convened 26 annual meetings and countless intersessionals. There have been two constants since then: the escalating warnings from scientists about the scale of the problem we're facing, and the weakness and ineptitude of the world's political leadership over those years in dealing with it. The more that science demonstrated that the planet was heading for a climate apocalypse, the less that seemed to be achieved.

There are myriad reasons for this failure that has led to the climate crisis becoming the monster it has, but the greatest responsibility lies with the fossil-fuel industry and the political leaders greedy for their financial support, the backhanders some have received and the lucrative jobs they hope to get via the revolving door when they leave office. This system of corruption manifests itself in many ways and Global Witness has lifted the lid on several of them over the years. It was time to lift it on another.

In December 2022, 30,000 delegates – including heads of state, government ministers and officials, NGOs, policy experts and scientists – converged at Sharm El Sheik in Egypt for COP27, the 27th annual meeting of the UNFCCC. Yet again, the world's governments failed to reach an agreement that would reduce carbon emissions and keep the global temperature rise below 1.5°C (2.7°F). What on earth was the problem? In the lead-up to COP26 in Glasgow the previous year, one of our climate-change campaigners, Murray Worthy, had had a good idea.

When the annual conference opens, the UNFCCC releases a list of all the delegates that attend the meeting. Murray's idea had been to find out what kind of people they were and who they represented. Following this, Sam Leon and one of our data-investigations advisers, Malina McLennan, together with sister organizations Corporate Accountability, Corporate Europe Observatory (CEO) and Glasgow Calls Out Polluters, had drilled down into the list and come up with some interesting facts. Of the approximately 36,000 COP26 delegates in 2021, 503 were fossil-fuel lobbyists representing 100 companies. Between the Glasgow meeting and COP27 in Sharm El Sheik, the team honed their art and decided to do it again.

Louis and fellow Global Witness data expert Ben Ayre had built a computer script so that when the UNFCCC published the delegate list – an unstructured database in PDF format – they could automatically turn it into a searchable database. That made things easier, but it was still 30,000 names to analyse. The five team members worked around the clock classifying each name, double-checking who was affiliated to what. Other organizations had tried this in the past but the lack of this computer script had held them back. This time, Louis and Ben had cracked it. The results of their investigation rushed down the wires of the world's media.

At least 636 of the 30,000 delegates registered for the meeting in Sharm El Sheik were linked to the fossil-fuel industry, a 25 per cent increase since COP26. Our analysis showed that this was more than the combined delegations of the ten countries most affected by climate change and twice the representation of indigenous peoples. But it got worse.

Of those 636 people, 200 actually had seats on the national delegations of 29 countries; that meant that representatives of the fossil-fuel industry were part of the rule-making process. That's rather like having a weapons trafficker at arms-control talks, or the tobacco industry at a health conference. Simply put, the industry contributing most to the climate crisis were cuckoos in the nest, with a role in decision making that could impact their companies' profitability. Judging by the industry's past record, the chances of them putting the planet before profit were slim. Among these fossil-fuel cuckoos was Bernard Looney, the CEO of BP. He was accredited to the Mauritanian delegation, where his company had recently acquired a gas field.

Patrick Pouyanné was in Sharm El Sheik too. Global Witness managed to video him as he walked through the crowded venue dogged by a handful of peaceful climate activists asking him questions. At one point, doubtless with the best of intentions, security hustled him into a room to avoid his pursuers. These besuited heavies then stood outside the room, hands folded in front of them, no doubt receiving instructions via the corkscrew wires connecting their ears to the world beyond.

Inside the room, Pouyanné discovered what his security had failed to notice: that the room had glass walls. He was imprisoned like a goldfish in a bowl with an amused audience looking on, like sharks, waiting for him to come out. When he finally exited the room looking sheepish and evidently wishing he was somewhere else far, far away, there was no escape. He was cornered by Svitlana Romanko of the Ukrainian anti-war environmental group Razom We Stand, who asked him: 'Will you use your Russian blood money to rebuild Ukraine?'

Among all the phones and other recording devices capturing this delightful scene, there was one that apparently captured the word 'probably'. I don't know whether that meant probably or probably not, but given Total's record so far I am not holding my breath. It was one of the highlights of an otherwise depressing meeting.

In September 2023, I was invited to the 40th Cambridge International Symposium on Economic Crime, a week during which the sleepy university town attracts a host of international law-enforcement agencies, experts in money laundering, ministers and officials from an array of justice and defence ministries and top lawyers from around the world.

I delivered a keynote speech based on the results of a new Global Witness investigation that showed how Russian tankers transshipped their cargos of oil in international waters in the Mediterranean, which is not illegal. In turn these newly loaded ships delivered the oil to a refinery in Turkey and three in India, where it was blended with oil from other exporters. Using the Indian refineries as an example, in the first six months of 2023 their feedstock included 146.8 million barrels of Russian crude. Unlike sanctioned Russian oil, a blend of this type is not caught by sanctions. The UK imported 6.2 million barrels of blended oil products from these refineries, to be used as jet fuel, which would have required 2.33 million barrels of Russian oil. A 'back of a cigarette packet' calculation showed that this means 1 in 20 of all UK commercial flights is fuelled by Russian oil.

My colleagues at Global Witness had then examined where the money went. US$112 million would be generated for Russia, of which the

Kremlin's tax take would be US$53 million. Enough to purchase 2,500 Iranian drones at a minimum.

We'd put these figures to the UK government, who'd responded that, 'The claim is not true – since the ban came into effect there have been no imports of Russian oil and oil products into the UK.' The government had also responded that blended oil doesn't count. So apparently the UK doesn't receive any Russian oil, except that it does, which is somewhat Orwellian.

The day after my keynote speech, I put the same figures, plus additional ones relating to the increasing EU imports of Russian LNG, to an expert panel that included NATO's director of operations and current and former senior NATO military experts who were talking about how the organization had performed in the lead-up to and in the aftermath of Russia's invasion of Ukraine.

During the Q&A, I pointed out that since Russia's invasion of Ukraine the EU – many of whose countries are members of NATO – had paid over €160 billion to Russia for fossil fuels and in the first seven months of 2023 had spent €5.3 billion buying over half of Russia's liquid natural gas output. Why, I asked, given NATO's admirable efforts to keep the world safe, were we funding our battlefield enemy?

The answer was that we can't just turn the tap off. It was an ill-informed response because there are plenty of other places we can buy fossil fuels from. More disturbingly, whether the world is faced by the climate crisis, war, economic chaos or any other catastrophe that has the fossil-fuel industry at its root, judging by past experience the only things we can be sure of are that politicians won't act and the oil companies will get richer. Unless, of course, something changes.

Since Russia's invasion of Ukraine, it has continued selling its fossil fuels all over the world, including to India, China, the UK, the EU and the US. According to the beyondfossilfuels.org live tracker, since the beginning of the war up until October 2023, when I'm writing these words, the EU has spent over €165 billion on Russian oil, gas and coal.

In October 2023, the annual Energy Intelligence Forum took place, as ever, at London's Intercontinental Hotel. Now, a year after Louis Goddard had been there raising Total's role in the Ukraine war, infuriating Patrick Pouyanné in the process, Greta Thunberg made the headlines. As the meeting between the luminaries of the fossil-fuel oil industry and government ministers took place, it was besieged by climate protestors. Outside, Thunberg told the press that '[. . .] spineless politicians are making deals and compromises with lobbyists from destructive industries, the fossil-fuel industry [. . .] Their plan is to continue this destructive search for profits. That is why we have to take direct action to stop this and to kick oil money out of politics. We have no other option but to put our bodies outside this conference and to physically disrupt [it].'

The press photos of the physically diminutive activist being hauled off by two large policemen tell the world what we need to know about where our politicians' sympathies lie.

2

PROJECT FAT CAT

VEĽKÁ MAČA, SLOVAKIA, FEBRUARY 2018

On a cold February afternoon, a message, transmitted via the super-secure Threema instant-messaging app, bleeped onto the screen of Alena Zsuzsová's phone.

50 → SOON 💀

Two hours later, Ján Kuciak and his fiancée, Martina Kušnírová, were drinking coffee around the kitchen table in the small house they were renovating. Martina got up to go to the toilet, leaving the screen of her MacBook displaying a page of wedding dresses – the couple were to be married in only three months. She must have heard the knock on the front door and, as Ján answered it, the muted sound of two shots. Rushing into the kitchen, she came face to face with the gunman, his face obscured under his hoodie. Calmly he raised his right arm, sighted down the silenced Luger pistol at Martina's head and squeezed the trigger one more time. It was exactly a week after Valentine's Day.

*

Shortly after the killings, the silence of the house was broken by the ringtone of Martina's phone. After a minute or two of it ringing out, silence returned. Her mother called again the next day and the next, but on the third day the phone went dead, its battery exhausted. The bodies lay where they fell until the morning of 26 February, when the police, alerted by Ján's and Martina's families, broke into the house. The police found Martina's body crumpled on the kitchen floor in a pool of blood. Ján was hunched forward on the bloodied basement stairs, having been shot twice in the chest. Both were 27 years old.

Whoever ordered this assassination on a quiet street of red-roofed houses in Veľká Mača, a small village in the southwest of Slovakia, could not have imagined the storm they had unleashed. It was perhaps the final salvo in a phoney war; the battle for the soul of Slovakia had begun.

That same morning, the country's police chief, Tibor Gašpar, held a press conference. At first glance, he cut a commanding figure as he walked across the room to the wooden lectern bearing the police emblem. Smartly dressed in his drab olive uniform, his shirt enlightened with his gold badges of office and his iron-grey hair cropped short, he appeared both relaxed and in control. He adopted a solemn expression as he surveyed the room, and then he told the gathered reporters what had happened on that quiet street.

'Allow me to express my deepest condolences to the relatives of the victims of this severe crime and to all those who worked with him, to the whole journalist community,' he said. 'And to strictly condemn this crime – because even though we do see severe crimes, Slovakia has not yet experienced the murder of a journalist, most likely motivated by his investigative journalism.'

The first question came from Monika Tódová of Slovakian newspaper *Denník N* and she didn't hold back. 'You say you'll do everything to solve the murder, but why didn't the police do everything they could to prevent it?' she asked. 'Ján Kuciak wrote mostly about VAT scammers and tax frauds and we've been asking you about the same people and suspected tax frauds for years now, yet those people are still free. It ended with Ján being dead today.'

The question had the effect of a ball from a siege cannon thudding into the fortress walls. Gašpar's face remained impassive, but somehow, almost imperceptibly, the edifice rocked. Gašpar managed to hold onto his cool and tried to deflect Tódová's line of enquiry, without much success. 'With all due respect, I will not have a discussion about whether the police did or didn't do something.'

'We report on tax frauds but you don't investigate,' Tódová responded, 'so journalists continue to write about it. Journalists wouldn't write so much if you did your job.' The walls began to crumble.

Gašpar started shifting from foot to foot, looking down and from side to side as if trying to find an escape route. But stuck in front of the cameras, Slovakia's chief of police wasn't going anywhere. He was beginning to lose the argument and the conversation had only just begun. Evidently, he decided to step further into the mire.

'I'm not going to have this sort of discussion with you today. I don't understand why we are searching for connections between things that are probably unrelated . . .'

'*You* said that it was probably related to his work,' Tódová flashed back.

'Ján was threatened by Marian Kočner,' another journalist chimed in, putting a name to one of the underworld figures at the centre of their thoughts. '[Kočner] threatened him with obtaining information relating to his family – what do you think about that?'

No sooner had Slovakia's top cop ducked the question, responding that everything was subject to investigation, when someone landed the next volley: 'Ján Kuciak said that he himself wrote and filed a complaint and the police ignored it.'

Another chimed in: 'Mr Gašpar, we don't trust you . . .'

'It may sound a little weird to say after these events,' said Gašpar, struggling to retain control and appearing increasingly angry, 'but we are not living in a mafia state.'

However, as the next few days were to show, a mafia state is just what Slovakia had become, right under Tibor Gašpar's nose.

Slovakia's prime minister, Robert Fico, was also quick to condemn the killings. 'If the journalist's work was really the motive, I consider it a severe attack on democracy and the freedom of the press,' he told waiting reporters, while his minister of the interior, Robert Kaliňák, assured the worried citizens of Slovakia that his teams were on the case. But this would do little to halt the political maelstrom that was brewing.

Opposition leader Igor Matovič delivered his own press conference, during which he stated that both Gašpar and Kaliňák had been the subject of Ján Kuciak's journalism and therefore were embroiled in a deep conflict of interest.

The following day, flanked by Gašpar and Kaliňák, the prime minister first condemned the Opposition for making political capital out of the killings. And then made what he may have intended to be an important gesture: 'Ladies and gentlemen, in front of me lies one million euros. This reward is intended for anyone who comes forward to the police or provides information about this crime.'

Sure enough, there on a table in front of him were fat stacks of tightly bound euro notes. Fico and his team couldn't have looked more mafia if they had tried.

Marian Kočner was one of the chief players in this mafia state. A short, arrogant and heavy-jowled man with a bullish chest and spindly legs, Kočner wore his thick black hair combed back and was given to wearing designer clothing that served mainly to accentuate his thuggishness. He had already made it into police files more than once, accused of mafia connections and VAT fraud, among other things, and into Ján Kuciak's articles around 25 times. It was known that he had threatened Ján, and many journalists had no doubt that Kočner had also commissioned the hit on him and Martina. And so, while the police continued to do nothing, Ján's colleagues began to rally.

The editor-in-chief of Aktuality.sk and Ján's boss, Peter Bárdy, first heard about Ján's killing from his deputy. This thoughtful man was stunned and almost refused to believe it, but in his heart, he knew it was true. Any doubts he may have had were dispelled by a call from the minister of the interior, and a great sadness descended on the editorial office. Ján's killing really hurt. But for Bárdy, as with others of Ján's friends and fellow journalists, the effect of the murder was the opposite of what the killer or killers had intended.

Peter was consumed by worry for his other colleagues, but that also gave him the motivation to push on despite the terrible shock that the murder had caused; to deal with the dozens of interviews and meetings with journalists and the interrogations by the police. Out of that process grew a deep determination to carry on the work that they were doing.

Ján's murder had brought home a new reality. 'None of us thought that they could threaten us physically,' Peter said. 'We expected lawsuits and court hearings. But a physical attack, or murder, was not tolerated by anyone.' Ján Kuciak was the first journalist to be murdered for his work since Slovakia had emerged from the ashes of the Soviet Union, and the shockwaves hit hard. Groups of people started gathering around the country. They lit candles outside the office where Ján had produced so much of his work, while more gathered in Slovak National Uprising Square.

Slovakia's president, Andrej Kiska, was quick to condemn the killing; and the executive director of the International Press Institute, Barbara Trionfi, said that, 'The murder of a journalist is a crime not only against the victim, but also against society as a whole.' In calling for a thorough investigation, Antonio Tajani, president of the European Parliament, must have been acutely aware that Ján's murder followed the car-bomb assassination of investigative reporter Daphne Caruana Galizia in Malta just four months before. Tajani had cause to be worried. The EU, of which Slovakia was one emerging economic star, evidently had a serious organized-crime problem. Perhaps no one had known that better than Ján himself, and his death released years of pent-up frustration among the Slovak population, long sick of the corruption they knew was pervading their country.

Nine days after the killings, mass demonstrations took place across the nation, with 20,000 people gathering in Bratislava alone. A black-and-white headshot photograph of the smiling couple, showing them with their heads nestled together and obviously very much in love, became an emblem of the All For Ján campaign, forming the centrepiece of makeshift candlelit shrines and lapel badges. The white writing on a long black banner carried by numerous people bore the message 'An attack on a journalist is an attack on all of us'.

Among these heartfelt tributes, one group of people carried a larger-than-life poster featuring a very different image – a young female model dressed only in a pair of sunglasses and the briefest of knickers, who was looking alluringly into the camera while eating a banana. Above her head were the words 'HLAVNÁ ŠTÁTNA RADKYŇA' – Chief State Adviser.

Sadly, for Slovakia, this wasn't a joke. When he was killed, Ján had been working together with a Czech journalism outfit, Investigace.cz, and the Italian Reporting Project Italy (IRPI) on a story that linked the 'Ndrangheta – one of the most powerful arms of the Italian Mafia – with top politicians in Slovakia. Twenty-seven-year-old model Mária Trošková was a former business partner of the Calabrian mafia boss in question, Antonino Vadala of the notorious Vadala clan, which had captured much of Europe's cocaine market. Mária had gone on to be appointed by Slovakia's prime minister, Robert Fico, as one of his advisers, but her exact job description was somewhat unclear.

In the face of this outbreak of public fury, the political system began to unravel. Eleven days after the killings, siding with the demonstrators, President Kiska publicly broke with Fico, whose only response was to accuse Kiska of being involved in a George Soros-inspired plot to bring down the government. Unsurprisingly this did nothing to quell the public fury.

Sixteen days after the murders, 60,000 people filled the Slovak National Uprising Square, with thousands more gathering across the country, all chanting 'No more Fico'. At that point, the whole house of cards began to fall. The first to resign was the vice prime minister and minister of the interior, Robert Kaliňák, followed three days later by Robert Fico himself.

Evidently under pressure, the following day, Police Chief Tibor Gašpar, resplendent in his glittering dress uniform, called another press conference and said that he didn't 'think the protests represent the opinion of the whole of society'; that if people were expecting him to resign they were in for a disappointment. He vowed to fight on. As it turned out, he didn't have to fight for long: just five hours later, this time dressed in an ordinary suit, Gašpar was hauled into his second press conference of the day by the new prime minister, Peter Pellegrini, who publicly sacked him.

The All For Ján campaign was gathering momentum, demanding an end to the endemic corruption at the heart of the Slovak state and the corrosive power of organized crime. But Pavla Holcová, the founder of Investigace.cz, with whom Ján had collaborated on the 'Ndrangheta story, did not attend the rallies. She didn't attend Tibor Gašpar's press conference either, because the morning of 26 February had changed her life.

In addition to the terrible shock and sorrow of her friend and colleague's brutal killing, Pavla and the police knew that she too was at risk, and so she and her family were immediately taken out of circulation. The next two weeks saw them being shuffled from safe house to safe house, permanently guarded by four heavily armed police officers. But this was taking a toll. The police guard was a constant reminder that she could be the next victim; so, armed only with a panic button, she and her family went into hiding in a remote forest region.

Pavla was also the European editor of the Organized Crime and Corruption Reporting Project (OCCRP), a dynamic umbrella organization for investigative journalists, based out of Sarajevo. Initially focused on organized crime in Eastern Europe – not a job for the faint-hearted – OCCRP's network has become a real force for investigative journalists worldwide. Following Ján's murder, one of the first calls Pavla made was to one of the OCCRP's founders, Drew Sullivan. Although he didn't know Ján personally, the news hit Drew hard. He was always worried about the dangers investigative journalists faced.

'You expect bad things to happen when you cover organized crime in Eastern Europe [. . .] it's like war,' Drew told me. 'You don't have a problem until you have a problem. And we suddenly had a problem.' The OCCRP began to rally its resources.

Drew continued: 'When somebody kills a journalist [. . .] the only thing we can really do is to make people pay as big a price as we possibly can. And so, we report, we finish their work; we demonstrate that, if you kill somebody, then 20 people will take their place. In the end, they're going to be sorry that they did it.'

Ján, with a master's degree in journalism from the University of Constantine the Philosopher, in the picturesque city of Nitra, was introduced to Pavla by a mutual friend, Eva Kubániová, in 2013. From then on, Ján became Prague-based Pavla's primary contact when she needed someone on the ground to work on cases in Slovakia.

'He was not this typical investigative journalist that you know from TV. He was very silent and very modest,' Pavla recalled. 'He was very analytical and he preferred documents to people; not the sort of person that meets his sources in an underground car park. He was able to build a story on numbers and documents, and [only] then he would talk to the people.'

*

Through my own experience of investigating bad guys, I have long been aware of the risks of being spied on. Probably overly paranoid, I have been careful about what I said on the phone and have searched my hotel rooms with a bug detector. At Global Witness we would vet our staff and volunteers as best we could to prevent infiltration – which has been tried on us – and we would hold the most confidential conversations outside of our office, walking on the street or sitting in a park. So when I saw Matt Sarnecki's brilliant documentary *The Killing of a Journalist*, which premiered at the Hot Docs Canadian International Documentary Festival in Toronto in May 2022, one of the things that chilled me most was the deceptively innocent scene of Ján and Martina pushing their loaded shopping trolley into camera shot in a supermarket car park, unloading their purchases into their car and then Martina walking almost right up to the camera as she returned the trolley to the storage area. At that point, whoever was filming them was just 2–3m (6–9ft) away from her. The camera captures Ján and Martina getting into the car and driving off, and then either the same person or another tail follows the car as it drives away.

In another rolling shot a concealed camera – carried at hip height and probably hidden in a bag of some sort – takes in the wide arc of a quiet suburban street and then rests on Ján and Martina's house. Ján is in the drive using some kind of heavy power tool. In order to keep filming him without raising too much suspicion, the spy bends over – probably to adjust a shoelace – and continues filming, capturing his own head and ears and the peak of his baseball cap. The very ordinariness of the scene is sickening, because in hindsight we know that this was part of the preparation for an assassination.

What was perhaps more shocking was that this surveillance had been organized by an unusually experienced operative. Peter Tóth was the former head of counter-intelligence at the Slovak Intelligence Service (SIS), but he wasn't doing this for the state. Marian Kočner paid better than the state.

Ján Kuciak had become a painful thorn in Marian Kočner's ample side. Known as 'The Belly' for not-very-subtle reasons, Kočner was one of Slovakia's best-known businessmen. He regularly appeared in the gossip columns attending some lavish party or other; his tanned face beamed out of the pages of the tabloids alongside some celebrity, or he was photographed leaving designer shops loaded with yet more expensive tat.

Over the years, he managed to deflect numerous accusations of corruption and dirty dealings, ranging from his involvement in dodgy property deals, through to VAT scams and the controversial takeover of a popular TV station. Apparently, Kočner was Teflon-coated.

Eva Kubániová – Pavla and Ján's mutual friend – was waiting for a delayed plane in Paris when she saw her boyfriend approaching across the concourse. 'His face was absolutely pale, and I [knew] something had happened,' she told me. He asked her to sit down, and there in the terminal building he told her that Ján had been assassinated.

'And then I saw it on the TV screen. It was already breaking news and I saw a black-and-white photo of Ján and Martina. I couldn't speak; I was just crying.'

Eva's first thought was that the murders may have been connected to Ján's investigations into the 'Ndrangheta, and she also feared that Pavla could be a target as well. Like most people in Slovakia, Eva didn't think the murders would be investigated properly; and she offered to do whatever she could to help.

'Pavla asked me to go to Slovakia [. . .] to act as a fixer for the journalists from OCCRP, to take them to Ján and Martina's house,' she remembered. 'I thought it was going to be for three days, but I ended up staying in investigative journalism full-time for five years. We felt that we owed it to Ján and Martina.'

As lead investigator into Ján's and Martina's murders, police officer Peter Juhás and his team had been quick to seize CCTV data, 16 terabytes of it; and, as they painstakingly pored over the thousands of hours of footage, they were transported along the main streets and down the quiet suburban lanes of Veľká Mača, examining the weaving traffic and the countless nameless people going about their daily lives under the unblinking stares of the cameras. Among them, someone was on their way to commit murder.

Eventually, something stood out. Grainy black-and-white footage captures two men, one in a pale hoodie, the other in a darker one, walking side by side towards the camera along a quiet street close to where Ján and Martina had lived. They are flanked by a low fence and some trees on their right, with higher buildings on their left, where the camera is positioned. Their heads are bent forward, obscuring their faces, and their hands are thrust deep into their pockets against the winter cold. The date embedded into the film was 15 February 2018; the time was 20:11. Almost exactly one week before the killings, to the hour.

On 21 February 2018, the man in the darker hoodie was filmed striding purposefully under the same camera on this deserted street. The time was 20:21 – close to the time the police believe the murder was committed. But that wasn't all.

'Based on the time data, we were able to identify a vehicle that behaved in a way that supported our hypothesis of two perpetrators,' Peter Juhás said when he was interviewed for Matt Sarnecki's film. 'One being the shooter, the other being the driver.'

The challenge now was to connect this suspect vehicle, a silver-coloured Citroën Berlingo, to these suspects, but the cameras had not managed to catch the registration number. Police officers all over the country were tasked with patrolling the streets, covertly looking at thousands of Citroën Berlingos, their owners unaware of this sudden, peculiar interest in their cars. Photographs were taken of hubcaps, the scratches and bumps that accumulate over time, the design of the door-handles and any other clues that might set one car apart from the others, and gradually the search narrowed down to 3,000 vehicles – still a significant haystack in which the needle was hidden.

Into this mix, the police were cross-referencing the vehicle information with, as Juhás put it, 'a massive amount of telecommunications data'. Over time, the fog began to clear.

'We were able to identify a transmission between two burner sim cards,' Juhás said, 'and we were able to connect one of the burner sim cards to a specific person who was already connected to the assassination of a businessman in 2016.' Staring out of one of the documents in the police files was the heavy-set face and shaven head of Tomáš Szabó, himself a former cop. Tomâš's father was the proud owner of a silver-coloured Citroën Berlingo, registration number KN-434 BG.

Juhás put Tomâš under close surveillance. Footage taken from the windows of unmarked cars showed him shopping in a supermarket and chatting with friends, while wiretapping evidence led to the identification of the user of the other burner phone. Miroslav Marček, whose powerful physique had stood him in good stead as a former soldier and then as an armed guard helping to protect merchant ships navigating the pirate-infested waters off Somalia, was Tomâš's cousin.

The police had also identified the middleman who they suspected had recruited Tomâš and Miroslav to assassinate Ján. His name was Zoltán Andruskó. Finally, seven months after the murders, the cops went in.

Police footage of the night-time raid shows heavily armed officers smashing open the door of one house, pushing one of the rudely awakened suspects – dressed only in his undershorts – to the ground and cuffing his hands and feet. Newsreel footage showed these men being hustled out of their homes, faces hidden or blinking in the daylight as they were led away for interrogation.

Zoltán Andruskó began to cooperate with the police almost immediately. He claimed he had been hired by one of Kočner's close allies, Alena Zsuzsová, to kill Ján and had hired Szabó and Marček to do the job. The fee was €50,000. Just 24 hours after Andruskó's arrest, Zsuzsová, dressed entirely in black, was led from her house to the waiting police car. Her head was bowed so that her long, jet-black dyed hair concealed her face, and her arrest turned the spotlight glaring on to one man: Marian Kočner.

It's hard to know how someone as unlikely as Alena Zsuzsová was so good at her job – and it was a very odd job. Devoted to Marian Kočner, she supplied him with kompromat on some of the most powerful people in the country, which gave him an inordinate and corrosive power – a power he used to great effect. Apparently obsessed by her own appearance, one of her main talents was to alter it: this proved to be an effective methodology. Using Photoshop like a digital Botox to give her lips some extra pout or accentuate her cheekbones, she would superimpose the finished product onto photographs of nude models she had downloaded from the web and send them to Kočner's potential victims. She would then follow up these images with the offer of a meeting in the flesh.

'I could leave the car at the parking lot at the airport,' she told then speaker of the National Council and chair of the Slovak National Party, Andrej Danko, in one phone call.

'I can't wait a second more,' his voice cracked urgently. 'Lots of kisses all over you.'

'Uh-huh [. . .] same here,' she breathed back.

'Finally, you'll be mine for the whole night,' he said.

However, like all the other powerful men she ensnared, which included a veritable roll call of prosecutors, members of parliament and ex-ministers, Andrej Danko was to be disappointed, because Alena Zsuzsová always cancelled the date at the last minute. Disappointment usually turned out to be the least of her victims' problems.

Alena's conversations, sometimes accompanied by intimate photos and even videos of her subjects masturbating, were carefully recorded and categorized in order of the men's importance: 'Sheep Class 1' earned Alena more money than Sheep Classes 2 or 3. The recordings were then forwarded to Marian Kočner, to join his vast archive. But at this point, Kočner's methodology was unknown to most people in Slovakia beyond Zsuzsová, Kočner and the victims themselves.

So, while Kočner knew that there was not much chance that anyone in authority would dare pursue him for his crimes, the pesky young journalist Kuciak always seemed to be on his tail, firing question after question at Kočner's press conferences, or calling him up to interrogate him further. Marian Kočner hated Ján Kuciak.

And this hatred had already manifested, not least in a phone call where Ján was questioning Kočner.

'You're not a journalist; you're just a hired hack,' Kočner spat down the phone at Ján. 'You're far from being a journalist. Be sure that I will give you my special attention. To you personally, Mr Kuciak.'

'Is this a threat?' Ján asked.

'No. Why? I'm telling you calmly. I'll pay special attention to you personally. Your mother, your father and your siblings. As soon as I find any dirt, any missteps, on you or anyone in your family, I will publish it in the same way as you do.'

Ján was a good journalist. He had recorded Kočner's threat and submitted a complaint to the police; but, like most complaints submitted to them at that time, it was not acted upon. And unfortunately for Kočner, Ján was completely clean. Which left Kočner with a problem: how was he going to shut him up?

Perhaps one of the most important people in Kočner's orbit was Peter Tóth, a former journalist who had switched sides to become an intelligence officer with the SIS before changing employers once more, placing his skills in the more lucrative service of Marian Kočner.

As Tóth later testified in court, in the summer of 2015 or 2016, Kočner told him that killing one or two journalists in Slovakia would silence the rest. This didn't turn out to be very good advice and hadn't stopped him spying on up to 20 journalists, including Ján Kuciak and Monika Tódová.

'Kočner trusted [Tóth] fully,' Pavla told me. According to Pavla, the arrest of Alena Zsuzsová led Tóth to suspect that his patron was linked to the murders, and, as the police investigation became more intensive, he probably realized that his close relationship with Kočner would be unearthed. Whatever his motivation, he gathered together all the treasures that Kočner had entrusted him with – enough to fill the assortment of suitcases which he stuffed into the boot of his black Kia Rio car – and drove them to the police. Among the material he packed into the boot that day were two of Kočner's mobile phones, one of them a black, gold-trimmed Bentley limited-edition iPhone.

Meanwhile, by June 2018 Kočner's various scams were catching up with him. Dressed in designer gear and delivering his usual barbs to the journalists gathered outside, Kočner swaggered into court for a hearing on charges relating to the forging of promissory notes. News footage captures his surprise as he was placed in pre-trial detention and unceremoniously cuffed and led away down a corridor by a group of well-built police officers.

The police took advantage of his absence to search his house. Their own footage of the raid shows a number of plain-clothes officers opening the electric gate of the house on a hill in an upmarket part of Bratislava and making their way inside.

They entered room after room, from the marble-clad hush of the indoor pool through to the rest of the bland (although no doubt pricey) interiors, with their flatscreen TVs, a wardrobe the size of a London bedsit and the white Bentley in the garage. And then there was the safe room.

Shelves crammed with handbags, designer shoes and a plethora of expensive stuff lined one wall, but the police images of the drawers were more interesting. In one lay a submachine gun, a sawn-off pump-action shotgun, five pistols and a profusion of ammunition. In another lay something far more dangerous.

'It was a USB key,' Pavla told me.

*

Please be available

The message flashed up on Pavla's phone one morning as she was on her way to the office, around 20 months after Ján's and Martina's murders. Intrigued, she said she would be free at around 10am.

The caller was prompt and told Pavla what was on offer: 'We want to give you a copy of the police-investigation file, with all the annexes.'

Simple as that. This is the sort of call that is usually confined to an investigative journalist's dreams and Pavla was excited, but she was cautious too. 'I started to think about the motivation of the source to give me it,' she said. 'During the call we talked about this, and it was somehow believable that I couldn't be part of some game between politicians or [. . .] the Secret Service or whatever. So I agreed.'

This was what Slovakian journalists came to term 'The Breakthrough'. Pavla found herself in possession of a vast archive comprising 70 terabytes of data. But what on earth did it contain, and how do you deal with 70 terabytes of data?

Pavla waited until she was in possession of the haul and then she called Drew Sullivan at OCCRP. Drew is a laconic veteran journalist but he must have been less than laconic when he took Pavla's call that day.

'Seventeen terabytes?' Pavla remembered Drew saying. 'That's bigger than Aleph!' Aleph, OCCRP's mega database with its 3 billion records containing information from countless data leaks, the web-scraping of public databases and, critically, the findings from hordes of journalists across the world. Aleph, with the details of over 97 million companies, 20 million contracts, 492,000 bank accounts, 73 million legal entities and 40 million properties. Aleph, which as it turned out, was several times smaller than Pavla's data leak.

No, Pavla told him. Not 17 terabytes; 70 terabytes. There was silence on the line for a few seconds, then Drew said, 'You need Fred.'

If you didn't know Friedrich Lindenberg you might think that one of journalism's best data wranglers would turn out to be the archetypal data geek who doesn't get out much. In fact, with his shock of red-blond hair and beard, Friedrich looks like a rugby player, deploys a wry sense of humour in most of what he says and is very, very good at what he does. When I first asked to talk to him about his role in investigating Ján's murder he was remarkably self-effacing. 'You've got Pavla, who's the Christiane Amanpour of this matter . . . I'm just the sound guy.'

Friedrich was being overly modest. Not only had he designed OCCRP's Aleph database, but in the investigative journalism world his reputation is near unparalleled. I asked him why he had embarked on the career path he had. 'Curiosity,' he told me in his soft German accent. 'It's probably more accepted to say that you are in it because you're trying to save democracy or something like that. But I'm just really curious about all the ways the world [is] broken.'

Friedrich's curiosity had led him to become one of the early and leading advocates for open data. 'I got involved in German politics by scraping the budget information from the finance ministry's website, and then discovered I was the only person outside of the finance ministry who now had an Excel version of the budget, and I started receiving inquiries from various parliamentary factions asking, "Can we have that too?"'

Friedrich ended up in possession of a lot of government-related information but with no outlet for it, which led him into the world of journalism and eventually to OCCRP. 'I was trying to bring together both a sense of what's technically possible and also an actual interest in the topics of the investigations and then building technology that would help people actually access it.'

Everything he had done up to now was vital preparation for one of the biggest tasks he had ever dealt with. Not long after Pavla's call to Drew, she and Friedrich travelled together to Slovakia. The quantity of material was the first of many technical problems Friedrich would have to deal with. 'Copying 10 terabytes takes maybe three, four days, and I didn't really want to move to Slovakia for two or three months to make this happen,' he told me. 'And so we built this weird contraption that would let us go there with ten micro-computers and copy ten different source hard drives over the course of the weekend.'

As Friedrich put it, 'Data has gravity.' He described how he stuffed these hard drives into a very large backpack and caught the night train back to Berlin, where he began to find out exactly what this vast data trove contained. 'There was one hard drive that we already knew was the core of the information, the immediate court case and related information, and we spent some time going through it. But the big problem was how do we find what's interesting in there?' he explained.

'[We had] an entire police case. Some of it was well-organized evidence – items and photos from the crime scene, a lot of CCTV footage from places that have been surveilled, but also from the workplaces of suspects,' he continued. 'The weirdest aspect was the seized digital assets. The police had gone in and raided the homes [. . .] of quite a few people and made digital copies of their phones and of their laptops, and we ended up with complete copies of probably 30–40 computers. And that then became an interesting thing to sift through.' Friedrich was a master of understatement.

The team he was building examined the chat histories of the various suspects and began to get a broader understanding of what kind of figures these were. 'One of them was running a pizzeria [. . .] and I remember we found on the desktop all these everyday insights in the midst of a criminal conspiracy,' Friedrich told me. 'Little documents where he calculated how to most deeply bake a pizza and what ingredients he could buy. Just very everyday stuff.' The big problem was that the sheer amount of information was itself an obstacle. But Friedrich had begun to see the way forward.

'I was in this very awkward position where I neither speak Slovak and nor do I really have the full background on these people,' he said. 'Slovak politics to me feels like this: everyone has a history of 20 years that you need to know, and everybody knows everybody. It's a relatively small country and everybody knows that this person used to be involved with this thing then previously was involved with that thing and then went into politics. And I was missing all that context and yet trying to prioritize the information became the biggest thing that I had to do. And I realized that I had to get myself out of the line of fire and let people who understand this stuff get to it.'

The team realized that because of the sheer scale of the data leak they needed to have some kind of focus, and they homed in on the chat histories of three or four people who were at the centre of the conspiracy.

'And so it became a little bit of a bounty hunt,' Friedrich said. 'The opposite of what often happens with investigative-data software [where you might] have a corporate registry [. . .] and you're trying to find out who's in there. This was the opposite. We knew what we were looking for, and the question was [. . .] can we find the hard drive of so and so as quickly as possible and then make the key material on that accessible?' But how to deal with password-protected files?

This was not a question that fazed Friedrich, who had drafted a security expert onto his team. 'You just go through all the passwords that have been used in the past and you form them randomly, computing clusters on a super-computer [. . .] and it will run as many passwords as possible through these files.' And so, Friedrich's team accessed computer after computer, phone after phone . . .

The creation of what was to become known as 'Kočner's Library' was revolutionary in the world of journalism. It was the blueprint of a captured state and the data it contained penetrated deeply into the top levels of government, law enforcement and the judiciary. It was a database that would be invaluable to Slovakia's journalists working to expose the country's deep corruption. It would also be a gold mine if it fell into the wrong hands, and also many people would go to any lengths to destroy it. For these reasons, the source wanted the data out of the country.

Friedrich Lindenberg was of the same mind. 'The sentiment that I got out of Slovak conversations I had around the time was that everybody was feeling that what had happened to Ján Kuciak and his partner was the boiling over of a whole culture of corruption [. . .] And this was an opportunity to actually really react. I think the source and everyone [else] realized that finding this material was a chance to seize the moment,' he explained. 'And even if you assume that the Slovak investigators working on this case were fully goodwilled, the question was: did they have the capacity to work through all of this? Did they have the capacity to find everything in there? So, I think there was a civic interest in making sure that this window of opportunity would not be wasted.'

Friedrich continued: 'The decision was basically that if we work on this by ourselves we're not gonna get anywhere, because it's too much information, and whatever we produce is going to be seen as filtered and partial and biased towards wherever we are seen as standing politically. And so it's just not going to have the same impact. So, the idea was to involve all the other media organizations that had good journalist practices. The way this worked is that we wanted to make a room where journalists could access the material and we wanted to impose some sort of rules around that. Basically, we wanted to avoid the material just being leaked online, because it was from the personal computers of dozens of people and bulk data releases couldn't have done any good.'

By December 2019, Friedrich's team had installed a series of computers in a nondescript room in Bratislava, and Kočner's Library now had a home. It was far more than the simple room it appeared to be, not only technically but also – more importantly – in the philosophy it embraced.

Friedrich ensured that the computers were ultra-secure. USB ports were physically removed so no one could download files or install any software that might modify the computers. 'At the time, we told people that the data was in the room,' Friedrich told me, 'but that that was never the case.' In fact the data was located on a server at a secret location in Germany; so if anyone had broken into Kočner's Library in the hope of stealing the data, they would have come away empty-handed.

Finally, like all good libraries, it was presided over by a librarian; documents or pictures a journalist wanted to take away were duly noted so that there was an audit trail.

And this was how the Slovakian population began to learn, in tremendous detail, just how the corruption that had pervaded their country actually worked and who was running it.

'It was a very unique moment in Slovak journalism,' Eva Kubániová recalled. 'First of all, the journalists were collaborating together, publishing the same day, the same hour, the same story. So the outreach was amazing because it really reached all media across Slovakia. It was the legacy of Ján.'

'Because we understood the sensitivity of the material,' Pavla remembered. 'We understood that if more people would have access to this data it's going to be safer for all of us.' Pavla also knew that a major collaboration would bring many different talents to the team, from skilled investigators to the paparazzi of the tabloids, well versed in capturing photographs of unknowing or unwilling subjects.

KOČNER'S WORLD

As they pored over the data over the next few months, the journalists began to realize the importance of what they had. The contents of the two phones Kočner had entrusted to Peter Tóth, together with the USB key from Kočner's house, began to yield the vast scale of kompromat he had gathered and the degree of control he exercised on some of the most important arms of the state, and it became a dragnet enmeshing the great and the good – or rather – the not-so-good of Slovakia.

Among this vast archive were the honeytrap recordings Alena Zsuzsová had forwarded to Kočner. It's hard in this morass of top-level corruption to decide what is the most egregious example, but the case of Norbert Bödör ranked high. A prominent oligarch with high-level police connections, Bödör acted as an intermediary between Kočner and the top management of the police. In one example, the leaks showed that Bödör asked a police investigator to go on medical leave in order to postpone an investigation into Kočner by a couple of weeks. In fact, when it came to police corruption, there was more scandal to come.

The police investigation led by Peter Juhás discovered that Ján Kuciak's file in the police internal database had been accessed prior to his murder. 'Can you pull the files on two more people for me?' one text message read. 'It shouldn't be a problem to get passport copies,' said another. Juhás expresses little doubt that 'the person who ordered the file to be accessed may be associated with the top management of the police force'.

Daniel Lipšic, the Kuciak family's lawyer, was more explicit: 'All the cases in which Marian Kočner was involved were handled by two investigators from the National Crime Agency,' he said, and he outlined that while the investigators themselves didn't have the power to ensure these cases landed on their desks, there was one person who did.

'We know someone from the top management of the police force was assigning these cases,' Lipšic continued. 'We know, from the communications of Marian Kočner and Norbert Bödör, that he [Bödör] had a direct link with Tibor Gašpar.' Police president Tibor Gašpar – the man who at the press conference following Ján's and Martina's murders had put on his sincere face and said that Slovakia was not a mafia state – was a close friend and relative of Bödör.

'The police itself was the most powerful organized criminal group,' Pavla said at a February 2023 event organized by OCCRP to commemorate the fifth anniversary of Ján's and Martina's murders. Indeed, virtually the whole top management of the Slovak police, around 12 to 15 people, were charged with corruption and being part of an organized criminal group. 'There were messages between Marian Kočner and some of the judges and it was very revealing how cheap it was to run Slovakia,' Pavla told me.

Trawling through the lives and practices of some of Slovakia's most influential citizens also produced another rather unexpected emotion in Pavla: disappointment.

'If you're an investigative journalist, sometimes you can really admire creativity,' she said. 'You can [. . .] admire if a money-laundering scheme is really sophisticated and really smart. I know it's twisted, but you can appreciate the thought and the skills that were put into a money-laundering scheme. But [. . .] it makes you kind of embarrassed [. . .] that such a guy [as Kočner] had such a power over people. Because although he was smart, he was definitely not an evil genius that you can study to learn more about how the world works. This was just someone who was not afraid to bend the laws and bypass them. It was just basic. There was nothing to admire.'

For Ján's and Martina's parents, friends and their colleagues, the importance of the massive data leak that Pavla received in October 2019 was that it laid bare not just Kočner's seedy criminal life and the brutally simple and bizarre way he had got away with it for so long, but also the chilling circumstances that led to the cold-blooded assassinations that took place on that cold February night the previous year.

It was against this backdrop of a corrupted judiciary and a bent police chief – all with high-level political connections – that the trial of those accused of Ján's and Martina's murders took place.

I have never met Ján's and Martina's parents but I have watched their interviews in *The Killing of a Journalist*. Sitting side by side on a garden bench as the rain drips off the awning above, Ján's parents seem to be the mirror of what everyone says about their son; they come across as loving, quiet and reserved, thrust into a spotlight that their worst dreams could not have envisaged. Gaining strength from each other they speak fondly about their son and Martina, the jokes they told and the wedding they had been planning when they died.

'The main difference between those two families is that Ján's parents are very, very good people, very peaceful people, and I think very humble; like everything you can imagine about Ján,' Eva Kubániová told me. 'And I really believe that without Martina's mother – she is very wild; she is a fighter for justice – [Ján's parents] would just be in mourning. They wouldn't even talk to media about the murder. They kept it to themselves. But Martina's mother – she wanted justice. And I think that was a good combination because then [Ján's parents] started talking with media,' she continued. 'I saw them at the court hearings and it was really heartbreaking because they [had] to sit in front of the people who killed their children, and they [had] to see their faces every time, every single time.'

THE TRIAL, PEZINOK, DECEMBER 2019

Since the killings almost two years before, the wheels of justice had been grinding slowly and inexorably towards a trial that would transfix Slovakia. The middleman, Zoltán Andruskó, had already entered into a plea bargain and been sentenced to 15 years, and the shooter, Miroslav Marček, had confessed. The chilling footage of this confession was nestled among the thousands of hours of video recordings in Kočner's Library.

'At first, we were supposed to kidnap and kill Ján Kuciak so that he couldn't be found,' Marček told the court. But instead he decided to kill the journalist in his home.

In the police film of his confession, Miroslav Marček is sitting on a chair in a small room, the walls flanked by various men in plain clothes and two black-clad, heavily armed police officers in balaclavas. Marček leans forward as he recounts the events of that tragic evening in February 2018. Shaven-headed and matter of fact, dressed in a dark-blue Reebok hoodie atop camouflage trousers, he is calm as he describes being dropped off just after dark had fallen, next to a playing field not far from Ján and Martina's house. Concealed on his person was a 9mm Luger automatic.

Marček recounts walking past a bar, then along a dirt path and through a hole in a fence, emerging on Ján and Martina's street. 'There was nobody at home,' he says, his voice stark in the otherwise silent room. 'I walked into the yard, the gate was unlocked, and I waited in the garden shed [. . .] the annex.' After an hour and a half of waiting, he recalls, Ján and Martina arrived home. 'I could see two people, he was there with his girlfriend [. . .] I didn't leave the annex, not until his girlfriend went to the toilet. That's when I decided to act.'

Also in Kočner's Library is a video recording of the police reconstruction of the killings that took place at the crime scene. In this, surrounded by a group of huge police officers, flak jackets over their camouflage uniforms, Marček is holding an automatic pistol with a long silencer. It's not a Luger, but would doubtless suffice for the final act of the play he was now acting out.

Marček knocks on the front door. A figure appears, its vague form blurred by the frosted glass – much as Ján's must have been on the night of the killing. As the door slowly opens Marček raises the gun.

'Boom,' he says quietly. 'That was the first shot.'

Inside the house, he tells the forensic experts how Ján hit the wall and then collapsed down the basement stairs, as they measure the direction of fall and mimic Ján's final position.

'I went on,' Marček tells his audience, walking into the kitchen. 'Perhaps right here I cocked once or twice [. . .] I aimed with the suppressor.' Then he raises his straightened arm, with the gun pointed at the balaclava-clad head of a policewoman playing Martina. She falls to her knees and slowly collapses backwards, head close to the bookshelves on the wall behind her.

'Did she react to the shot?' he is asked.

'She didn't react at all. I saw her being hit.'

Marček's calm narrative and the silence of the room seemed a million miles from the bloodied bodies of two young lives cut so tragically short. The final moments of Ján Kuciak's and Martina Kušnírová's lives had been played out, but not the final act.

The remaining three suspects continued to protest their innocence, and on a cold December morning a few days before Christmas, Alena Zsuzsová, Marian Kočner, Tomáš Szabó and Miroslav Marček, barely visible behind a wall of more black-clad, balaclava-wearing, machine-gun-carrying police, filed into the courtroom in the Judicial Academy building in Pezinok, near Bratislava, for the pre-trial hearings. The public gallery was filled with reporters, the noise of their cameras clicking away like a swarm of cicadas.

Outside the court, Ján's and Martina's parents and their legal teams, all wearing their now iconic 'All For Ján' badges, were also negotiating the press scrum. 'It's difficult to talk. We'll have a tough day,' Zlata Kušnírová, Martina's mum, told reporters, echoing what the others must feel, sitting in the same room as those accused of assassinating their children.

'The people were on the squares in 2018 because they felt there was no justice in this country,' Ján's lawyer, Danial Lipšic, reflected when interviewed for *The Killing of a Journalist*. '[. . .] The legacy of this decision of the court may be that people will start slowly to feel that justice is coming back. That may be the legacy of the outcome of the trial.'

On the first day of the trial proper, 13 January 2020, the former soldier Miroslav Marček publicly confessed to killing Ján and Martina, and was subsequently sentenced to 23 years in prison. The next day, the man who arranged the killing, Zoltán Andruskó, also pleaded guilty in a plea bargain and went on to testify against his fellow defendants. But Marian Kočner, Alena Zsuzsová and the driver on the night of the killings, Marček's cousin Tomáš Szabó, had decided to fight it out.

Kočner, who in the meantime had been sentenced to 19 years in prison for forging promissory notes, said, 'I am not a saint, but I am not a murderer either. I'm certainly not a fool who wouldn't realize what a journalist's murder would lead to.'

A fool or not, Kočner was returned to his prison cell for the long months until the verdict was due, but his impact on Slovakian society was far from over.

'A storm like we've never seen,' the presenter on TV station TA3 told her viewers on 11 March 2020. 'Judges in Kočner's phone in handcuffs. Janovská, Maruniaková, Hajtová, Cviková – all connected to Kočner's fraud case,' she continued against the backdrop of film footage of Slovakia's legal elite being bundled into police cars. 'Police detained thirteen judges, two former judges and three others.'

The information contained in those two phones that Kočner had entrusted to Peter Tóth, that Tóth had in turn handed over to the police and that had subsequently been leaked to Pavla Holcová, were shaking the nation.

One grainy video shows Kočner and Slovakia's prosecutor general,

Dobroslav Trnka, setting up a secret camera in Trnka's own office, presumably to collect kompromat on those unfortunate enough to divulge anything sensitive to him as they sat together, centre-shot, on the red L-shaped sofa. But this was only scratching the surface.

'What now? Grant or dismiss the charges?' read one text message from Judge Vladimír Sklenka to Kočner, one of many messages he sent asking for Kočner's decisions and advice on what to rule in a particular case. This was dwarfed by the 6,000 messages exchanged between Kočner and Deputy Justice Minister Monika Janovská, who had intervened with two other judges to decide ongoing cases in Kočner's favour.

'I suppose you'll split Zuzana's reward with Denisa?' Kočner wrote in one message.

'No, Deni gets part of mine,' Janovská wrote back. 'I promised that cunt something and I must keep it.'

Another exchange that took place just a few days after Ján's murder was even more chilling. 'She should do what she is required to do,' Kočner wrote about one of Janovská's subordinates who was ruling in a case concerning him. 'Or she will end up like Kuciak 😳 😳 😳.'

It was against this backdrop that Slovakia nervously awaited the verdict, which came on Thursday 3 September 2020. Marian Kočner was dressed in a dark suit and, like the other defendants, wore an orange armband. Finally, his fate was delivered by Judge Ružena Sabová. 'The Special Criminal Court, at this hearing on 3rd September 2020, has decided as follows: the accused, Marian Kočner, born May 17th 1963, and Alena Zsuzsová, born June 13th 1974 [. . .] Not Guilty.'

Before the judge had finished speaking, Ján's and Martina's families rushed from the courtroom, holding back their tears. 'I had started to believe justice finally had come to Slovakia,' Ján's father told the press throng waiting outside. 'But now I see we're still at square one.' Asked whether she felt Kočner and Zsuzsová were guilty, Zlata Kušnírová answered a curt 'Yes'.

In an interview for *The Killing of a Journalist*, Kočner's lawyer, Marek Para, said, 'Everybody wanted Mr Kočner to be the one. They wanted the police to get him. Nobody was looking at the evidence in the whole. Just pieces of evidence were shown to the public, in order to convince them he's guilty.' Was he right?

'Slovakia is in the process of a revolution that was started after Ján's murder,' Pavla said. And the fight wasn't over yet.

The case was referred to the Supreme Court and nine months later, on 15 June 2021, Kočner, handcuffed and dressed in his prison garb of an open-necked blue shirt and blue trousers, listened as Slovakia's Supreme Court overturned his and Zsuzsová's acquittals and ordered a new trial by a different panel of judges. The ruling stated that the Specialized Criminal Court had made various mistakes and cited that new evidence had come to light, including text messages between Kočner and Zsuzsová.

Perhaps the cryptic '50 ⇒ 💀' received by Zsuzsová on that February afternoon 40 months earlier – 2 hours before Ján's and Martina's young lives were cruelly taken from them – would be part of her and Kočner's undoing. The suspects and the friends and families of the victims would have to wait until May 2023 to hear the Supreme Court's ruling. In the meantime, Ján's former boss, Peter Bárdy, pulled no punches in his view of Kočner: 'A disgusting crook, a cynical, heartless, self-absorbed monster.'

The city of Trnava in southwest Slovakia, about 30 minutes' drive from Bratislava, has been nicknamed 'Slovak Rome' because of the number of churches there, but on 11 November 2019 the Italian connection took on a new significance. While the townspeople might not have noticed the snipers taking up position on the roof of the local theatre, there was no avoiding the thudding rotors of the helicopter hovering overhead, nor the 30 or so heavily armed police that sealed off the area as a limousine with blacked-out windows drew up outside. Dapper in his blue suit and matching polka-dot tie, the diminutive, balding and moustachioed man who got out was quickly hustled into the theatre, surrounded by bodyguards.

Federico Cafiero De Raho, now a politician, was one of Italy's leading national anti-mafia prosecutors and had been invited to speak at an Against the Mafias event hosted by the city of Trnava and the Italian Embassy in Bratislava. He warned about the spread of the mafia throughout Europe, and the 'Ndrangheta – the Calabrian mafia – in Slovakia in particular. De Raho was here at the behest of Ján's and Martina's parents: Ján's last story for Aktuality.sk, published posthumously, had focused on the 'Ndrangheta and the inroads it was making into Slovakia.

De Raho was there, he said, to show solidarity, but that wasn't the only reason. There was an urgent need for anti-mafia legislation throughout the EU, he argued, and with a track record for bringing dozens of mafiosi to trial – and earning himself a pocket army for protection in the process – he was happy to help. It is an offer the European Parliament is yet to take up.

My colleague Simon also spoke on a panel that day, invited by one of the organizers, the leading Italian anti-Mafia journalist, Maria Grazia Mazzola. 'State capture doesn't happen in a vacuum,' he said and went on to highlight the roles of the enablers – what I call the Pinstripe Army of lawyers, accountants, PR companies, company formation agents and others who are the service industry of organized crime, providing a seamlessness between a mafia state and corporate behaviour.

In the aftermath of the trial, Pavla was talking to a member of the European Parliament. 'He was telling me you should do more as a journalist to guard the subsidies,' Pavla told me.

'No,' she had spat back. 'We are already dying for being the guardians of the subsidies and reporting on it. It's not our role to do the work of police or prosecutors. We are here to inform people.'

Pavla is right. Investigative journalists play a vital role in democracy, by highlighting where politicians, government officials and institutions fail. In an ideal world we wouldn't need them – but ours is far from an ideal world.

On Friday 19 May 2023, the judges of the Specialized Criminal Court in Pezinok finally delivered their verdict. Alena Zsuzsová had decided to stay in her cell so was not in court to hear Judge Sabová convict her for murder and sentence her to 25 years in prison. Her reaction was probably muted compared to the reaction of Ján's and Martina's parents after what came next.

For the second time, Marian Kočner was acquitted of the murders of Ján and Martina. For the second time, Ján's and Martina's parents hurried out of court in tears. According to the verdict, Kočner was unaware of Zsuzsová's assassination plot and hadn't funded it.

Drew Sullivan's view was succinct: 'The Slovak system doesn't deal with circumstantial evidence very effectively. He was the only one involved with a motive. His close confidante was found guilty of the murder. He was found with surveillance video and pictures of Ján in his house. He sent a cryptic message that read "50 ➡ 💀" on the day of the murder – the people said they were paid €50,000. So that gets you the electric chair in the US. In Slovakia you need more proof.'

The families are appealing the verdict.

EPILOGUE

'When you kill a journalist, you're not only killing the stories he was working on, but you kill a career,' Drew Sullivan told me. 'You kill 30 more years of experience digging into these issues; you kill a mentor who would likely develop 20 or 30 more investigative reporters, and then their work. You really cut out a whole family tree of people who would have done public-service journalism in a country. There's very few investigative reporters in Slovakia to this day, and there are still stories that are not getting done.'

Investigative journalists in Slovakia had amply demonstrated their crucial role in tackling the crime and corruption that was eating the heart out of the country's democracy, and they had demonstrated the courage to do this – but had they succeeded?

In early January 2021, Monika Tódová, the *Denník N* journalist who had also been a thorn in Kočner's side, was with her family at their cottage in the High Tatra Mountains in northern Slovakia when she noticed that an SUV had been parked outside for around eight hours, its occupant surveying the cottage and photographing her. She also noticed a second car with Bratislava plates outside the house and saw it again as she returned to Bratislava.

She reported these incidents to the police, who fined one of the men for breaking a curfew and launched an investigation into this 'dangerous surveillance'.

When I interviewed Ján's former boss, Peter Bárdy, he was distinctly downbeat about the future. 'Politicians attack us more than before, the mood in society is terrible, we see no hope or vision for change. And Ján is not here,' he told me.

'People are tired, disappointed with developments in the country and angry,' he continued. 'They want revenge. And Fico is supposed to be the bearer of revenge. If he forms a government, it will be a serious problem. Slovakia needs the world to know about this. The world must know that we exist, that we are still a democratic part of the EU and NATO, but that the fight for democracy here is very difficult and brings sacrifices.'

Peter Bárdy's words were prophetic. On 30 September 2023, Slovakia held its national elections. Robert Fico's Smer party took the lead and within a month he had formed a coalition government, once again becoming prime minister and adding another pro-Putin populist leader in the heart of the EU, alongside Viktor Orbán in Hungary. Like Orbán, Fico wasted no time in targeting the independent media, who had contributed so much to his previous downfall.

'I announced actions against enemy's media – TV Markíza, Denník N, SME and the portal Aktuality,' the *Guardian* reported Fico saying in early November. Claiming that these outlets 'openly declare hatred and hostility against Smer and spread these trends with joy', Fico banned them from any access to his office. He wasn't stopping there. In early December he announced that he was planning to abolish the office of special prosecutor, run by his bête noire, Daniel Lipšic. 'The special prosecutor's office cannot be fixed,' he told Aktuality.sk, the former journalistic home of Ján Kuciak. 'The evil in the form of Lipšic must end.'

Even taking into account populist politicians' seemingly ubiquitous cosy relationship with corruption and criminality, this looks a lot like an act of revenge, but perhaps it was also an act of bed-feathering designed to hinder any inconvenient graft investigations in the future. While on the subject of bed-feathering, it isn't yet known whether Fico is planning to hire any Mafia-linked topless models as senior advisers, but on this he does have previous.

3

THUNDER

THE SOUTHERN OCEAN, DECEMBER 2014

There was a slight swell as the fishing captain gave the order to set the nets. The first buoys, three red and one yellow, were cast off the aft deck and plumped into the sea, followed by the gill net itself. The net, some 15–22km (9–14 miles) long, snaked out for over an hour as the ship moved through the water. Weighted down by the sinkers attached to its lead-line, the net began to sink down to the seabed 1,500–2,000m (4,900–6,650ft) below. Once there, the floats attached to the top of the net – the float-line – held it up, forming a fence along the ocean floor. The second set of buoys marked the other end of the net, and they too bobbed on the surface as the ship prepared to set another net. Steaming at 6 knots, it could deploy around 10km (6 miles) of net per hour. In total the *Thunder* probably carried 400–600km (250–375 miles) worth of nets – walls of death that would indiscriminately ensnare any fish unless they were smaller than the mesh.

The *Thunder* had become the most notorious of a fleet of pirate fishing vessels known as the Bandit 6. It had eluded international law enforcement for a decade and was the subject of countless international conferences on illegal, unreported and unregulated (IUU) fishing, yet no government had seen it for years. It was estimated to have made an illicit profit of US$60 million in its 10-year poaching career so far.

The Southern Ocean girdles Antarctica and comprises around 15 per cent of the world's seas. Despite, or perhaps because of, being among the most remote and hostile fishing grounds on the planet, the Southern Ocean's rich living natural resources have been plundered on an industrial scale for over two hundred years. The whalers and fur-seal hunters of the 19th and 20th centuries brought some of these species to the brink of extinction and even penguins were killed for their oil. Fish stocks were seriously depleted and the over-harvesting of krill, the foundation of the Antarctic food chain, threatened the entire ecosystem.

In response, an international treaty, the Convention on the Conservation of Antarctic Marine Living Resources, was opened for signature in May 1980 and came into force on 7 April 1982. The Commission for the Conservation of Antarctic Marine Living Resources (CCAMLR), currently comprising 27 member states, was created to protect the critical ecosystems of the Southern Ocean. The harvesting of marine resources in the CCAMLR area is strictly regulated, but the Southern Ocean is far from the eyes of law enforcement.

IUU fishing is one of the most lucrative arms of organized crime, worth some US$23 billion per year. It devastates the way of life of fishing communities worldwide and destroys entire ecosystems. Extraordinarily rich pickings, coupled with an almost non-existent risk of being detected, have turned the Southern Ocean into bandit country.

*

I first met Alistair Graham at the annual UN Climate Change Conference at Poznań, Poland, in 2008 and immediately liked him. He is an unorthodox, irreverent genius and troublemaker and what he doesn't know about illegal fishing probably isn't worth knowing. With his mass of long grey hair and beard, he looks a little like a benevolent Father Christmas – but has a turn of phrase that would make a vicar blush.

A graduate of Oxford University, Alistair initially worked on forest conservation in New Zealand during the mid-1970s, got interested in albatrosses and eventually ended up in Hobart, Tasmania, focusing on a different arena altogether.

He told me: 'A friend of mine who was involved in CCAMLR, which has its secretariat here in Hobart, came to me and she said, "Hey, Alistair, we've got this problem." ' The problem was that Spanish fishing vessels operating from Chile were reporting themselves as being outside the CCAMLR area, when they were actually inside it. Alistair's friend asked if he could help. 'So, I took over being the NGO representative on the Australian government delegation to CCAMLR and set to work trying to work out how to go after these pricks.'

A polymath, Alistair explained to me the problem on the high seas. 'This was the general culture of the time, that came from [Hugo] Grotius, back in the 17th century,' he said. 'His Mare Liberum treaties basically consolidated current thinking at the time into a norm for trading partners, which was: it is a serious fucking offence to interfere with someone on the ocean, and that's where the whole piracy thing came from. So, there's this culture that when you're out there on the high seas, you could do what the fuck you like and no one could tell you what to do, and even if you did do something wrong, then they might just charge you a bit of money and send you home. There was a general culture of free-for-all.'

As a result, Spanish fishing boats that had been displaced by the EU Common Fisheries Policy were looking for new fishing grounds. One option was the cold waters around Chile. Originally targeting hake, the Spanish boats were coming up with another kind of fish altogether.

The Antarctic and Patagonian toothfish live at a depth of between 1,500–3,000m (4,900–9,850ft), grow up to 2m (6.5ft) long and can weigh 200kg (440lb). These fish were pretty much unknown on the international market until a clever marketeer decided to call them Chilean sea bass. They quickly became a costly favourite in high-end restaurants and soon attracted the attention of organized crime – in this case, a fishing mafia based out of Galicia in northern Spain. Once more, the Southern Ocean's resources would be subject to industrial-scale plunder.

OPERATION ICEFISH, HOBART, NEW ZEALAND, DECEMBER 2014

On 3 December 2014, the MV *Bob Barker*, a 52-m (170-ft), 488-ton Norwegian-built former whaling ship, slipped its moorings in Hobart, Tasmania and set course for the Southern Ocean, the most remote fishing ground in the world. As the sun broke through the clouds, it lit up the ship's jagged blue, grey and white ice-camouflaged paintwork. Its captain, Peter Hammarstedt, looked from the bridge down to the black flag flapping from its pole on the bow. Emblazoned on it was a white skull above a crossed shepherd's crook and a trident. A pirate's flag.

Six days later, the *Bob Barker*'s sister ship, the *Sam Simon*, painted in the same camouflage and flying the same flag, left Wellington, New Zealand and also headed for the Southern Ocean. It's captain, Siddharth

Chakravarty, known as Sid, had learned his trade captaining chemical tankers, but had chucked that in for a far more worthwhile and – as it transpired – exciting cause.

These two ships and their volunteer crews were part of Operation Icefish, a mission planned by Sea Shepherd, a free-thinking, maverick, non-violent private navy whose goal is to protect the marine environment. Their reputation terrifies whaling fleets and the illegal fishing industry alike; because although their operations are calculated, strategic and meticulously planned, their external image gives the impression of being angrier than a bag of cats. Their guiding ethos is that it takes a pirate to catch a pirate, and their goal in that Antarctic summer of 2014 was to catch the *Thunder*.

Peter Hammarstedt and his chief mate Adam Meyerson stared in turn at the radar screen and then back through the heavy windows of the bridge at the seemingly endless Southern Ocean. The screen cast a gentle glow around the room, and the shark's-mouth emblem emblazoned on the bow just above the waterline nosed through calm waters like a hunting dog sniffing for a scent. Icebergs as big as apartment buildings dotted the horizon and they caught the odd glimpse of a whale's back as it briefly broke the surface. Peter was exactly where he wanted to be and doing exactly what he wanted to do. Somewhere out there in this expanse, he knew, he just knew, lay his quarry.

It would take the two Sea Shepherd vessels two weeks to get to their hunting ground. Like their prey, their transponders were switched off, so none of the ships could detect the other by satellite. The one difference was that they knew what they were after, while the *Thunder*, if it was there, knew nothing about the target on its back.

It was Peter who had christened the Bandit 6, a name that had stuck. And *Thunder* was now the focus of international attention. In December 2013, on behalf of the New Zealand government, the international criminal police INTERPOL issued a Purple Notice to its 190 member states. A facsimile of this notice, in laminated plastic, was affixed to one of the walls of the bridge. It sought

> [. . .] information about the individuals and networks which own, operate and profit from the suspected illegal activities of the vessel, currently believed to be called 'Thunder' [. . .] The vessel is currently believed to be operating in the Southern Ocean around Antarctica where it may be fishing illegally for Patagonian toothfish, also known as Chilean Sea Bass, a highly sought after protected species.

Sea Shepherd were looking for a very small needle in a very big and very wet haystack. The Southern Ocean covers just under 22 million km² (8.5 million square miles) of some of the planet's most inhospitable seas.

Peter Hammarstedt was 14 years old when he saw a picture of a dead whale being pulled up the slipway of an 8,000-ton factory whaling ship in the Antarctic, and he was sickened by it – he thought whaling had been confined to the dustbin of history. He was 17 when he volunteered for Greenpeace and heard that their more radical offshoot, Sea Shepherd, was going to send a ship to Iceland to directly intervene and block the whaling ships. Peter knew he had to be on that ship.

He phoned Sea Shepherd every day for a month. On Monday he asked to speak to someone and they said call back on Wednesday. On Tuesday he phoned to remind them that they would talk to him on Wednesday. On

Wednesday he called them before they found a reason not to take his call. Eventually his persistence paid off. He was told to report to the Port of Seattle in Washington State, USA, to join the RV *Farley Mowat*, an aging former Norwegian-fisheries enforcement vessel launched in 1985.

Peter didn't mind what he did – which was just as well, because any aspirations of standing in the bows of a speeding vessel with the wind in his hair were soon to be dashed. He was appointed as an oiler and found himself in the guts of the ship, up to his knees cleaning out oil sludge. He had never been happier – he was contributing to getting the ship ready to go to sea to save whales.

Peter never looked back. After spending a decade chasing the whaling ship he'd seen a picture of when he was 14, he became what the US Navy calls a hawse-piper.

'The hawse pipe is the pipe on the ship that the anchor chain goes up and is how the rats get on the ship,' Peter explained. 'There are two routes that seafarers can go to become a captain. One is that you go to a maritime academy as a cadet. The other is where you accrue tremendous amounts of sea time. I got a lot of sea time as an oiler, a deck-hand, then as a helmsman up on the bridge, and then I went to school and got the qualifications.'

He became a captain at just 27 years old.

After spending the southern winter cleaning and preparing their ships, Peter and Sid had been ready to embark on that year's anti-whaling campaigns when Japan announced a one-year hiatus from whaling, the result of an unfavourable decision at the International Court of Justice in the Hague. The *Bob Barker* and *Sam Simon* were all revved up with no place to go.

'It gave us the opportunity to focus on a different conservation issue in the Antarctic,' Peter told me. 'I knew that illegal fishing was a problem there because in years past we'd come across unmarked fishing buoys while pursuing Japanese whaling ships; but we were never able to stop and confiscate that gear because they were not the prime focus of the mission. So, when the news came through that the whalers weren't going to go down that year, it gave us the opportunity to go after the *Thunder*.'

Peter travelled to Vermont in the United States to meet with Sea Shepherd's founder, Paul Watson – he wanted to get his blessing. When Paul asked Peter if he thought he really would find the *Thunder*, he replied, 'Absolutely. Yes, 100 per cent we can find them.' But he had no real idea whether that was true – it was a punt. Now, he had to deliver.

THE SOUTHERN OCEAN, DECEMBER 2014

'Good morning, everyone – welcome to the Shadowlands.' The youthful-looking captain of the *Bob Barker* looked across the mess at his crew, 30 men and women clad in various assorted versions of their black uniforms – T-shirts, sweatshirts and hoodies – all emblazoned with Sea Shepherd's name and skull-and-crossbones logo.

'Our mission is to find these bandits, shut down their illegal fishing operation, confiscate and destroy any illegal fishing gear that we find and measure our success by the number of criminal operations we shut down.' Peter paused and looked directly from one of his crew to the other, letting his words sink in. 'OK, thank you. Let's bag a poacher.'

The question was: how to find one ship in 22 million km² (8.5 million square miles) of ocean?

Peter took out a big nautical chart of the Antarctic and shaded the underwater topography – the depth contours where the water was deep enough to find Patagonian and Antarctic toothfish – around 2,600m (8,500ft). The *Thunder* would have to be there if they were fishing for toothfish, but it was still a very big area. Then he looked at a chart of the ice conditions to see where the ice edge was at that time of the year. The *Thunder* wouldn't be able to fish where there was 'fast' ice – in this case, ice that is fastened to icebergs. Peter was now looking at water that was deep enough to find toothfish and that was ice-free. Finally, he looked at where legal fishing vessels were known to operate, like in the Ross Sea: if they had seen the *Thunder* they would have reported it, but there hadn't been any reports. There was only one area that remained.

The Banzare Bank is the most remote area of the Southern Ocean and therefore the most remote area of water in the world, two weeks' sailing from the nearest ports in Western Australia and South Africa. Peter set up a grid-pattern search field and estimated it would take them between two to three weeks to cover the search area. Successive watches on the bridge of the *Bob Barker* kept their eyes glued to either the radar screen or their binoculars as they scanned the seas. Crew members clad in their waterproof survival suits took turns in the crow's nest, sweeping the horizon with their binoculars. Often the message over the ship's intercom to the bridges was, 'All I can see are icebergs . . .' But then, just two days after they began their search, there was a blip on the radar. One of the icebergs was moving at a speed of 6 knots.

DAY 1

Peter plotted a course through the thickening fog towards the blip and they came across four buoys floating in the sea on their starboard side. Given this was in the CCAMLR area, whoever's net it was was fishing illegally, and they couldn't be too far away. The *Bob Barker* was not equipped to retrieve nets, so the crew noted its position and carried on with their search. Their eyes strained through their binoculars and then, in the distance, a ship emerged out of the rain and the fog. As they closed in on it, its high grey hull and pale upperworks were clearly visible. Peter grabbed a pink file off the bookshelf and opened it. Images and the basic dimensions of the Bandit 6 stared out of the pages like a collection of marine mugshots. Peter compared the size, hull shape and superstructure of the vessel in front of them to the pictures.

'It's the *Thunder*.'

Peter took the *Bob Barker* astern of the vessel, where a crudely painted sign read 'Thunder Lagos'. The crew on *Bob Barker*'s bridge was jubilant, but Peter was just relieved, remembering his commitment to Paul Watson six months earlier. Unfortunately, the sense of relief didn't last very long. He grabbed the marine VHF radio and called *Thunder* up on Channel 16. He told them that they were fishing illegally and should report to the nearest Australian port to turn themselves in.

'*Nosotras no hablamos inglés, solo español,*' came the reply. ('We don't speak English, only Spanish.')

'That's very lucky, because we speak Spanish as well,' Peter responded, handing the mic to crew member Alejandra Gimeno, who repeated the message.

'Of course, they recognized my complete absence of any kind of lcgal authority to order them to do go anywhere or do anything,' Peter smiled ruefully. But it had been worth a try. Then he radioed the news to Sid Chakravarty on the *Sam Simon* and gave him the position of the buoys they had sighted. The *Sam Simon* was fitted with net-hauling gear, and the net was valuable hard evidence of *Thunder*'s illegal fishing.

As Sid took the call on the bridge of the *Sam Simon* and relayed it to the crew members around him, they spontaneously clapped and cheered – nailing the Bandit 6 was what they had volunteered for. They were 1,250km (777 miles) from the *Bob Barker* and it would take them 9 days to reach the position of the buoys.

Next, Peter emailed INTERPOL, as any member of the public can do if they have information relating to one of INTERPOL's Purple Notices. He notified them that he had found the *Thunder* and gave its position. He sent the same email to the authorities behind the Purple Notice: the Australian Federal Police, the Australian Fisheries Management Authority, the Norwegian Directorate of Fisheries and the New Zealand Ministry for Primary Industries. From that point on, he emailed position updates twice daily.

The only other thing that the *Bob Barker* could do was to stay on the *Thunder*'s tail. If the *Bob Barker* was there, the *Thunder* couldn't fish; and every day that passed would cost the illegal fishers money and deplete their supplies of food and fuel. A battle of wills had begun.

INTERNATIONAL CRIMINAL POLICE ORGANIZATION (INTERPOL) HEADQUARTERS, LYON, FRANCE, 17 DECEMBER 2014

Peter's message was just one of numerous emails sent daily to INTERPOL's public email address; but it was quickly passed to two criminal intelligence officers (CIOs) in the operations room at the Lyon headquarters, Alistair McDonnell and Mario Luís Alcaide. The message was short and to the point. The MV *Bob Barker*, operated by Sea Shepherd, had located and positively identified the fishing vessel *Thunder*, which was subject to an INTERPOL Purple Notice. The message detailed the ship's position and the time and date of the sighting.

INTERPOL is not permitted to interact directly with the public or civil-society organizations like Sea Shepherd, other than acknowledging receipt of tip-offs like this. All Peter knew was in the brief response he received: 'Thank you very much for your message. We're listening.'

However, behind the scenes, a hardened bunch of law-enforcement officials got very excited. 'The mechanics of the operation kicked into action, big time,' Alistair McDonnell recalled. 'This was a great opportunity because there was somebody on *Thunder*'s tail.' INTERPOL doesn't control any assets of its own, so one of the first priorities was to set up an evidential exchange group so they could work through their member countries.

For Alistair McDonnell as INTERPOL's project manager, it was critical to understand their quarry. He knew that the *Thunder* was one element of a sophisticated and virtually risk-free business model. 'You put in between £600,000 and £1,000,000 to buy a boat, the buoys and nets, hire a crew, set off down to the Southern Ocean and make £5,000,000 in six months,' he told me. 'Like all forms of organized crime, it requires networks to launder the catch through the documentary systems in ports, health paperwork, etc., and then sell it to the richest people you can in Beijing, or US and British restaurants.' Alistair's job was to massively ramp up the risk, to prevent people converting their fish into money.

Mario had only just joined INTERPOL. As the son and grandson of fishermen, fishing and the sea were in his veins. After nine years in the Portuguese Navy, he had joined the maritime police and from there had joined INTERPOL. He was in no doubt about what he wanted to happen: 'Sea Shepherd found the vessel; we need to go and fetch it.'

They knew the *Thunder* would try to keep to international waters. There, on the high seas, they were effectively beyond any country's legal jurisdiction. They knew what they were doing because they had done it before, but now they had someone stuck on their tail and badly needed to lose them. Doing that would depend on outwitting the captain of the *Bob Barker*. Abandoning the costly nets they had already set, an occupational hazard for a pirate fishing vessel, the *Thunder* steered a course heading roughly northwest. The *Bob Barker* followed.

During that first day, the two ships cut through a placid mercurial sea that mirrored the leaden sky. Massive icebergs dwarfed the ships as they steamed in unison just hundreds of metres apart, the captains sizing each other up. *How does my ship compare to the other? What tactics and strategies do I have to better my opponent? Which crew will prevail?*

For around a day, Peter Hammarstedt and Adam Meyerson maintained a vigil on *Bob Barker*'s bridge, trying to second-guess their adversary. Staring at the horizon, Adam got an inkling of the *Thunder*'s first move. 'I think they're leading us into the ice.'

The two ships neared an ocean of pack ice and the *Thunder* began to carve its way in. The *Bob Barker* followed, its shark-nose trying to find a route through the ice. Designed as a Norwegian whaling ship, the *Bob Barker* had been built for these waters and had a thick, strong hull, but that didn't make it invincible. Ships had disappeared in these waters before.

This was Alistair Allan's first voyage as *Bob Barker*'s boatswain, using the skills he'd learned over the years as a deck-hand with Sea Shepherd. His team of around seven people were responsible for everything that happened on deck, from cleaning the toilets to mopping the deck and making sure everything was ship-shape inside the vessel. They were also in charge of operating the small boats – the RHIBs* – with their powerful outboards. Right now, Alistair's role was certainly not dull and not very comfortable either. Dressed in hoodies to ward off the cold, he and his colleagues stood at *Bob Barker*'s bow, radioing instructions through to Peter on the bridge about how to navigate through the growlers.

'Growler is ice that isn't quite an iceberg, but is bigger than an ice cube in your glass,' he told me in his laconic Australian accent. Alistair was Queensland-raised and had during every year of his life watched the migration of humpback whales along Australia's eastern coast; he was committed to protecting the oceans. When backpacking around Europe he had visited a Sea Shepherd vessel moored in Barcelona and never looked back.

'When we hit the big ones you could sort of see the ship moving a little bit, the hull would flex a little bit as you push through the ice, and you just check that everything was holding together,' he told me.

From the bridge there was a seemingly endless vista of ice. Adam Meyerson knew that they had to get it right the first time. 'One thing to

---

* Rigid-hulled inflatable boats.

worry about is that the ice can close in behind you and that can happen pretty rapidly,' he remarked on the bridge. 'And you can't back up.' The most vulnerable parts of the ship, the propellor and the rudder, are at its stern.

Alistair reflected that while the ice might look harmless it was actually as solid as a rock. Peter felt it was like being bounced around in a pinball machine. 'You can hear the ice grinding down the side of the ship, a sound that gets right into your stomach.'

This vigil continued through the Antarctic summer night until, after a few painstaking days, the ships began to come through the other side of the pack. On the *Bob Barker*, tensions began to ebb and Peter handed over the bridge to the second mate, Paola Sanz, wishing her goodnight and heading to his cabin for some well-earned rest. The *Thunder* had banked on getting through the ice faster than the *Bob Barker* and increasing the distance between them by the time they reached open water. It had failed, but the *Thunder*'s captain had another card to play.

The Southern Ocean is home to some of the most ferocious winds on Earth – the Shrieking Sixties, the Furious Fifties and the Roaring Forties – and the *Thunder* began to lead the *Bob Barker* into a storm. The wind rose to around 40 knots – gale force – which screamed as it whipped the sea into mountains of crashing, crushing, 8-m (26-ft) waves. Water cascaded down the windows of the bridge like waterfalls and the ship heeled first 45 degrees one way and then 45 degrees to the other, its bows crashing down into the waves, seemingly on a one-way trip, before rising again and then crashing down once more.

Priya Holmes had been crewing for Sea Shepherd for two and a half years and was chief cook when the *Bob Barker* had left Tasmania. The storm was just one of many challenges she would face on this voyage. Like

Alistair Allan, she had grown up on the eastern coast of Australia, and the migrating humpback whales were a fixed part of her childhood memories. She began 'rattling the tin' for Sea Shepherd on the streets of Byron Bay, but a move to Melbourne, where the Sea Shepherd ships were based, allowed her to help out more directly, rust chipping and painting the ocean-battered boats. When she was invited to join one of the ships as crew, she didn't hesitate.

'I think there were several days where we were going through seas that were up to 10m [33ft], so everything was flying around, but people still needed to eat. So, to cook we would have everything bolted down,' she remembered. 'You would have to just move slowly. And as you were chopping things you'd put your elbow on the chopping board, try and support yourself and keep hold of everything, because otherwise things would just be flying off as you were trying to chop them. It was incredibly frustrating. But often, there would be two of us in the galley together, so at least we had some solidarity and would try and make it a bit of fun.'

She downplayed the danger of dealing with cauldrons of hot food, the pots held in a big frame. 'We'd fill a massive pot only a third full, otherwise it would be sloshing out.' Thanks to her and her fellow cooks the crew wouldn't go hungry.

Alistair meanwhile had challenges of his own. One of the ship's fenders, two or three times the size of a person, had broken loose and began whipping around on the deck below the windows of the bridge. It had the capacity to damage valuable equipment as well as being a danger to anyone on deck. Peter looked anxiously on as Alistair and his team donned high-visibility survival gear, hooked their safety lines onto the railings and braved the walls of water to wrestle the massive fender back into place.

'It was a trial by fire on that trip,' Alistair told me. 'If I hadn't seen rough weather before, I certainly got my fair share of it on the *Thunder* chase.'

'It was like working on an elevator that suddenly dropped and climbed six stories every 10 seconds,' Peter subsequently told *The New York Times*.

INTERPOL HEADQUARTERS, LYON, FRANCE

It was crucial that INTERPOL had an effective line of communication with Sea Shepherd, but their protocols dictated that this could come only via a CCAMLR member state. Norway was happy to help. Mario Alcaide eagerly awaited the daily emails from the *Bob Barker*, which reported the *Thunder*'s position, course and speed, and he relayed these to the other CCMALR member states.

'We didn't know what *Thunder*'s intentions were,' Mario told me. 'We thought they would try to get into the nearest port, so we were assessing which ports were close to them.'

Their other priority was to gather evidence that could be used in a court case if they could apprehend the ship. Without that, everyone's efforts would ultimately be in vain. Via Norway, Mario asked question after question of Peter, particularly regarding what technical level of communication equipment the *Thunder* had on board. He knew that they would not be transmitting VMS* information as commercial fishing boats are required to do, precisely because the *Thunder* was a rogue vessel and didn't want to advertise its presence to anyone. 'But I was wondering

---

* Vessel-monitoring system.

if there were any older transponders still mounted on board, so that we could reach out to the provider and find out if that transponder was still being updated. If so, then we would ask the provider to pull the information on the position of the vessel,' Mario told me.

At the same time, Alistair and Mario took part in daily calls with their evidential exchange group – their counterparts in the CCAMLR member states – maintaining the flow of intelligence.

MY *SAM SIMON*, CHRISTMAS MORNING, 2014

The *Sam Simon*, named after the co-creator of *The Simpsons* who had paid for the ship, reached the position Peter had given them for the abandoned fishing net and the crew began to scour the sea's surface through their binoculars.

'We should be able to see them by now,' Sid said, almost to himself. Shortly afterwards a cry went up – 'We've got them.'

The boat crew looked for all the world like riot police as they donned survival suits, balaclavas and visored crash helmets while the deck team rushed to launch the black-hulled RHIB with its powerful twin 90-hp Suzuki outboards. Dwarfed by the heavy swell that prevented them getting a clear view of anything much other than walls of dark sea, the boat crew relied on radioed directions from the bridge as it plunged through the water, down into troughs and climbing up the other side.

One of the crew hooked the yellow buoy, secured the line and returned it to the mothership. The next phase of the operation, hauling in the line, was going to be the most delicate one. They knew it could be tens of kilometres long and that it had been in the water for way longer than planned by the fishing captain of the *Thunder*, so it was likely to be heavy with its catch. They also knew that the whole point of the operation was gathering this evidence – the instructions from INTERPOL, relayed via Norway, had been explicit in what they needed to ensure a successful prosecution. There was a lot at stake.

Once they had got back to their ship, the boat crew passed the line to the deck crew, who gave it several turns around the hauling winch, and the slow process began to bring the net on board. As they had expected, the net was incredibly heavy, but under Sid's watch they began to bring the line in, inch by inch. The line was super-taut and a sudden release of tension as a knot gave way saw it slide back a few inches. The crew froze in case it snapped; no one wanted to be in the way of the whiplash that could result from that. After a brief pause, Sid instructed them to give the line another turn around the winch – but with a sudden thud, the line snapped and the net fell back into the sea and disappeared. 'Fuck,' someone said.

Sid decided to try to find the set of buoys at the other end of the net. It would be like looking for a needle in a haystack but he had an idea. He asked the helm to go round the next iceberg and make for the point where the *Thunder* first spotted the *Bob Barker* and presumably ditched the net in the first place.

He knew that these nets could be up to 130km (80.7 miles) long, which was around the same distance his ship could sail in one day. Sid radioed an update of the situation to the *Bob Barker* while his crew got back to work scanning the sea for any sign of the buoys. Fortunately, after only a few hours one of the lookouts called, 'I've got them!' And sure enough, one yellow and three red buoys were floating ahead of them. 'This is our last shot,' someone said.

The RHIB was launched and took a line from the *Sam Simon* to connect to the buoys, but this time the sea was against them with a mounting swell. They connected the line from the ship with the one from the net but it ran under the RHIB and got caught. Krystal Keynes, the ship's second mate, tried to free it but it was stuck fast. She had no choice but to lean over the stern and reach under the port outboard, barking back a warning in a not-to-be-misunderstood Australian twang: 'Make sure no one touches the throttle.' She still couldn't free it and had to plunge her head into the subzero water, her head camera capturing the moment from the clear-eyed drama above the surface to the translucent freezing blue below.

She managed to free the line but in so doing flooded her survival suit and lost all feeling in her arms. 'So numb it burns,' she gasped and was in agony by the time they got back on board. She would be in trouble if she didn't get warmed up quickly and was rushed to her bunk, wrapped in blankets and given a hot drink while a fellow crew member massaged the life back into her frozen hands.

Once more the line was wound around the hauling winch; very slowly, the net appeared over the side of the ship and its grisly catch began to arrive on board. They reckoned the net had been in the water nine days and it was heavy with the large silver toothfish in varying stages of decay. Just like the crime scene that it was, as the toothfish arrived on the conveyor belt they were photographed against a mini-blackboard marked TF1, TF2 and so on. They also photographed the by-catch – the red spidery king crabs and grenadiers, a common Antarctic fish.

Hauling in the line was grim, cold and exhausting work and the only respite was when a crew member noticed one toothfish on the conveyor belt flapping a fin. 'It's alive!' he cried. As his crewmates looked on, he quickly cradled the heavy fish in his arms and dropped it over the side.

The fish remained stationary for a moment, its silver scales glinting just below the surface, and then it flipped its tail and made its way to the depths. The crew around the line whooped and one danced a jig. It was just one fish, but it was a symbolic glimmer of hope as they got back to the slaughterhouse.

The crew worked day and night in driving sleet and snow to bring in the net, sliding on a deck awash with blood and decaying fish flesh. 'This is the worst thing I've ever done,' someone remarked, speaking for everyone.

The work went on for nearly a fortnight before Sid decided to call it a day, worried about the strain on the crew as well as on the equipment they were using.

'We've hauled in over 70km [43.5 miles] of line,' he told his crew. They had documented 700 toothfish weighing roughly 21 tonnes and worth around US$210,000. The net itself would have cost the owners of the *Thunder* another US$120,000. Then he gave them some good news.

'What we do have to look forward to is that we're heading straight for the *Bob Barker* [. . .] we should be there in six to seven days.' The crew were delighted – not just to meet their fellow seafarers but also to get their own view of their elusive prey.

THE GREAT DRIFT

By late January, the chase had been going on for over 40 days and had already exceeded the longest pursuit of an illegal fishing vessel in history. The *Thunder* was still heading northwest with no one but its officers knowing where they were headed. The weather grew hotter the further north they sailed and then, around 500 nautical miles off the southernmost tip of South Africa, the *Thunder*'s captain did what no one expected. He shut off the ship's engine.

'We described this time as the period of the Great Drift,' Peter said, 'where for days and days, we just drifted together, our engine also shut down in order to conserve fuel, just staring at them across half a mile of water with binoculars, endlessly speculating as to when they would start moving again. Are they waiting to meet up with somebody? Are they trying just to wait us out? What's the plan?'

When he left Hobart, Peter had estimated that this trip would last for two months and that's all the crew had signed up for. He had not reckoned on drifting for weeks off the southern tip of Africa and he needed to take stock.

'The *Bob Barker* was a former whaling ship and the big holds that had been used for storing whale meat had been converted into fuel tanks, so we had a tremendous endurance. We could carry about 470,000l [104,000 gallons] of fuel on board. If we drifted indefinitely we could potentially be out at sea for two years.'

The ship also had a reverse-osmosis water maker so they could produce their own water. From a logistics perspective the ship would be fine. That left the issue of food and the wishes of the crew. Priya Holmes said they had enough rice and beans to last them for two years, although she knew that that would be pretty grim.

Personally, Peter badly wanted to stay on *Thunder*'s tail, but he could not force the crew to make this kind of commitment – they had already done more than anyone had asked of them. If the crew wanted out, then Peter would have no choice but to return to their home port.

He asked the crew to assemble in the canteen so he could put the situation to them, and in so doing would be making probably the most important speech of his life.

Meanwhile, the *Sam Simon*, with its cargo of 72km (44.5 miles) of *Thunder*'s gill net, was on the way to hand over the evidence to the Mauritian police, the nearest place where INTERPOL had jurisdiction. As they would be sailing close to the Great Drift, they planned to meet the *Bob Barker* and share the vigil for a few days. Peter took advantage of this moment. He stood with his back to the bulkhead and surveyed the sea of faces looking expectantly towards him.

'In 24 hours, the *Sam Simon* will be here and there is an opportunity for you to disembark and for the *Sam Simon* to take you back to port. But I do need you all to know that we have enough fuel to stay here for two years. There's no guarantee of outcome. We could, after a year of this, suffer some kind of mechanical breakdown that means that the *Thunder* gets away. Or, at the end of two years, we could be escorting the *Thunder* into port and the port authorities could end up arresting us and letting them go.' He paused to let the information sink in.

'But there is one certainty, which is if you look outside you'll see the *Thunder* sitting there drifting and not fishing. Every single day that we're with this vessel, they're not able to fish; and every day that we're with them, we're saving toothfish. And that has to be good enough, right? We can talk all day about the big issue of illegal fishing, but we are making a difference every day we're with this ship, and that means we cannot leave them.

'If you want to disembark, I completely understand.' He gave them 24 hours to think about it. Privately, Peter prayed that if anyone left, the chief engineer wouldn't be among them.

Peter needn't have worried: everybody got back to him in less than two hours. And out of 30 crew, just 4 decided to leave and 26 stayed – including the chief engineer.

The next day, the *Sam Simon* joined the *Bob Barker*, boosting the morale of both crews as much as it must have dented the morale of the captain and crew of the *Thunder*. Up until now they had had no idea that there were two Sea Shepherd ships on their tail. Worse, Sid took the *Sam Simon* close by the *Thunder* so that its officers could clearly see the 72km (44.5 miles) of net they had hauled out of the sea at the Banzare Bank. Hard evidence of their illegal fishing. In case there was any doubt, Sid radioed the *Thunder* and told the captain he was taking the nets to Mauritius to be handed over to law enforcement. The *Thunder*'s captain denied they were his but Sid said simply, 'That's for law enforcement to decide.'

DAY 78

On Day 78 of the Great Drift, the monotony was broken by the arrival of the legal Australian longline toothfisher the MV *Atlas Cove*. This was a slick, 68-m (223-ft) vessel, its freshly painted royal-blue hull and white trim in stark contrast to the *Thunder*'s rust-streaked grey hull. Its captain radioed the *Thunder*.

'We've taken up position with Sea Shepherd to show support for their actions,' he began. 'These guys behind you won't let you go peacefully. Their reputation precedes them, so do yourselves a favour. Go back home and stay there.'

There were a few minutes of radio silence before the *Thunder*'s captain gave his answer, which was to turn his ship and steer between the *Atlas Cove* and the *Bob Barker* with barely a cable's length between them. Only then did he switch on his radio.

'Tell the captains of the *Sam Simon*, *Bob Barker* and *Atlas Cove* that I'm not frightened.' But his actions belied that. With three ships on his tail and the *Thunder* becoming increasingly conspicuous, he was getting desperate.

MAURITIUS, 5 MARCH 2015

For Mario Alcaide of INTERPOL, conducting a forensic analysis of a fishing net was like a homicide cop examining a bloodstained carpet; every piece of fishing gear was unique. Having grown up watching his fisherman father and grandfather, he knew that every fisherman has their own way to stitch the nets together, to tie on the buoyancy ropes and marker buoys. He remembered his grandfather telling him that any fisherman can recognize his own gear in the blink of a second.

With that in mind as he arrived in Mauritius to meet the *Sam Simon*, Mario structured a way to collect evidence regarding the fishing gear which would be put into a forensic report for INTERPOL to disseminate. The crew of the *Sam Simon* stretched the nets out on the quay while Mario meticulously recorded the details of the nets' construction.

Once this work was done, Sid steered the *Sam Simon* back out to sea to rejoin and resupply the *Bob Barker*.

With the *Bob Barker* alone again, the crew's show of dedication and loyalty couldn't be taken for granted, and Peter had to walk a thin line between keeping morale high and preserving discipline. He also had fears of his own. They were dealing with a faceless adversary and being unable to picture even what they looked like encouraged his imagination to wander and caused him to assume the worst. What he did know was that he was dealing with criminals, the Galician mafia, and there were rumours about their connections with narco-trafficking that haunted him. The burning question for Peter concerned when the *Thunder* would start moving again – and he figured that the *Thunder*'s captain was thinking the same about them.

Then something happened that changed the dynamic; something that began to tip the scales. 'After about 60 days or 70 days, the media determined that this was a long enough chase to warrant their attention and they started reporting what we were doing,' Peter told me. 'And every article that was written I would print and post for the crew in the mess. And that gave everybody the feeling that the world was paying attention to what they were doing and that this was important, not just for the toothfish we were saving on a day-to-day basis.'

THE FIRST MONTHS OF 2015

Alistair and Mario were also trying to get inside the criminals' heads. They noticed that every day for three weeks, at precisely the same time in the morning, the *Thunder* started circling. Alistair thought they were picking up a satellite signal. If he was right then it was likely the *Thunder*'s captain was in daily contact with the ship's owner, keeping them updated.

Mario and Alistair felt that he was looking at escape routes and they began to model the options open to him. Would he go south of Madagascar, then head northeast and try to get through the Malacca Strait? Or was he planning to go through the Mozambique Channel, or round South Africa to try to get up to the Gulf of Guinea?

'We were putting massive pressure on, because this chase was now being followed. Updates were going out from us, from NGOs and the press,' Alistair told me. The *Thunder* had gone from an elusive, almost mythical predator to an extremely conspicuous pirate fishing vessel. If Alistair had got it right, these daily satellite conversations between the captain of the *Thunder* and his boss must have been becoming very uncomfortable.

The crew of the *Bob Barker* passed their days playing board games, reading and speculating.

'It got so bad that certain crew members would leave the bridge if other crew members started talking about what would finally happen. Half the crew didn't want to talk about the future at all and just resign themselves to the present, while the other half were obsessed about the future and speculating as to how it would end,' Priya remembered.

The captain of the *Thunder* amused himself by getting drunk and radioing the *Bob Barker* at all hours – 'Mostly saying bad things about my mother in Spanish,' Peter remembered.

As one day much like the day before went by, the few American crew on the *Bob Barker* began to look forward to watching the Super Bowl and the final battle between the Seattle Seahawks and the New England Patriots. They had settled down in the mess to watch the game when suddenly, Peter was called urgently to the bridge.

The *Thunder* had turned on their fishing lights. Peter knew the drift had taken them close to a sea-mount, an underwater volcano. In their location it was the only place that wasn't too deep to fish. Peter ordered the chief engineer to start the engines and the *Bob Barker* made for the *Thunder*'s starboard side.

The ship had set a short net, perhaps a couple of kilometres (a mile or so) long, and then turned off their fishing lights. The crew on the *Bob Barker* didn't know whether this was a test to see whether they would block them from fishing, or if it might be subsistence fishing because they were running out of food. Either way, Peter radioed across to the *Thunder* and told his adversary that he would block him.

As soon as dawn broke over the choppy sea, Peter asked Alistair Allan to get the deck team ready as the *Bob Barker* headed for the buoys marking the net that the *Thunder* had set overnight. The *Thunder* had only a limited number of buoys and couldn't afford to lose them; and, guessing Peter's intentions, she turned and steered directly towards the *Bob Barker* at speed. Peter urged the deck crew to hurry as one of the crew threw a grappling hook over the side and caught the line. One after the other, the crew hurriedly brought in all four buoys and cut them away from the net, which sank down into the sea. As the *Thunder* came closer, the *Bob Barker* repeatedly sounded its horn and the warning went out over the ship's tannoy – 'Stand by for possible impact.'

As soon as the last buoy came in over the side, Peter put his engines full astern; then, as the *Thunder*'s high hull passed their bow, he swung his ship astern and to starboard. The full length of the *Thunder* passed in front of the windows of the *Bob Barker*'s bridge as the Sea Shepherd ship slid away backwards and then, with just a metre (3ft) to spare, Peter's ship was in the clear. The crew on the bridge laughed in relief, happy that they had got the buoys on board – one more piece of evidence that could tie *Thunder* to the nets that the *Sam Simon* had offloaded in Mauritius.

'Let's let them calm down a bit . . .' Peter joked. But the *Thunder*'s captain didn't want to calm down. He radioed the *Bob Barker* and said he was going to get his fishing gear back – either the easy way or the hard way.

'Once they passed us, I put more pitch on and we picked up speed; and for the first time they started chasing us,' Peter told me. 'I remember turning to the crew and saying that it felt like being charged by an angry bull running down the streets of Pamplona.'

The *Thunder* chased the *Bob Barker* for three hours. Peter knew he could outrun her but kept his speed at just enough to give the *Thunder* the illusion that they could catch them. 'I wanted to give him hope that he could catch us,' he remembered, 'knowing that if he's moving at least he's burning fuel, and that brings us closer to ending this ordeal. You might think being chased by this criminal enterprise would be scary, but we were high-fiving and cheering because finally we were moving. Just the fact that we were making way and the fact that we were burning fuel again was like, finally the Great Drift is over.'

Three hours later it must also have occurred to the *Thunder*'s captain that he was using valuable fuel, because he shut down the engines once more. And so began the Great Drift Part 2.

The *Thunder*'s officers always wore balaclavas when on deck, wise to the fact that the less Sea Shepherd knew about them the better. They didn't want their faces on any law-enforcement database. The crew were less concerned, occasionally even taking photos of their own and waving through the *Thunder*'s windows at the *Bob Barker* and the *Sam Simon*, which had returned from Mauritius on 25 March to resupply their sister ship.

The illegal fishing industry is notorious for its role in human trafficking and using forced labour, and Peter and Sid decided to see what they could find out about their circumstances. The crew of the *Sam Simon* wrote down various questions that they stuffed into sealed plastic jars before launching the ship's inflatable. The boat sped across the heavy swell to bring them under the *Thunder*'s stern, and from there they lobbed some of the jars onto the ship's aft deck. Watching from the *Sam Simon*'s bridge, Sid could see one of the *Thunder*'s crew, his red overalls standing out against the darkness of the doorway he came from, as he picked up one of the jars and opened it.

He read: 'You have done nothing wrong. The captain and the owner must be brought to court to answer for their illegal fishing. Any information relating to the owners and officers of this ship will greatly help us. Yours sincerely, Peter Hammarstedt, Captain, the *Bob Barker*.'

One of the crew scribbled a message, placed that in the bottle and threw it back to the inflatable as it kept pace with the *Thunder*. Back on the *Sam Simon*, Sid opened the message. 'It's in Bahasa,' he said. The *Thunder*'s crew were Indonesian. Sid got the message translated and it said that the crew were worried – they didn't know they were fishing illegally.

Sid and Peter decided to send a second message to see if the crew were OK, and this time Alistair steered the *Bob Barker*'s inflatable towards the *Thunder*. As they neared its stern, a heavily built man in a grey T-shirt, his face obscured by a black balaclava, came onto the aft deck. He went to the stern and purposefully picked up a heavy length of chain. This he swung over his head and threw it at the launch, narrowly missing it.

Persistent as a wasp around your breakfast, Alistair steered the launch alongside and they threw their second message. Simon Ager, long-term crew member and the *Bob Barker*'s videographer and photographer, filmed the big man as he picked something up from the *Thunder*'s deck and hurled it at the RHIB. Simon's film captured the moment when the missile, a large bolt, some 7.5–10cm (3–4in) in diameter and heavy, hit Simon in the groin, causing him to grunt in pain, almost losing the camera. The launch beat a hasty retreat.

They've tried to ram us, Peter thought. *They've thrown chains and bolts at us. They're beginning to crack.*

DAY 110, 16,095KM (10,000 MILES)

Once the Great Drift had taken the two ships around the Cape of Good Hope, the *Thunder* turned on her engines and they began steaming northwards up the west coast of Africa and into the Gulf of Guinea, around 148km (92 miles) off the coast of the tiny country of São Tomé and Príncipe – the second-smallest in Africa, with a population of just over 220,000.

The night had started normally enough and the *Bob Barker*'s bridge crew, their faces dimly lit by the night lights, were maintaining their usual vigil when they saw a fire on the *Thunder*'s stern. Flames leaped high against the blackness and they could see the dense oily smoke, but it was too dark to make out what was happening.

As dawn broke, the crew saw that the fishing buoys that had been stowed on the *Thunder*'s decks had disappeared; then they realized something else was going on. Some of the *Thunder*'s crew began gathering on the aft deck wearing their life jackets. Then suddenly a sound like a car alarm began wailing over Channel 16 on the *Bob Barker*'s bridge radio – the international distress signal. This was interrupted by the *Thunder*'s captain himself.

'He says he's got a problem and they're sinking,' Alejandra translated. There was a stunned silence and sense of disbelief on the bridge. The ship didn't look any different than usual, but a life raft was lowered and some of the crew climbed down a ladder from the bulwark and started getting into it. Peter's first reaction was that this was a feint – that he would be obliged to rescue the crew in the life raft while the *Thunder* high-tailed it away, manned by a skeleton crew, and made for a West African country to offload their catch of toothfish before INTERPOL could arrive. That way there would be no evidence of the *Thunder*'s illegal fishing.

He called Sid in the *Sam Simon*, which by this time was steaming nearly 67km (41.5 miles) away, and asked them for their assistance. Sid urged caution – it was possible the *Thunder*'s crew could be armed – and told Peter they would be there in three hours. In turn, Peter told the *Thunder*'s captain that he would not pick up the crew until they were all in the boat, including the captain and chief engineer.

'You have to rescue the people,' was the response.

'Tell the son of a bitch,' Peter told Alejandra, 'tell him that his crew have attacked my crew and we can't take them on board until all 40 of them are in the life rafts.' But still the captain delayed.

'Tell him to get off his fucking boat so we can take him on board.'

Finally, all of *Thunder*'s crew were in the lifeboats and the *Bob Barker*'s RHIB approached them gingerly, well aware they could be overpowered at any time. They tossed a line to the life raft and towed them back to the *Bob Barker*, but didn't yet allow them on board. At this point the sea was lapping just below the *Thunder*'s aft hatch, around halfway between the deck and the sea, where the net-hauling gear is located. Peter knew that when the sea reached the hatch the *Thunder* would certainly sink. By now he had developed a new theory: that the captain had scuttled his ship in a bid to destroy the evidence of their illegal operations and to claim on insurance. He couldn't test that theory right now, nor stop the ship going down, but he could put a couple of his crew on board to see what they could find.

Meanwhile, as the *Sam Simon* drew nearer to the sinking ship, Sid was worried about bringing the 40 crew from the *Thunder* onto his ship. It would outnumber his own crew 2 to 1. 'It's hard to imagine how this day will end,' he said to himself.

With that he ordered that the stairs to the rear deck be cordoned off, and immediately his crew began putting plywood barriers in place. Sid had no intention of giving *Thunder*'s crew free reign over his ship.

The *Thunder*'s crew looked apprehensive and the officers sullen as they began absorbing their new reality; and the captain's mood soured further as he saw three of the Sea Shepherd crew climb on board. He hadn't bargained on that.

Peter and Adam kept their binoculars fixed on the *Thunder* and tension mounted – poking around a sinking ship is not for the faint-hearted.

The *Bob Barker*'s chief engineer, Erwin Vermeulen, and third mate, Anteo Broadfield, along with the ubiquitous Simon Ager, wearing a head camera and carrying a GoPro, carried out a rapid survey of the neat wood-lined bridge, grabbing a few box files and a computer hard drive. Then, with Erwin wondering whether they could find a way to stop the ship sinking, Simon's cameras captured their mad rush through the empty corridors and down clanging metal ladders into the darkness below. The sea had already flooded the engine room, so they diverted their attention to one of the holds – and there, shimmering in the beams of their flashlights, were stacks of white packages.

'It's all toothfish,' Anteo shouted up the ladder. 'Bags and bags of it.' And with that he reached underwater and grabbed one of them.

'Give them another five minutes then get them off,' Peter ordered as he continued watching from the *Bob Barker*. Finally, after what felt like an age of silence and no signs of movement, his crew members appeared on the deck and came down the ladder, clutching their spoils.

'All crew are back in the inflatable,' Alistair radioed.

Meanwhile, Priya Holmes woke to the announcement that the *Thunder* was sinking and had made for the *Bob Barker*'s aft deck. The ship looked the same as it had every day for the past 110 days. But when it began settling in the water she was filled with adrenaline and quiet, jittery and buzzing. 'I was imagining this multimillion-dollar vessel being scuttled for the sake of these Patagonian toothfish. It was really hard to swallow and it made me realize the scale of the industry, the amount of money that was involved; because it was such an incredible vessel, so for them to treat it as disposable was really quite shocking.'

After just a few hours, the *Thunder*'s stern began submerging into the calm sea while the bow began to rise, exposing the bulbous bow. Almost gracefully, the grey hull, so familiar now after their epic three-month pursuit, slid slowly into the water. Its Indonesian crew and their officers sat on the sides of their life rafts looking silently on. Simon Ager was filming the whole scene – conscious, I wonder, of how rare a thing it is to film a ship sinking. The officers of the *Thunder* shouted at him to stop.

'Keep filming,' Peter ordered.

One of the officers, a heavily built, shaven-headed and tough-looking man, looked towards the camera and gave it his middle finger, and then glanced away. For all his bravado, he looked defeated and humiliated.

The bow rose higher and higher, framed by the calm sea and the cloudless sky, and then the *Thunder* finally slipped below the waves. After 110 days, the longest chase of an illegal fishing vessel in maritime history had come to an end.

A moment passed and then the air trapped inside the ship frothed to the surface and foamed for a minute or so. The *Thunder*'s officers cheered. The evidence would soon be at the bottom of the sea.

'It's counter to every narrative you have in your head of what a shipwreck would be like,' Alistair recalled. 'You don't imagine people celebrating it as their ship sinks beneath the waves.' There was no sign left on the ocean's surface that anything had ever been there.

Only then did Sid allow the rescued seamen to board his ship, one by one. Each one was registered and searched as they came on board and then confined to the rear deck. The officers were asked what had happened and either gave evasive answers or claimed they'd been asleep. Once everyone was accounted for, the two Sea Shepherd ships sailed for São Tomé.

'I remember asking myself: why, out of all the places where the *Thunder* could have sunk their ship, why did they choose the waters of São Tomé?' Peter told me. 'They could have sunk it anywhere. They could have sunk it off Argentina, they could have sunk it off the east coast of Africa. But when I saw the São Toméan coastguard boats, with a range of just 20 miles [32km], it was clear to me that the captain of the *Thunder* knew that the São Toméan coastguard wouldn't have the resources to come out with submersible pumps and salvage his boat. He knew the ship would go down.'

Peter figured that the captain of the *Thunder* sank his ship in São Toméan waters for the same reason that the Gulf of Guinea is beset with piracy, narco-trafficking, human trafficking and the transshipment of illegally caught fish. These West African countries didn't have the resources to monitor and control their territorial waters. The realization gave Peter the germ of an idea, but right now there was more pressing work to do.

By an unfortunate fluke, the captain of the *Thunder* could hardly have chosen a worse place to sink his ship. São Tomé is a former Portuguese colony. Mario Alcaide was a native Portuguese speaker and as soon as news of the *Thunder*'s scuttling reached him he leaped into action. He contacted the regional Maritime Rescue Coordination Centre (MRCC) in Abuja, Nigeria, which would in turn coordinate with its counterpart in São Tomé.

Mario had been worried whether São Tomé would be interested or able to prosecute the officers of the *Thunder*. 'One of those cases of it's not my monkey, not my circus,' he told me. *Thunder* was not a São Toméan vessel, the crew were not São Toméan, the company that owned the *Thunder* was not São Toméan and the ship had not fished in São Tomé. Moreover, São Tomé was not a party to CCAMLR. Mario needed to find some legal hook.

His next step was therefore to examine São Tomé's penal code to find laws that the authorities could use to prosecute the crew of the *Thunder*. He settled on the 'Al Capone strategy': in the end, the infamous American gangster had been jailed for tax evasion rather than murder; so, Mario now came up with charges of pollution, reckless driving, forgery and negligence, and he found a willing collaborator in a young São Toméan prosecutor. Mario also brought with him a colleague who focused on human trafficking and another person from INTERPOL's National

Central Bureau (NCB) who spoke Bahasa. This gave the investigators a distinct advantage, because the *Thunder*'s officers could not.

Mario's next job was to assist the São Toméan prosecutors interviewing the officers and crew of the *Thunder*. Mario's interviewing technique was one of the skills he was most proud of and he dedicated a lot of time to it. 'For me, it's crucial,' he explained. 'The type of chairs, the angle between the natural light and the eyes of the suspect, my position facing the door, the type of table that we have between us and the disposition of the team in the room. But everything was the opposite of what it should have been. The suspects should have a very hard and very uncomfortable seat; the walls need to be as sterile as possible. It's very psychological.'

One of the most important suspects was the fishing master Juan Manuel Patiño Lampon, the man who had thrown a chain and the large bolt that hit Simon Ager as he filmed from the RHIB. 'This guy was very aggressive,' Mario remembered. 'He was 1 metre 90 [6ft 2in] and a very strong fisherman. I remember when he came to the room he had tears in his eyes – full of rage at his being there. He didn't recognize any rights of São Tomé to be interviewing him or interrogating him, let alone INTERPOL.'

Lampon, still aggressive, sat on the edge of the chair. Mario looked at him analytically, noting his body language, and thought to himself that this was a guy who was not expecting to be there that long. This was not where Mario wanted him – he was unlikely to give anything away in this mood. Mario handed him a bottle of water, the same as he did with all the suspects they interviewed, but Lampon swept it aside. 'I don't need it,' he spat out.

'I'm done with this guy,' Mario thought to himself. 'I won't get anything out of him.' He knew he had to change tack and decided to play nice cop. Mario asked Lampon if he had ever been on board the *Thunder* before, or if this was his first trip. It was a question he already knew the answer to. He knew from the *Thunder*'s documented port calls exactly where the ship had been and when. For good measure, he also knew all about Lampon, his life, his home address and his family. Mario pressed him further, asking whether he had been in this particular port on specific dates. The answer was always no. And then Mario played his trump card.

He took out a sheaf of papers and started riffling through them. Then he turned to the prosecutor and said they would need to start a new criminal case against the captain of the *Thunder* because, based on Lampon's denials, the captain had evidently presented false declarations to the relevant maritime authorities on all these port visits. 'This means we can jail the captain,' Mario said.

Lampon, trapped by his lies, slumped into his chair, reached for the bottle of water and started mumbling to himself. *Got you*, Mario thought. Gradually Lampon began 'remembering' his previous trips and even smiled a few times. By the end of the interview, he had admitted they were fishing for Antarctic toothfish.

'Everyone has their own breaking point. Everyone has their own point of rupture,' Mario reflected.

With the sinking of the *Thunder* came the disappearance of any hard evidence that would allow the investigators to forensically examine the fishing gear on the ship with the nets recovered by the *Sam Simon*. The last-minute boarding of the *Thunder* by Erwin Vermeulen, Anteo Broadfield and Simon Ager would be crucial to the case.

The rules of evidence demanded that to preserve the chain of custody, evidence should be handed over to the authorities of either the ship's flag state or its first port of call. Nigeria had already revoked the *Thunder*'s flag, which left only one option. The *Bob Barker* would forgo a well-deserved victory tour that Sea Shepherd's founder, Paul Watson, had arranged for the *Sam Simon* and the *Bob Barker* in Paris and instead make for their home port of Bremerhaven, Germany. There, the evidence was collected by the German police and handed over to the São Toméan prosecutor, Kelve Nobre de Carvalho, who INTERPOL had flown in. Carvalho then took it to the nearest São Toméan consulate, in Amsterdam. The chain of custody was unbroken.

The consulate facilitated a secure office and, with a digital-forensics team provided by the Canadian Department of Fisheries and Oceans, the investigators extracted and analysed key evidence from the computer seized from the *Thunder*'s bridge.

Mario meanwhile began examining the film footage taken by the cameras of the *Bob Barker*'s boarding party during *Thunder*'s final moments. He noted the layout and contents of the bridge, the crew members' courageous descent into the flooded engine room and the holds containing the white-wrapped packages of toothfish. But something else caught his eye too.

'They passed in front of the whole electric board of the vessel and you could see that the batteries still had power,' he recalled. 'That was important for the prosecution, because they were saying that they could not save the vessel, that the engine room was flooded and that the pumps were not functioning because the vessel had no power. But the indicators showed that the ship did have power. That indicated that they did it on purpose.'

*

On 12 October 2015, Alistair McDonnell was leading a panel on the role of INTERPOL in tackling IUU fishing at the first International Symposium on Fish Crime, held in Cape Town, South Africa. On the same day, the verdicts were due at the trial of the officers of the *Thunder*. Just as Alistair was wrapping the session up, Mario rushed to the podium and handed over a piece of paper. Alistair looked at it and then read it out.

The Chilean captain of the *Thunder*, Luis Alfonso Rubio Cataldo, together with the ship's chief engineer, Agustín Dosil Rey and the first engineer, Luis Miguel Pérez Fernández, were charged with pollution, reckless driving, forgery and negligence and placed under house arrest. Cataldo was sentenced to three years in prison while his two fellow Spanish crew members received jail terms of two years and nine months and two years and eight months respectively. Together they were fined, in total, more than €15 million. It had been an expensive trip.

There was a moment's silence and then everyone in the room began cheering and clapping. For the team at INTERPOL and for all the countries that had played such a crucial role, this was a tangible moment of success. 'This isn't just a victory for our country,' Frederique Samba Viegas D'Abreu, the attorney general of São Tomé and Príncipe, told *The New York Times*. 'It's a victory for the oceans and against these international crime syndicates that have operated for too long above the law.'

But had the architects of the crime – the owners of the *Thunder* – got away with it?

A few weeks after *Thunder*'s sinking, Peter was telephoned by an insurance investigator in Spain. 'He told me he was representing an insurance company that had received a claim from a guy called Florindo

Gonzáles, based out of Galicia in northern Spain,' Peter recalled. 'This guy was claiming about US$1.7 million for the total loss of his vessel, a ship called *Thunder*, including 33 tons of Patagonian and Antarctic toothfish.'

I imagine a wry smile must have passed Peter's lips as the investigator said someone had given him his number and asked if Peter had ever heard of the ship or had any information about it.

'How much time do you have?' Peter asked.

In 2016, in cooperation with the Ministry of Agriculture, Livestock, Fisheries and Food of Gabon, Sea Shepherd intercepted a shrimp trawler. Only 0.3 per cent of its catch were shrimps, the rest being other marine life. The fisheries minister ordered the arrest of the ship and suspended the shrimp fishery. This set Peter thinking.

A three-hour inspection, carried out in cooperation with government authorities, had shut down three ships, while it had taken him 110 days to shut down the *Thunder*. These countries had the authority and the will to enforce the law, but not the means. Sea Shepherd had the means: their ships and volunteer crews, their engineers and deck officers. Sea Shepherd's donors even provided the fuel.

The collaborations that began in Gabon spread to other countries, including Liberia, The Gambia, Sierra Leone, Namibia and Tanzania, and over the next few years these combined operations led to the arrest of 85 illegal fishing vessels. 'I credit the captain of the *Thunder* for those arrests,' Peter reflected. 'Had it not been for him taking us to the Gulf of Guinea and sinking his ship there, those 85 vessels would not have been arrested.'

When I interviewed Peter in the summer of 2023, he told me: 'Eight or nine years have passed since the chase and it still blows my mind that there were twenty-six people on board, with mortgages and families and homes, many of whom were volunteers who weren't being paid to be on board the ship. And they were willing to commit to just being on the ship and being at sea for two years. That just blows my mind. That's the kind of dedication and passion that I think is rare to find in any organization. I think it's very special that I had that on my ship.'

In conjunction with INTERPOL, the Spanish authorities raided several Galician fishing syndicates linked to the *Thunder*. The *Thunder*'s owner, Florindo González Corral, was fined €8.2 million. In addition, the syndicates were hit with a 12-year fishing ban and cut off from government fishing subsidies.

'We would never have known who the actual beneficial owner was had it not been for him claiming insurance on the loss of the vessel and its illegal cargo,' Peter said. 'It's remarkable how arrogant, how brazen, how confident these guys are that they're going to get away with it.' He added that he'd always thought the *Bob Barker* had a 'karmic debt to pay', as a former whaling ship. 'After the *Thunder* sank, that debt had been repaid.'

4

LEAVE NO TRACE

'But you have to understand one thing. Who is a Wagner soldier? He's someone who isn't accountable, has no legal existence, no clear status. He acts with absolute impunity. He will never answer for his actions, for his crimes in a court of law. So everything depends on his personality.'

—Marat Gabidullin, former Wagner mercenary
interviewed by Radio France Internationale, 21 May 2022

In 2014, Dmitry Utkin, a tough-looking, shaven-headed and highly decorated former lieutenant colonel with the Russian military intelligence service (the GRU), together with the oligarch (and close ally of Vladimir Putin) Yevgeny Prigozhin, formed the private military company (PMC) Wagner. Many believe Utkin named it after his own military callsign, which in turn was Adolf Hitler's favourite composer.

In its early years, this mercenary army saw service during the Russian invasion of Crimea and then in Libya, Syria and Mali. Although technically illegal in Russia, Wagner became a deniable arm of Russian foreign policy and has committed atrocities wherever it has set foot, most recently in the Russian attack on Ukraine.

In late 2017, Wagner set foot in the Central African Republic (CAR). What happened there gives a chilling insight into the direction of both Wagner's and Putin's global aspirations.

NATHALIA

I first met the then 30-year-old Nathalia Dukhan in 2013 when she joined Global Witness as an investigator, and she was adamant about what she wanted to investigate. Timber from the rainforests of the CAR was flowing into European ports in contravention of EU laws and was funding the brutal Séléka regime, a coalition of armed groups, including Chadian and Sudanese combatants, which had recently seized power in CAR and plunged the country, once more, into a brutal, grinding conflict. Nathalia knew the CAR well and also knew the sad truths behind so much foreign investment in Africa, from 19th- and 20th-century colonialism to the present day.

Diving deep into this bloody business, she and her colleagues at Global Witness carried out numerous undercover investigations into the timber trade, which resulted in the launch of our 2015 report 'Blood Timber'. The undercover footage Nathalia shot in the office of Nice-based French timber importer Tropica Bois captured the underlying problem. She asked the manager whether the war in CAR was a problem for their operation. 'There will always be threats,' the smartly dressed and urbane woman on the other side of the desk told her. 'But it's Africa. It's so common we don't really pay attention. It's not really a concern; it's not a war where they attack white people.' Nathalia was honing her skills as an investigator.

CENTRAL AFRICAN REPUBLIC, 1 JANUARY 1966

'This is Colonel Bokassa speaking to you. At 3am this morning, your army took control of the government. The Dacko government has resigned. The hour of justice is at hand. The bourgeoisie is abolished. A new era of equality among all has begun. Central Africans, wherever you may be, be assured that the army will defend you and your property [. . .] Long live the Central African Republic!

The words that crackled over people's radio sets that morning marked the beginning of decades of violence for the CAR, led first by Jean-Bédel Bokassa's infamously brutal and corrupt regime and then one despot after another. After Bokassa's downfall in 1979 by a French-led intervention, the country suffered six coups d'état, four of which were successful. The Bush War ran between 2004 and 2007 and then – following a brief interregnum – in 2013 the mainly Muslim Séléka rebel movement ousted then President François Bozizé. Reprisals by predominantly Christian militias known as the Anti-balaka took the form of massacres, torture, mass rapes and looting, and these armed groups ended up controlling most of the country, with the Séléka forces pervading in the north and east while the Anti-balaka exerted influence over the rest. The government effectively controlled nothing, but thanks to multiple UN interventions another coup was prevented.

In response to Bozizé's overthrow, the UN Security Council imposed an arms embargo on CAR. The task of trying to keep the peace fell to the African Union's International Support Mission to the Central African Republic (MISCA), the UN Multidimensional Integrated Stabilization Mission in the Central African Republic (MINUSCA) and France, the former colonial power.

This was the unenviable legacy Faustin-Archange Touadéra inherited when he was elected president in 2016. Eyeing the country he must now govern, Touadéra evidently felt that he needed more support. It was in this frame of mind that, in September 2017, he packed his bags for a trip: first stop, the United Nations General Assembly (UNGA); second stop, Russia.

SOCHI, RUSSIAN FEDERATION, OCTOBER 2017

Having said farewell to the Big Apple, President Touadéra, together with a small delegation that included his chief of staff, Firmin Ngrébada, arrived at the Russian Black Sea resort of Sochi. They were not there for a holiday.

Sergei Lavrov, Putin loyalist and Russia's minister of foreign affairs, welcomed the Central African delegation to a meeting that would not only change CAR but also be a key plank in President Putin's ambition to reclaim some of the former glory and power of the Soviet era. The official photograph of the meeting shows Lavrov, slouched in his chair, looking at his African guests over a small coffee table topped with a bowl of flowers; behind them is a backdrop of the flags of their two countries in what looks like a film-set library.

As its name suggests, CAR is about as close to the centre of the African continent as it's possible to get and covers a land area equivalent to France and Belgium combined. It is bordered by Chad to the north, Sudan and South Sudan to the east, the Democratic Republic of Congo to the south and to the west by the Republic of the Congo and Cameroon, which provides CAR's main route to the sea. The country's rich deposits of uranium, gold and diamonds, together with its forests, have over the years made it a magnet for a host of adventurers – most of them bad – and its long history of insecurity and conflict mean that CAR has always been ripe for exploitation by the unscrupulous. As it happened, the unscrupulous were well represented that day at Sochi.

The Central Africans and the Russians had a busy agenda ahead of them. Top of the list was the establishment of a Russian-owned gold-mining company in CAR, together with the allocation of the necessary licences and permits to exploit the country's riches. Russian mining specialists were to arrive in less than ten days.

Item two was security. The blandness of the minutes belies the significance of the subject matter: '[. . .] the parties agreed that the presence of "armed specialists of foreign origin" [. . .] could be justified in this context for the purpose of protecting mining areas. These specialists could be disguised as employees of a Sudanese security company.'

To enable this to happen, Russia requested a relaxation of the UN Security Council's arms embargo and noted that it would despatch 170 civilian instructors to CAR and that these would be '[. . .] of Russian nationality and were recruited by the Ministry of Defence of the Russian Federation from an association of primarily former military officers called the Officers Union for International Security [OUIS].'

The OUIS is run by former soldier Aleksandr Aleksandrovich Ivanov. Its logo depicts – in a fetching blue – two hands gently cupping the world; not a million miles away from the UN Refugee Agency (UNHCR) logo – an irony that would become palpable. The OUIS website describes them as '[. . .] an association of people advocating for peace and stability.' But the OUIS would prove to be not all that it seemed.

'Sensitizing' the population and making the president coup-proof also ranked high on the agenda, and the meeting's minutes record the Russian intention to help CAR with the dark arts of propaganda and surveillance. On the hardware side, armoured vehicles and the provision of snipers were promised.

The transference of funds was a problematic issue for both sides because all the banks in CAR used correspondent banks in France to make transfers, which would allow French scrutiny of all transactions. Not very helpful when you might have something to hide. Happily, the Central African side suggested an acceptable solution, which was to fly cash in by private jet – a methodology in which Putin's corrupt regime would undoubtedly be well versed.

The private jet would need somewhere to land, of course, and the parties agreed to an operating contract that would allow for a secure airport capable of handling heavy aircraft such as the huge Ilyushin Il-76 and Antonov military transports, meaning that private jets shouldn't have any problem at all.

Meanwhile, according to open-source intelligence outfit T-Intelligence, the arms shopping list included 900 Makarov pistols, 5,200 Kalashnikov assault rifles, 840 Kalashnikov light machine guns, 140 sniper rifles (mostly Dragunov), 270 rocket-propelled grenades (RPG), man-portable anti-tank rocket launchers, 20 man-portable anti-air defence systems and ammunition. All in all, enough to equip a small army – which was exactly the plan.

Pleased with their work, the Central African delegation returned home. On the Russian side there was a great rubbing of hands: Wagner, the mercenary army co-founded by Yevgeny Prigozhin, had secured their first foothold in the Central African Republic.

'Often people say there's no money in CAR; it's not interesting,' Nathalia told me. 'Well, actually, there are a lot of people travelling there and making a lot of money. The country is poor, but not for everyone.' Now that Wagner had a foothold, they were about to dip their toe into the water. The ripples they created were gentle at first. They began analysing the environment without trying to change anything; and they began to understand at a deep level how the country worked and what opportunities that may provide for them. And then they began to infiltrate.

NATHALIA

When Nathalia finished university in Belgium and the time came to think about the future, there was never any doubt in her mind about *where* she wanted to be; the trickier question was *what*. She had grown up and spent all her life in Africa and that was where she belonged. Equally, she wasn't blind to the problems and threats facing the continent she loved, and she passionately wanted to contribute in some way.

'I got the sense of some kind of shadowy forces threatening the freedom I'd experienced as a child and young adult moving around Africa and that was really painful to see,' she remembered. She could see a new colonialism in foreign powers, multinational corporations and a whole array of buccaneers that came to loot the continent, and it filled her with resolve.

'I thought that projects and programmes implemented by foreign development agencies, NGOs, etc., were failing to understand the dynamics,' she told me, 'and therefore failing to tackle the root causes of violence and insecurity. They were using dressings on a massive haemorrhage. I wanted to help unravel truth, help reshape some of the narratives and support a change in mentalities, both at local and international level.'

It was then that she decided that she would become an investigator and start to poke around some of the murky networks bent on exploiting the continent. She had no idea that this was a journey that would lead her to get a glimpse into hell.

BANGUI, CENTRAL AFRICAN REPUBLIC, 2010

Nathalia's plane touched down in Bangui at 10pm on a Saturday. She sniffed the night air as she got off the plane and sucked it in, her first breath in a new country. However, she could feel the tension as the car drove her through the low-rise streets, through police and army checkpoints, to where she was staying. She was struck by the darkness and the silence. No shops and, worse, no bars were open; no one was on the streets. It was as quiet as a morgue. For her, it was unheard of for an African city to be so dead in the evening; like a phantom city, she thought.

Nathalia had come to Bangui for a three-month stint helping a humanitarian agency. As the next day was a Sunday, she wanted to play tourist and asked her host to take her to the centre of town.

When they arrived in the city centre, 'My world collapsed,' Nathalia remembered. Bangui brought to her mind's eye the dusty desolate frontier towns in Western movies. 'I was silent as we were leaving and I thought to myself, "No way. I'm not going to spend one week here." I had been raised in Africa but I had never seen anything like it. It was like you were transported 40, 50 years back in time and nothing had changed.'

But within a week she had totally fallen in love with the place.

She had discovered the day clubs, where people arrive in the early afternoon and dance until midnight. 'I met young people like me, including Central Africans, and we started to go out,' she told me. 'And I felt that this country wasn't developed but it was so warm. People were extremely welcoming.' Nathalia and her new friends would dance as music from Central Africa, Congo and Cameroon thumped out over the central dance floor and people crowded together, gyrating to the rhythms, drinking beer and eating eggs with chilli sauce. She began to make lasting friendships, and when you talk to Nathalia today, despite the horrors that have taken place in CAR, it's no secret where her heart lies.

The nonprofit Nathalia was working for specialized in forest governance and forest community rights in Central Africa, covering Cameroon, CAR and Gabon. Over the next three years she travelled throughout western CAR and its rich rainforests. 'By the time I joined Global Witness I had visited all the logging companies operating in CAR and spent time in the rainforest with communities like the pigmies,' she said. 'I was working on how the timber trade between CAR and the EU could help forest communities, but then the Séléka took power.'

Nathalia took the last commercial flight that left Bangui's tarmac one afternoon in March 2013, landing in Douala, Cameroon. The Séléka took control of Bangui the next day at 7am, and nine months of chaos ensued.

The Kimberley Process Certification Scheme suspended the export of diamonds from CAR, but timber continued to flow through EU ports and elsewhere. 'And suddenly, I realized that I was fighting the wrong battle. That's when I decided to start investigating and expose some different dynamics: corruption, war profiteering, repression and violence,' Nathalia told me. 'And that's when I joined Global Witness.'

She worked with us for a couple of years but the pull of Africa was too strong. In 2015, Nathalia left to join the Washington, DC-based Enough Project, and then its sister organization, The Sentry, an investigative anti-corruption and conflict prevention organization co-founded by John Prendergast, a former director of African Affairs at the US National Security Council, and the actor George Clooney. As their CAR expert, Nathalia got down to the business of investigating the armed conflict that was tearing her adopted country apart.

Over the next few years, her detailed reports for The Sentry – made possible by the extensive networks Nathalia had built over years – were among the most authoritative available. In summarizing 'Fear, Inc.', her devastating 2018 exposé of one of CAR's most notorious warlords, Abdoulaye Hissène, Nathalia told the press:

'Mass violence is a billion-dollar business in the Central African Republic. Unscrupulous political and economic actors, including foreigners, fuel and perpetuate warfare for personal gain. By capturing the country's rich resources with the complicity of perpetrators of mass atrocities like Abdoulaye Hissène, these networks have sunk the people of the Central African Republic into a terrifying realm of deep injustice, crushing poverty, and overwhelming fear.'

In one of the poorest and most violent countries on the planet, where people could be massacred for no reason whatsoever, getting people to talk at all was an incredible feat. But this was Nathalia's special skill. These detailed dossiers represented years of painstaking work building relationships and, perhaps most importantly, empathy. Everything she had learned before was now going to be put to the ultimate test.

BERENGO, BOBANGUI, CENTRAL AFRICAN REPUBLIC, JANUARY 2018

Three months after Touadéra's fateful meeting with Sergei Lavrov at Sochi, an Ilyushin Il-76 military cargo plane touched down at the country's capital, Bangui, taxied to a halt and disgorged the first 'armed specialists of foreign origin', together with the first shipment of arms. A contingent of these specialists made their way to the tiny village of Bobangui, an hour's drive southwest of Bangui and home to Bokassa's palace, abandoned as of his overthrow in 1979. The building had gradually succumbed to the heat, humidity and tropical rains of equatorial Africa; now, a green carpet of algae floated towards the rusting slide in the rain-filled swimming pool, and black mould stained the once-white facades of a wider complex of rotting buildings.

Nathalia had been to Berengo before. She told me that as she explored the desolate place she stumbled across the two escape tunnels leading from the palace to the bush – a must-have for a dictator who might have to flee the next coup. She saw the rough drawings on the walls scribbled by a rag-tag of people that included the fighters of the Séléka and Anti-balaka armed groups, both of whom had used the palace as a training camp. It was a popular location. 'The Russians decided to use Berengo because it had its own tarmac runway where they could land heavy planes,' Nathalia told me. 'So, this is where they set up their military base. They wanted to be outside Bangui because they wanted to create a fortress, a place where you don't know what's going on.'

The former imperial palace began its reincarnation as a Wagner-run military training centre for Les Forces armées centrafricaines (FACA) – the Central African Armed Forces. The crumbling outbuildings and overgrown gardens and fields of the palace became home to FACA soldiers, dapper in their new Russian-supplied combat fatigues. Wagner's white instructors, clad in camouflage uniforms and baseball caps, with their holstered pistols at their sides, drilled their recruits in the dark arts of war: wielding their knives in hand-to-hand combat or charging towards the treeline, diving to the ground to spray hundreds of rounds from their Kalashnikovs and 12.7mm heavy machine guns at an imaginary enemy in the encroaching forest, then up again and forward. The old buildings provided a perfect stage set to practise street fighting – a useful skill, it would transpire – as these forces were to be sent on operations to villages and townships outside Bangui. Torture featured high on the curriculum as the students learned how to remove finger- and toenails, slice people's flesh or even hack off limbs. It was a master class in terror.

Wagner's first job was to provide security for the president, who was now a valuable Russian asset. From then on, when Touadéra appeared at political rallies and other public outings he was surrounded by masked and heavily armed Wagner mercenaries in full combat gear. This was just the beginning.

Nathalia knew that the game had changed, that something really serious was in the offing – but she didn't know exactly what. She had been reporting on Wagner for The Sentry and had exposed a proxy war between France and Russia in the CAR. The question for her now was: what does the world need to know that they don't know?

Her plan was to put together a seminal dossier on Wagner's business model, which was a simple one: state capture. She knew that obtaining first-class intelligence would be even more important than it had been before. The trouble was, it was going to be even harder to get. The security situation in CAR meant she could no longer travel there, but she could still work her sources. She could still travel to Cameroon, CAR's only trade route to the sea, through which heavy imports and exports are likely to route and which, with CAR's porous borders, was a natural bolthole for people fleeing the country. She could also talk to the Central African diaspora in Europe, plus her diplomatic contacts.

'What kept me motivated to keep working on CAR was because there were so few journalists working there, and I felt that the quality of the information that was leaving that country and sent to the world was relatively poor,' she told me. 'Many advocacy and research groups left after the big crisis in 2013 and 2014. Human Rights Watch published a few reports from time to time. Funding became difficult to obtain. But The Sentry persisted and with a small team and limited resources, we continued to investigate conflict motives and shed lights on dynamics that very few were exposing in such depth.'

Nathalia's earlier investigations had begun not when her plane landed in Africa but in the departure lounge in Paris. She was used to the flights to Cameroon and the mix of fellow passengers – Cameroonian families, businesspeople, a few aid workers, NGOs and tourists – but travelling to

Bangui was different. Here, the majority of passengers were foreign: Americans, Europeans and Russians.

The more trips she made, the more adept she came at working out what these people might do for a living. She noted the relaxed attitudes and casual dress of the humanitarian workers; that person might be a missionary, whereas others acted more privately – perhaps someone hired to gather intelligence for a company or even a state. And then there were those working for UN agencies, who live by their own codes. 'They don't need to wear a blue helmet for you to know they're working for the UN,' she said. Even in civilian clothes, the soldiers were obvious; whether regular armed forces or mercenaries, the tattoos and muscles usually gave them away. Two groups of people were almost totally absent on the Bangui flights: tourists and Central Africans themselves.

'This gives you first a taste of where you're going, then when you arrive you realize that this country is very special,' Nathalia told me. She described Bangui as a bubble in the middle of an ocean. 'You have the UN – thousands of people coming from the outside with big salaries, living in buildings built by the Lebanese community that are rented out for thousands of dollars per month. And then you have the Central Africans living side by side, doing their own thing. Then there's the rest of the country, bigger than France and Belgium combined, and mostly empty.'

Security was always a key concern for Nathalia when she travelled around the country, but one thing bothered her more than almost anything else. 'I was worried at night,' she told me. 'When you sleep, you're vulnerable. The days were OK because you're awake, you're on alert, you look at everything that is going on around you. But when you sleep that's when anything can happen, so it was always key for me to move. Never sleep for too long at the same place and choose a place that will keep you safe.'

She would only stay in places that had multiple escape routes, and her backpack was always ready to go. 'You also need to have friends, people you know, who will open their door and give you the space you need to organize your thoughts. So this all becomes part of who you are – in your DNA,' she said. She also had a practised modus operandi to help her work as well as she could with her sources, who could be either the victims or perpetrators of violence.

'You need to create an environment, an atmosphere so that people don't feel used. Some journalists can be quite extractive and some may not consider the consequences of their reporting,' Nathalia explained. 'It's hard to get someone to talk from the heart straightaway; you will need maybe two or three meetings, especially with the victims. You need to spend time and show that you're interested in them, not just their story,' she continued. 'So, when you start the interview, you're more kind of, "How are you feeling? Where do you live? Do you have children? What's their name?" It's important to be human, because it's a human story. Very often people told me that it was the first time that they had the opportunity to speak about what happened to them. And I could tell that it felt good, like a release in some cases.'

ABDOULAYE IBRAHIM

Abdoulaye Ibrahim is a friendly but serious-looking man. He had lived in France since 2003 but returned to his homeland, CAR, every couple of years. In 2014, he had looked on in horror when the Anti-balaka slaughtered Muslims in a spate of ethnic cleansing; and in 2016 he was in Bangui as Faustin-Archange Touadéra was campaigning to be president. Abdoulaye had not been involved in politics but found himself close to the heart of power by dint of his marriage: his wife's big brother was Sani Yalo, a wealthy but controversial businessman and an adviser to Touadéra.

Abdoulaye was there when, in the lead-up to the elections, Touadéra spoke at the central mosque in the battle-scarred Muslim neighbourhood known as PK5 that had been the scene of ferocious fighting during the recent war.

'Listen,' Touadéra told the people gathered there. 'I am a Christian, but if I take power and it is to massacre you, to order that you be massacred, may God prevent me from taking power.' The Muslim community, who had been living in fear and terror for years, lapped it up. 'That's what motivated us to say that this is the man we needed, we had to support him, even if he is not from our community,' Abdoulaye told me.

When Touadéra's campaign prevailed, Abdoulaye was there in the crowded sports stadium for the inauguration and cheered along with the rest of the crowd when the newly elected president theatrically grabbed the national flag and tugged it away from the military officer presenting it to him – a gesture both proud and defiant. Abdoulaye felt he could no longer remain just an onlooker over his country's misfortunes.

'I entered politics because of the war between Muslims and Christians that took place between 2013 and 2016,' he said. 'There were few Muslim intellectuals who could protect this community; when I was in Bangui between 2014 and 2015 I saw the atrocities against the Muslim community, when too few people stood up to denounce the crimes. It was a break from the old political class because he (Touadéra) was not in a political party; he was working class and a former university professor. I thought perhaps a new political class will change the mentality and the system that is in place.'

Abdoulaye's sense was right: the system would change beyond recognition. And, although he didn't know it then, he would find himself at the heart of that change. Little did he realize what a dangerous journey this was going to be.

Valery Nikolayevich Zakharov, a former official of the GRU, arrived in Bangui in 2018 as chief security adviser to Touadéra. He was also the de facto head of Wagner's CAR operation and it was his job to spread the organization's tentacles throughout the country.

Tall, balding and paunchy, Zakharov gave the appearance of a cheerful, affable man – and a talented one too, judging by his media interviews. Whether claiming to an Al Jazeera TV crew at Wagner's Berengo training base that the civilian instructors busily engaged in simulating the slaughter of their opponents in the middle distance over his left shoulder were in fact Russian reservists and certainly nothing to do with Wagner, or claiming that Russia's interest in the country was humanitarian, he demonstrated he could ward off awkward questions and shamefacedly lie without batting an eyelid.

One of his main tasks was to implement the Sochi agreement, and the first item on its agenda was the key focus: Wagner's takeover of the country's natural resources.

As Abdoulaye became further enmeshed in CAR's political scene, he began to get an unparalleled fly-on-the-wall view of Wagner's unfolding strategy. A key part of this strategy was the manipulation of CAR's political system and business environment for their own ends.

'According to the constitution of 2015, before setting up a mining company in CAR it's necessary to present a convention to the National Assembly for approval,' Abdoulaye explained to me. 'But the president of the National Assembly, Abdoul Karim Meckassoua, blocked the mining conventions, so Zakharov simply "bought" the deputies.' Meckassoua was duly ejected from his post in October 2018, later impeached and eventually fled the country. Zakharov had got rid of an annoying obstacle and laid one of the crucial foundation stones for the Russian takeover of CAR. 'Once they ejected Meckassoua,' said Abdoulaye, 'they installed Laurent Ngon-Baba, and that's when they got it all [. . .] The National Assembly had come to their cause and laws were passed, in haste, even at night. Then, once Wagner had installed their system, they started to show their face.'

With the annoying hurdle of the National Assembly taken care of, Zakharov was free to oversee the creation of a network of CAR-registered companies. Among them, Lobaye Invest, Midas Resources and Diamville controlled gold and diamond mining; while the varied portfolio of Bois Rouge and Maison Russe included brewing beer, teaching Russian and acting as an economic hub for Russian investors. In addition, as per the minutes of the Sochi meeting, which noted that the civilian specialists 'could be disguised as employees of a Sudanese security company', Wagner's troops came under the umbrella of Sewa Security Services. All of these operations were ultimately linked to Yevgeny Prigozhin. The skeleton was now in place; the next job was to flesh it out.

Having laid the foundations for Wagner's venture into Central Africa, Zakharov's tenure ended in 2021. He was replaced by his former assistant Dmitry Sytii and Vitalii Perfilev, the respective bosses of Lobaye Invest and Maison Russe. Sytii was also alleged to be a veteran of the Internet Research Agency, the Prigozhin-founded troll farm that interfered in the

2016 US presidential election, and his particular skill was the manipulation of public opinion. Perfilev took control of security and defence. Between them, these two men controlled Wagner's main portfolios of security, economics, politics and propaganda.

The third member of the triumvirate was the boss of the OUIS, Aleksandr Ivanov. In addition to the OUIS's stated mission of advocating for peace and stability, Ivanov oversaw spying on mobile phone and satellite communications to ensure coup-proofing and to help bolster Wagner's growing political and military repression.

THE MIDAS TOUCH

Gold had long featured in the CAR's traditions, with farmers sometimes splitting their year between mining – which enabled them to pay for imported goods like soap, oil and wheat – and farming. The ability of ordinary citizens to augment their income from gold was about to change.

On 4 April 2018, just six months after the Sochi meeting and with the National Assembly's blessing, Wagner affiliate Lobaye Invest obtained permits to exploit gold and diamonds at seven sites in the remote mining area of Yawa. Young men perched precariously on a series of earthen ridges that separated the gigantic water-filled pits they had dug by hand, feverishly shovelling away at the yellow-brown soil in search of treasure they would be forced to hand over to the Russians.

Wagner gradually took control of gold and diamond mines all over the country and by 2023 their mining operations were earning the group around US$1 billion per year, with the gold and diamonds being flown out on Russian military transports helping to alleviate the sanctions that hit

Russia following their invasion of Ukraine. The US TV station CBS News tracked one of these transports, a massive Ilyushin Il-76 military freight plane. Shortly after taking off from Bangui, it turned off its transponder and 'flew dark' across Africa. It turned up again when it landed in the United Arab Emirates, coinciding with the arrival of another Russian freight plane out of St Petersburg. The planes shared eight hours together on the tarmac before returning to their starting locations. Plenty of time to swap cargos, you might think. Next, Wagner turned their eyes towards CAR's rich rainforests.

On 9 September 2020, Société industrie forestière de Batalimo (IFB), headed by one Laurence Nassif, applied for a permit to exploit the Ngoto forest in CAR's Lobaye region. The permit was subsequently cancelled, only to be immediately replaced by another with the same coordinates – this new concession being allocated to a company called Bois Rouge. This caught the attention of a small group of volunteers working with French organization OpenProject, operating under the banner All Eyes On Wagner (AEOW), who had made it their collective mission to uncover as much as possible about Wagner's global activities. They decided to dig deeper into this deal.

On paper, Bois Rouge was owned by a businesswoman from CAR, but the team at AEOW noticed that when the company exhibited at a trade fair in Shanghai called 'Together Towards Global Green Supply Chains: A Forest Products Industry Initiative' in October 2019, it was listed as a Russian company and was represented by sales manager Artem Tolmachev.

Photos from the timber concession show a preponderance of white men and Russian-made machinery. The team at AEOW analysed 2021 and 2022 trade data that showed that there were 28 transactions between

Bois Rouge and a company called Broker Expert, located at 196084, St Petersburg, Tsvetochnaya. AEOW also discovered that Broker Expert was trading with other Wagner/Prigozhin entities, including Meroe Gold in Sudan. Broker Expert's phone number is also linked to several other entities, including a company called Concord LLC, which listed Yevgeny Prigozhin as its ultimate beneficiary.

In a May 2023 CBS News report, grainy footage secretly taken at night captures a checkpoint on the border between CAR and Cameroon. Old 205-litre (45-gallon) oil drums, filled with concrete, support a red-and-white striped pole road barrier manned by armed Wagner mercenaries. This barrier was raised as trucks loaded high with logs and sawn timber passed through on their way to the Cameroonian border town of Garoua-Boula and onwards from there for the 800-km (497-mile) journey to the port of Douala. As reporter Debora Patta discovered while posing as a timber buyer, each shipment carries a Sauf-Conduit International – a diplomatic free pass issued by the CAR government – ensuring no annoying searches at the border. Patta followed the trucks to Douala and learned from officials that the import of timber from CAR and export of it from Cameroon was a smooth, hassle-free operation and one that has become another key earner for Wagner.

ABDOULAYE IBRAHIM, 2018–2019

With elections due in December 2020, the end of President Touadéra's first term of office was approaching. But he faced a few significant snags.

'Touadéra was not a soldier, so he didn't have the loyalty of the army,' Nathalia explained to me. 'Nor did he have the support of a broad political class.' He had won the 2016 elections with the support of various political parties but didn't have one of his own. What happened next may have remained concealed in the shadows had it not been for one man who was close to the heart of power in CAR.

After Abdoulaye fled the country, Nathalia tracked him down. What she learned from him was confirmation of what many Russia and CAR watchers suspected but did not know. 'Wagner had a policy from the beginning,' he told her. 'It was long term, but I only saw things step by step; and it is only now that I can see the route they took, how they arrived, how they established their tactics and how they installed themselves.'

Zakharov was acutely aware that when Touadéra had taken power he had done so without a political party, and now Russia's candidate was weak. The backing he had received from other parties had dried up, he wasn't popular in CAR and he had lost the support of regional heads of state. With the next election on the horizon, this wasn't a situation the Russians could live with. So, with a remarkable pragmatism, Russia decided to create a party for him – and Abdoulaye Ibrahim was an important cog in the machine.

'Zakharov knew that for the Russians to perpetuate their contracts and stay longer in the Central African Republic, it was necessary for Touadéra to have a political party,' Abdoulaye told Nathalia. 'This is when Zakharov set up Le mouvement Cœurs unis – the MCU [United Hearts Movement]. He was the creator, the initiator. He set up the organization. Wagner sent key Central African figures to Russia to learn how to set up a political party, how to organize all the founding documents. The MCU began in Russia.' Inexorably the party became more influential, helped by the Russian-inspired removal of powerful politicians who were potential blockers to Wagner's ambitions. One of these was the president of the parliament, and another the president of the constitutional courts. The latter was crucial because, like so many before him around the world, Touadéra and his Russian backers wanted to remove presidential term limits – and here the constitutional court was the chief blocker. Both roles were replaced by people closer to the Russians.

'The Russians needed an ally so they literally hijacked the political institutions so that it served their agenda,' Nathalia explained. 'They also started to bring their military into the UN, the MINUSCA, and so they infiltrated the UN system. They've infiltrated almost every part of the country, so that they know precisely what is going on, where they can push the buttons and when.'

As a finishing touch, the server of the CAR National Election Authority was located in Russia.

Abdoulaye was tasked with setting up MCU political cells in France and didn't return to Bangui until August 2019. There he was given a new job. This fell under item three of the Sochi meeting agenda: the 'Sensitization of the population on the program of the President of the Central African Republic, strengthening a positive image to improve the investment climate.' If this sounds Orwellian, that's because it is.

'The nephew of the head of state, Arthur Piri, called me and told me to come to the MCU headquarters,' Abdoulaye recalled. He arrived there along with Ivanov and the two other key Wagner bosses, Vitalii Perfilev and Dmitry Sytii. The Russians wanted a spontaneous public demonstration of support for Russia's involvement in CAR. 'They told me to mobilize people in the Muslim neighbourhood of PK5 and to obtain some trucks. They wanted these people to go to the airport to celebrate the arrival of a shipment of Russian armoured vehicles. They would have to wave flags and demonstrate that they are very happy about Russia and everything,' he said.

Abdoulaye and his team mobilized around 750 people. 'We had to pay them and we provided them with T-shirts, baseball caps and Russian flags. Then, at 6am, we placed the people along the road where the tanks would pass. The Russians filmed all this and were pleased, and that's where my role as a mobilizer began.'

The next project he was given was to provide the crowds that would appear in a new movie that Wagner was putting together. Financed by Sytii's Lobaye Invest, *Tourist* would portray the mercenaries as the brave saviours of this grateful and conflict-ridden country. Sytii was, of course, the disinformation and propaganda specialist. 'For welcoming the tanks, Wagner gave us 15 million CFA francs and for the film *Tourist*, another 18 million CFA francs – approximately US$25,000 and US$36,000 respectively,' Abdoulaye recalled. The film turned out to be amazingly popular with the public, and in turn Russia had become popular, a key part of their strategy to turn the country against the West.

TURNING POINT, DECEMBER 2020

In the December 2020 national elections, former president François Bozizé was barred from standing as a candidate by the Constitutional Court, because he failed to meet the 'good morality' requirement. Given that the last time he took power had been by staging a coup, that he faced numerous accusations of torture and was also subject to UN sanctions, this probably wasn't an unreasonable ruling. Bozizé's next actions confirmed its wisdom.

He gathered together an alliance of six previously warring rebel groups under the umbrella of the Coalition of Patriots for Change (CPC) and embarked on a reign of terror. Polling stations were attacked and ballot boxes burned, but the elections took place as planned on 27 December. Touadéra was declared the winner with 53 per cent of the vote, but the CPC weren't finished. In January, Bozizé's rebel army launched a coup attempt, closing in on Bangui and taking several cities as they went. As the capital became increasingly threatened, Touadéra called on his allies for assistance, and a combination of FACA and UN forces together with Wagner fighters and Rwandan troops held them off. If Bozizé had been taught a lesson, Wagner had certainly learned one: if Bangui was at risk then so were their lucrative interests in the country.

'I think, for the very first time, Wagner realized that they were weak, that their system was weak and that had the coup succeeded they would be out of the country the next day,' Nathalia told me. A new phase of Wagner's gradual takeover was about to begin.

Over the next few weeks, the Antonovs and Ilyushins of the Russian Ministry of Defence disgorged hundreds more men onto the tarmac at Bangui. They had given up the pretence that these were civilian instructors – these were heavily armed mercenaries, and with them came an array of weaponry previously unknown in CAR. At Bangui, armoured vehicles and an assortment of other arms were unloaded as combat helicopters and other aircraft touched down. The UN Panel of Experts on CAR noted: 'deliveries of material in support of State security forces were observed at a pace unprecedented since the establishment of the arms embargo in 2013.'

Although the Kremlin had told the UN Security Council that the number of instructors never exceeded 550, they announced the deployment of 900 more, swelling Wagner's force in CAR to 2,600 troops. Wagner sensed their opportunity. The recruiting of troops by FACA was closely monitored by the UN, US and the EU, among others; but with Touadéra's support, Wagner avoided these restrictions and began to recruit a 5,000-strong parallel army to mount a counter-offensive against the CPC. CAR's military was morphing into a privatized force under Russian control. It was evidently time to seize the moment.

'These Wagner mercenaries were fighters, not instructors and were sent on military operations against the armed groups, backed by members of the FACA that they had started to train,' Nathalia told me. Her information was trickling in from what she calls the Arabic telephone network, but what she was hearing chilled her to the bone.

'The Muslim community is extremely well connected outside Bangui and we began hearing a lot of stories of villages being attacked, civilians being targeted; killed, tortured and raped on an alarming scale.' Nathalia talked of photos being circulated on social media showing prisoners of war being executed. 'We were seeing all the indicators that the situation was changing. For the first three years, Wagner had infiltrated the system and shaped it to work for them, and now they had started acting.' Wagner was now in full control of military operations throughout the country and from this point on their strategy was governed by a simple coda: leave no trace. With that simple guiding principle, Wagner launched a campaign of terror. The lessons learned at Berengo were about to be put into practice.

BAMBARI, CENTRAL AFRICAN REPUBLIC,
15 FEBRUARY 2021

On a main intersection of one of the predominantly Muslim gold-mining towns stands the Monument des Martyrs, an impressionist concrete sculpture of a man. The inscription marks the killings that took place there during the unrest that marked the dying days of former dictator Jean-Bédel Bokassa's regime in the 1970s.

A 15-year-old boy looked up as he heard and felt the thudding of the combat helicopter's rotor slicing through the heavy tropical air. He began to run but was cut down by a burst of machine-gun fire from the sky. His father ran to him but he too was shot. Claiming they were on the hunt for Séléka rebels, Wagner troops, comprising mercenaries from Russia, Syria and Libya – countries where Wagner operates – together with FACA soldiers, descended on the town.

A Muslim woman, Fatouma, gathered her two children and ran to what she hoped would be sanctuary inside the blue and ochre walls of the Taqwa mosque, joining other civilians sheltering there. But the same helicopter descended upon that sanctuary, machine-gunning it down in the belief that some of those in the mosque were CPC rebels. Wagner mercenaries and FACA soldiers burst in and opened fire indiscriminately. Fatouma's children were hit but survived; at least 12 people did not. Three men arrested outside the mosque were also killed. Locals claimed that none of them were connected to the CPC. Fighting continued all over the town well into the next day. CBS News reported that many of the bodies were taken to a pharmacy run by a man named Moubarak. He took on the grim task of counting the bodies and recording the names of those who had been killed. There were more than a hundred of them. Moubarak himself was abducted a few days later and neither he nor his list has been seen since. Leave no trace.

CBS News interviewed a woman called Madina in Cameroon, where she had fled with her son Usman and one of her daughters in the aftermath of the massacre. Usman told CBS how one of his sisters had been raped in the family home, which Wagner had commandeered, while another was taken to a Wagner base and suffered the same fate. 'She begged me for forgiveness and said she might as well be dead now,' Usman told the reporter. Meanwhile his brother had been shot by a sniper as he ran from the gold mine he was working at back into town to help his family. Madina, who had hidden under her bed for three days, concentrated on washing the bodies of the dead, according to Muslim ritual.

A subsequent UN report contained photos depicting the bullet-pocked and bloodstained walls of the mosque and the scorch marks that illustrated the intensity of the attack. A month after the massacre, a MINUSCA-led mission noted the grim checklist of a country that had become a living hell:

> Among the violations are reports of mass summary executions, arbitrary detentions, torture during interrogations, forced disappearances, forced displacement of the civilian population, indiscriminate targeting of civilian facilities, violations of the right to health, and increasing attacks on humanitarian actors.

The UN also expressed concern about the 'presence of "Russian advisers" at MINUSCA bases'.

Nathalia and a small team of investigators she had put together gathered information and worked with Clarissa Ward of CNN to put together a series of no-holds-barred news pieces reporting from deep inside CAR. Their filmed interviews with the survivors of these massacres and footage of those that were killed make grim but compulsive viewing. As Clarissa neatly summed up: 'Alongside Rwandan paramilitaries and CAR troops, [Wagner] are doing a lot less training and a lot more fighting, especially since a counter-offensive against rebel groups began in January.' CNN also noted that Russians had imported armoured personnel carriers, drones and combat helicopters, such as the Mil Mi-8 and Mil Mi-24.

The Russian government's response to a UN report detailing the atrocities committed by Wagner mercenaries during the massacre at Bambari was simply that 'Russian trainers are unarmed and not participating in hostilities.'

ABDOULAYE IBRAHIM

Up to now, Abdoulaye had willingly helped the cause and it felt good to be playing such an important role, but slowly and surely the atmosphere was changing. Gradually, as he began to see the Russian strategy materialize like a spectre taking corporeal form, Abdoulaye understood that he was a pawn in the Russian game – and that that was a dangerous position to play.

Abdoulaye Hissène, a notorious ex-Séléka warlord sanctioned by the UN, the US and others for atrocities he had committed, occupied (at Wagner's expense) the presidential suite at the Four Seasons Hotel, a clean and – for Bangui – affluent, Chinese-owned place, but one that still bore little resemblance to the swanky hotel group of the same name. It was there that he summoned Abdoulaye Ibrahim one day in April 2021.

Abdoulaye arrived at 4pm as requested and was directed not to Hissène's suite on the fourth floor, but instead through the ground-floor Chinese restaurant and then into the room next to the bar, which is where Hissène carried out his business trading gold and diamonds from the area his armed group controlled. The agenda would be different today. Abdoulaye entered to find Hissène with Ivanov, Sytii, another Russian and a translator. Whatever Abdoulaye had imagined, he wasn't expecting what came next. 'We want to make you a proposal,' they told him.

'They wanted to record my voice for a broadcast,' Abdoulaye told Nathalia. 'They said that I must pretend to be a general of the CPC rebels and that I was to call on all the armed groups to attack Wagner bases throughout the country and to kill as many mercenaries as possible. There was an agreement and a ceasefire between the CPC and the regime. This agreement had to be broken, they explained. This would allow Wagner to justify breaking the peace agreement.' He was referring to a peace and security mini-summit hosted by a regional intergovernmental body, the International Conference on the Great Lakes Region, in April 2021, in which the terms of the ceasefire had been made clear:

> The Heads of State and Government welcomed the results achieved and mandated the Government of the CAR to implement the conclusions of the Heads of State through a ceasefire that would create a climate conducive to peace and national reconciliation.
>
> The Heads of State and Government urge the armed groups not to carry out actions that jeopardize the ceasefire, which must be respected in its entirety.

It was a chilling insight into the creation of a 'false flag' operation, with Abdoulaye playing an unwilling and anonymous but key role. He tried as much as he could to refuse but, sandwiched between the mercenaries of Wagner and a feared warlord, had nowhere to turn. 'I told them my voice was known, but they said they would disguise my voice,' Abdoulaye explained. They gave me 500,000 CFA francs and then they left. I had no choice. We had become hostages.'

The day after he made the recording, Abdoulaye's electronically disguised voice was broadcast on the Wagner-funded Radio Lengo Songo. In addition to the radio, a very important medium in a country with poor internet access, Wagner bought 200 computers and established a troll farm based in the presidential palace. 'They specialized in social media,' Abdoulaye explained. 'They put out faked images like the French Army stealing gold bars, or the videos of happy crowds welcoming Wagner and cheering Russia.'

The final straw for Abdoulaye came in January 2022.

The predominantly Muslim Fulani people are traditionally cattle herders and one of their leaders in CAR was Issa Manou. Like Abdoulaye, Issa Manou was a strong MCU sympathizer and donor and, as the owner of a farm and large herds, provided the MCU campaign with meat, enabling them to invite many people to eat at their headquarters. Eager to help, when CPC rebels closed the only road between Bangui and Douala in Cameroon – the only road that supplies Bangui – Manou agreed with his fellow herders that he would take 200 million CFA francs to Douala by plane to pay various business partners to ensure the continuation of their business relationships. But as he waited for his plane in Bangui he was met by the director general of customs, Frédéric-Théodore Inamo – who is also one of Touadéra's nephews – and led away.

'I was in Sarandji's office,' Abdoulaye recalled, referring to former prime minister and current president of the parliament Simplice Sarandji, the executive secretary of the MCU, 'and we were taking stock of the political cells. Then Sarandji's director of cabinet, Male Payo, came in and said that Issa Manou has come to see you. Sarandji asked him to wait two minutes and then, in front of me, he called Touadéra's director of security, the feared Colonel Wananga. He told him that Manou had already arrived. We walked out of his office and I saw Issa Manou accompanied by two gentlemen in the reception room. Sarandji told me to wait. I was talking to someone when I saw a vehicle pull up. Members of the Presidential Guard got out and entered the headquarters, then took away three people.'

Abdoulaye recalled that when he returned the following day, Male Payo said they had discovered a bullet in Manou's pocket. 'They took him away and killed him,' Abdoulaye said, then paused. 'I didn't believe it,' he added, the shock of these events still in his voice.

Silence surrounded Issa Manou's disappearance and indeed the disappearance of the 200 million CFA francs, until Abdoulaye heard the official version of events on the radio some weeks later. According to the broadcast, Issa Manou had left home that day in his black Toyota Land Cruiser Prado, with a driver, saying that he had a meeting with his friend Sarandji – but Manou never arrived. When questioned, his driver said that the car had been stopped and he had fled while Issa Manou was kidnapped. Sarandji meanwhile said he neither knew nor had even heard of Issa Manou.

'I was an eyewitness to his arrest at the MCU headquarters,' Abdoulaye told me. 'I stopped going to the MCU office. I went back to France and in

January 2022 I submitted my resignation to leave the party permanently.' And that's when Abdoulaye became one of Nathalia's most important sources, laying bare the truth at the centre of power in CAR.

BOYO, CENTRAL AFRICA REPUBLIC, 6–13 DECEMBER 2021

One militiaman described a typical attack to Nathalia. 'When we go on a mission [there are] three Land Cruisers of Russians, two Land Cruisers of national forces, and three Land Cruisers with Anti-balaka and [UPC]. We're given the weapons and outfits, kalash and sometimes 12.7,' he said, referring to the 12.7mm heavy machine gun. 'The Russians tell us that drones flew over the villages and all the men in the villages are CPC rebels, they have just hidden their weapons in the bush [. . .] so we must kill them all.'

In the case of Boyo, the only variation from this theme was the make of the vehicle. According to the UN Office of the High Commissioner for Human Rights (OHCHR), in November 2021 around 240 FACA soldiers and Anti-balaka militia led by Wagner mercenaries climbed aboard six Russian-made Ural military trucks in their training camp at Bambari.

The convoy headed northeast through the bush to Tagbara, around 50km (31 miles) away. From there they headed southwest on foot through the village of Zoumako and passing through Atongo-Bakari before reaching their target, the town of Boyo. It was dawn on 6 December 2021. What happened over the next eight days was trademark Wagner. Carnage.

The Anti-balaka, led by a man named Edmond, leaped down from their trucks. They were dressed in civilian clothes, some little more than rags, and garlanded with lucky charms – rough squares of stitched multicoloured fabric and leather hanging from rope necklaces and headbands. Some carried battered homemade guns, others Kalashnikovs and grenades; most carried a knife or machete. Amid sporadic gunfire that killed one young girl, harsh commands were barked out as the Muslim men of Boyo were ordered to gather in the marketplace. There they had to present their ID and pay between 3,000 and 5,000 CFA francs to be released. For good measure, the Anti-balaka started looting people's motorcycles and demanding between 10,000 and 40,000 CFA francs for their return.

Later that day, Edmond and two fellow Anti-balaka leaders summoned the acting mayor and two other representatives of the Muslim community and accused them of being UPC rebels. Then, ominously, they vowed to stay in Boyo for a month.

At dawn the next day, UPC fighters attacked the Anti-balaka but were outnumbered and beaten back. Now the gloves were off. Houses belonging to Muslims were torched and at around 7am between 700 and 800 people were forced to gather in and around the mosque, where Edmond brandished a grenade and threatened to kill them all. The acting mayor fell to his knees and, waving the national flag, begged him for mercy. The Anti-balaka let the women go but 17 Muslim men were executed around the town, beheaded or mutilated with machetes. The bodies were buried by Christians at the behest of the attackers, some of them still alive. One man was decapitated by a woman acting as Edmonds' aide-de-camp.

On the night of 8 December, roving groups of Anti-balaka broke into Muslim homes and began gang-raping the women. The final toll was 19 confirmed dead, murdered with machetes, with further deaths outside the town. Twelve people were injured, some suffering amputations. Five women had suffered terrible injuries as they were gang-raped. Over the next few days Anti-balaka militias raided other villages and towns in the area, in one case with air support from Wagner, with the same grim result.

On 15 December, a MINUSCA peacekeeping force arrived at Boyo and the 1,000 or so townspeople who had fled gradually began to return.

'What shocked me was the massacres of the Boyo villages, hundreds of Fulani who were massacred in this attack,' a member of the Presidential Guard who took part in the attack told Nathalia when she talked to him. In another interview, a UPC militiaman said, 'The Russians say: "In this village, there are many mercenaries and informants, so when you enter, you have to commit massacres to influence people. We must slaughter women and children and men."'

'When we're on a sweeping mission, we kill everything that moves,' a member of the Presidential Guard told Nathalia. 'The orders, when we passed through the villages, were to sweep, cleanse, everything, without a trace.'

After the first three interviews with a mix of Presidential Guards plus regular army soldiers and militiamen operating under Wagner's command, Nathalia knew she needed to increase the pool. There was another problem. 'Soldiers don't like speaking. They listen to you but their responses are quite short.'

Nathalia had no sympathy for what the perpetrators did, but she had learned not to be judgemental because once she knew the background of some of these people – raised in brutality since their childhood – she realized that war and atrocities were their normal; they had known little else.

'Are you committing rape?' one of her team asked a soldier. 'And the soldier said, "You sit on your sofa and you ask questions like this? Where are you coming from? Obviously there is rape, mass rape." It was so obvious for him,' Nathalia said. 'Another person told me a story about a woman who was raped by a Wagner fighter and became pregnant,' she recalled. 'The family went to the UN, probably to request support, and it came to Wagner's ears. They came back, took the girl, opened up her belly, threw the baby in the rubbish and cut her throat, telling her family, "This is what happens to people who try to speak."'

In another example, Nathalia heard of how a white Wagner soldier hanged two villagers by their feet and cut their throats, catching their blood in a cup and drinking it in front of their family, who were forced to watch. 'Terror as a weapon of war,' Nathalia explained. 'It's a deliberate tactic to create fear so that nobody will speak, although everyone is a victim of this war. Everyone is afraid. Everyone.'

Spending your days listening to accounts of the worst things humanity is capable of takes a toll. 'I've been chasing war criminals for several years now. I think it was affecting me a lot in the first few years,' Nathalia told me. 'I was very anxious, processing all this information – all these stories can make you quite insane sometimes. But over time I thought, if I don't figure out how to manage my emotions I had better stop doing what I'm doing.' And she didn't want to stop what she was doing. If she didn't tell the stories she was hearing, then it was quite likely no one else would hear them.

The impacts of the war have been catastrophic: over a million people – a fifth of CAR's population – were displaced as they fled the mass atrocities that characterized the conflict. According to a study by the Columbia Mailman School of Public Health, in 2022 around 5.6 per cent of the population died – more than twice as high as any other country in the world. Despite its extraordinary mineral wealth, CAR hovers around the bottom of the UN Human Development Index.

On 25 June 2023, just two days before The Sentry's report was to be launched, Yevgeny Prigozhin and his mercenaries marched into Rostov-on-Don, took over the headquarters of Russia's Southern Military District and began their advance on Moscow. Wagner's relatively small number of troops, armour and anti-aircraft systems had suddenly become one of the biggest threats Vladimir Putin's dictatorship had faced. Within a day, the attempted coup was aborted, and over the next few weeks Prigozhin's private jet was tracked, flitting between Moscow, St Petersburg and Belarus. Wagner was declared illegal – which it technically was anyway – and senior figures among the Russian Army's general staff rushed to protect their own backs or simply disappeared. A horde of military experts and political analysts across the world began to analyse and theorize over what had happened and what was to come. Nathalia erred towards caution.

'Prigozhin is *the* master of disinformation,' she told me, referring to his brainchild, the Internet Research Agency troll farm. 'I cannot believe that what we're hearing about this isn't what he wants us to hear about this.'

In addition to CAR, Wagner is present in Libya, Syria, Burkina Faso, Sudan, Mali, Mozambique and Madagascar, but what will become of Prigozhin's nascent African empire is unclear. Was Wagner the deniable arm of Russian expansionism, or perhaps the mercenary group was using Russian hardware and logistics to pursue its own ends? Maybe it was a mixture of the two. Whatever the truth, what happens next in these strategic, troubled and resource-rich countries is of global significance.

On 27 June 2023, the day The Sentry published Nathalia's 'Architects of Terror' report, the US Department of the Treasury announced sanctions on four Wagner connected companies in CAR, the United Arab Emirates and Russia, citing that Wagner's gold business was financing the group not just in Africa but also in Ukraine. The department's under secretary for terrorism and financial intelligence, Brian Nelson, said that: 'The Wagner Group funds its brutal operations in part by exploiting natural resources in countries like the Central African Republic and Mali.'

The repercussions of Prigozhin's short-lived rebellion captivated Russia watchers across the globe and boiled down to one key question: would Putin dismantle the Wagner empire or simply take it over? In the immediate aftermath, the messages were contradictory. In a 28 June 2023 interview with Russia Today, Russian foreign minister Sergei Lavrov took the opportunity to send a message to Wagner's clients in Africa:

> In addition to relations with this PMC (Wagner), the governments of Central African Republic (CAR) and Mali have official contacts with our leadership . . . At their request, several hundred soldiers are working in CAR as instructors. This work will continue.

By early July 2023, cleaners of the multistorey, ultra-modern, glass-walled Wagner Center in St Petersburg, which had opened its doors only nine months previously, were seen scraping the group's logo from a window, while the large white 'W' that topped the building was dismantled. Oddly, at the time of writing, the Wagner Center's website appeared to be operational and the home page welcomed anyone who logs in with the legend: 'Today we break stereotypes. We know how to be the best and from this moment we are building the future together.' The photo gallery was still replete with Wagner's branding, although the rest of the site seems to concentrate on renting out the office space.[*]

Meanwhile, Nathalia found herself in high demand to give numerous press interviews. 'It's safe to say that no one can really predict what will happen tomorrow or in a few months,' she told ABC News. 'The situation is extremely volatile but what we have learned from investigating and analysing Wagner in Africa over the past five years is that the group is resilient, creative, fearless and predatory so it is less likely that the Wagner empire will instantly fall like a house of cards.'

A few days later, she reinforced this message, telling the *Guardian*: 'For the moment, it looks like Wagner's operations are on hold. But they are successful and not so expensive, so it is very likely Wagner will be rebranded [by Moscow] while maintaining most of its assets and systems. It is like a virus that spreads. They do not appear to be planning to leave. They are planning to continue.'

On 19 August 2023, Prigozhin was in Bangui; a selfie shows him in civilian clothes standing between two enthusiastic Central Africans in the grounds of Maison Russe. Four days later, his Embraer jet fell out of the sky and plunged into a field near Moscow, where it exploded. Its passenger list named Prigozhin, Dmitry Utkin and other members of Wagner's top leadership as being on board.

Putin's rule has been accompanied by an alarming number of his critics falling out of windows, being poisoned with radioactive materials and burning up in plane crashes. Even President Biden joked after

---

[*] Or so Google Translate tells me.

Prigozhin's aborted rebellion: 'If I were he I'd be careful what I ate. I'd keep my eye on my menu.' So no one was really surprised. Rumours swirled about whether or not Prigozhin had been on the plane. The Kremlin subsequently announced that DNA testing had confirmed him to be among the ten people whose bodies were recovered – the word of Putin's Russia confirming that Prigozhin, a master of disinformation, is no longer with us.

'When you go to CAR you don't see a lot of children smiling. When the children smile again that's when you will feel peace, but we're not there quite yet,' Nathalia told me.

And when there is peace, she fully intends to return. 'I was there before Wagner and I will be there after Wagner, if there is an after Wagner . . .'

BANGUI, CENTRAL AFRICAN REPUBLIC, 19 JULY 2023

In the presence of the diplomatic corps and representatives of international NGOs, Arnaud Djoubaye Abazène, CAR's minister of state for justice, condemned the 'Architects of Terror' report.

> These are still gratuitous and baseless defamations. The Central African government will draw all the legal consequences, and reserves the right to bring the NGO The Sentry to justice so that it can answer for its actions.

He was joined in his condemnation by the ministers of foreign affairs and communication, also accusing The Sentry 'of playing the game of Western powers in a geopolitical and geostrategic war.'

Talking of geopolitical and geostrategic wars, exactly a week after this gathering, President Mohamed Bazoum of Niger was toppled in a coup mounted by the leader of his Presidential Guard, General Abdourahmane Tchiani. Pro-coup demonstrators took to the streets of the country's capital, Niamey, many of them waving Russian flags.

5

THE BIG SLEEP

On 13 August 2018, quarantine officials at Kuala Lumpur International Airport gagged at the stench emanating from one of the countless shipments that passed through their hands every day. On opening the package, destined for Vietnam, the officials found the carcasses of several big cats – lions, leopards and tigers – with the remains of their decaying flesh still hanging from their bones. Among these skeletons were the horns of 50 rhinos, weighing 116kg (256lb). At that time, these horns were worth a shade over US$2 million. The wildlife traffickers who regularly used the KL route had been unlucky. Had the flesh been removed from the bones it's unlikely quarantine would have noticed anything untoward, which would have left customs as the only barrier to the cargo being shipped onward to Hanoi – and customs were no barrier, as long as the right people had been paid.

It was the largest-ever seizure of rhino horn in Malaysia. News of the seizure wasn't made public for a week, but the criminal networks behind this smuggling operation knew about it almost immediately and sprang into action. They needed to plug the massive hole in their finances that the Malaysian authorities had inflicted; once the information was public, they'd lose their chance. The snag was that these weren't issues that could be discussed over the phone.

Early the next day, a greying man in his fifties and his wife left their house in Johor Bahru, on the Malaysian peninsula just over the Johor Strait from Singapore, got into their top-of-the-range Mercedes sedan and set off along AH2 expressway and headed north. This was a complete break from their usual routine, which is precisely what attracted the attention of the watchers.

Dave Andrews couldn't recall the exact model of the car. 'But I know it definitely had a massive, supercharged lump under the bonnet,' he said, remembering that day as if it was yesterday. 'He liked to stick his foot on the carpet and we couldn't keep up with it. It just disappeared.' Dave was driving a 1.5-litre (0.3-gallon) Honda Civic, pokey enough around town but no match for a Merc driven by a man in a hurry on a motorway. 'It was a series of "we've lost them" and then – bang – ten minutes later we'd find them again at a service station or in the queue for a toll. Then we'd just become specks in his mirror again, which is a good thing. If you can't see the bad guy, the bad guy can't see you.'

In the end, Dave managed to stick with his target all the way to Kuala Lumpur. The Merc parked outside a hotel close to the airport and its two occupants lugged their bags inside. The fact that Dave was still on their tail was down to 'good surveillance procedure mixed with a shitload of luck'.

Dave hadn't wasted any time on the journey. He contacted the various surveillance teams at his disposal and booked them into two hotels close by. Working in shifts, they kept watch throughout the night until, at 4.30 in the morning, Teo Boon Ching and his wife – codenamed Jet and Ski by the watchers – came out of the hotel carrying their bags. Ready to follow the Mercedes once more, the team had to react quickly when their targets were picked up by a different car; and it was this one they followed to the airport.

'One of our foot units goes into the airport and sees him check in,' Dave said. Now in possession of the flight information, Dave managed to get one of the last tickets on the same Air Asia flight to Hanoi, Vietnam. Then he called up his Hanoi-based team and ordered them to provide a reception party. The Air Asia flight being full, the remainder of the Malaysian team boarded a Malindo Air flight that left five minutes later for the three-and-a-half-hour trip.

When they landed, Dave followed his quarry off the plane and watched as JetSki picked up their bags from the carousel and made their way into the arrivals hall; there they fell under the watchful eye of Dave's foot units. Outside, other members of the Hanoi team were deployed in the car park and at all the exits from the airport.

JetSki were met in the arrivals hall by a well-dressed Vietnamese man and were observed climbing into a people carrier, which then left the airport and took the motorway to Hanoi. This was a major complication for the hurriedly assembled surveillance team. They only had motorbikes, and motorbikes are not allowed on Vietnam's motorways. It seemed a cruel end to such a spontaneous but well-coordinated surveillance operation, but the fat lady hadn't yet stopped singing.

The next day, another man in Hanoi who had been the focus of Dave's team's attention for a while was also being tailed – an almost regular part of his daily routine, although he didn't know it. His name was Ah Nam. The team tracked him to a backpackers' hostel in the city's old quarter. There, he made his way to the restaurant and joined a group of other men among the babble of travellers' tales and the clinking of glasses. Shortly afterwards they were joined by another man and his wife – JetSki. It seemed an unlikely destination for a man as wealthy as Teo Boon Ching.

Surrounding them, Dave's foot units blended in with the multinational clientele, their video and audio recorders capturing every nuance of the group's conversation.

'It was probably the dirtiest meet of wildlife traffickers that we've ever seen,' Dave Andrews reflected when I talked to him in spring 2023, just over four years after these events took place. 'It was like all the godfathers of the wildlife trade converged on this backpackers' hostel, of all places. And we managed to get our team right on their shoulders.'

Dave's 20-year career in UK law enforcement had seen him working for the Metropolitan Police, New Scotland Yard and, after some 'squad-hopping' around London, what became the Serious Organised Crime Agency (SOCA), tracking down the crème de la crème of organized crime: drug dealers, human traffickers, counterfeiters and other top-level crooks. With his wry sense of humour and strong London accent, he reminds me of Carter, Dennis Waterman's character in the classic 1970s cop drama *The Sweeney*.

Following postings in Europe and Afghanistan, Dave took leave in Thailand and it was there that he decided to take a career break. After flirting with a couple of organizations, Dave worked for a while training officials of the United Nations Office on Drugs and Crime (UNODC), the UN agency charged with tackling serious organized crime and terrorism. It was there, in 2015, that he met Steve Carmody.

This hard-bitten Australian cop had joined the Australian Federal Police in 1988 and in his 30-year career had investigated the gamut of sexual assaults, break-ins, rapes, murders and drugs. Then, like Dave,

Steve started investigating serious organized-crime networks, particularly Asian organized crime. A stint at Australia's National Parks and Wildlife Service as a specialist investigator gave him his first insights into the wildlife trade, but he got frustrated at what he felt was a reluctance to go after anyone of substance. Eventually, he returned to his organized crime beat, probing the murky world of outlaw motorcycle gangs, but that wasn't to last.

'I was treading ground,' Steve told me, speaking from his holiday refuge deep in the Australian outback. 'I was starting to arrest and prosecute the children of the people that I was arresting and prosecuting when I first started [. . .] so I thought it's time to get out and see what else is out there. And from that, I jumped over to working for UNODC as a trainer.' Steve spent the next four years with UNODC in and around Southeast Asia, and it was there that he realized that the skills he had picked up during his long career investigating top criminals could have another outlet.

'It gave me a really good understanding of the landscape there, particularly around wildlife crime, because the last few years was focusing on that: the lack of political will, the openness of the trade, particularly in Vietnam, some of the law-enforcement agencies that are involved, their strengths and weaknesses.'

In the end it was a fluke that tipped Steve into the world of investigating wildlife crime. He was offered the job of director of programmes at the newly created Wildlife Justice Commission (WJC), an organization set up to tackle this branch of organized crime. The work looked interesting, with the bonus that the WJC was based in The Hague so he'd be only a stone's throw from the First and Second World War battlefields of Western Europe, providing an ideal opportunity for Steve to indulge his interest in military history. He took the job.

By his own admission, Steve was more cop than green. 'It was more about investigating crooks than the environmental side of it,' he told me. But once he got into the job he began to realize what he could achieve, and it grew on him. His initial brief was to produce a case file and present it to the WJC's independent review panel, which included, among others, former judges from the International Criminal Court. The WJC had two cases running: one was already hitting the buffers, and the other was focused on the village of Nhi Khe (pronounced *Knee Kay*), Vietnam, and Steve knew Nhi Khe. During some downtime when he'd been working for the UNODC he'd taken a taxi from Hanoi for the 40-minute ride south. He wasn't quite prepared for what he found.

Nhi Khe, once an important centre for the carving of religious objects from timber, is a small, picturesque and affluent village of just three or four paved streets, perhaps a hundred houses, surrounding the central temple – a typical Vietnamese commune. Steve found many of the properties were distinctly upmarket, speaking to the success of its new business model: the extremely lucrative and completely illegal trade in some of the most endangered species on the planet. But, unlike many places whose wealth derives from organized crime, there was no sense of tension or danger. As a Westerner, Steve Carmody didn't detect any particular interest in him when he visited, except perhaps as a potential customer. Nhi Khe was basking in the sunlight of impunity.

'It was industrial-scale trafficking like you've never seen. You could literally walk down the street and see rhino horn and ivory. There were carvings in the windows, and the police station was just 200m [650ft] away. Busloads of Chinese tourists rocked up when I was there. And it was like, "Wow, this place is just off the hook."' Steve is not the kind of guy who likes letting people off the hook. 'Since I've been exposed to the industrial-scale trafficking that's out there, like anyone else it disgusted me. The wholesale destruction of the planet is just nuts. It really is, and the money that people make is also nuts.'

WJC's first full-time executive director, Olivia Swaak-Goldman, joined the embryonic organization when it was being set up in early 2016 and brought a different set of skills; skills that demonstrated not only her commitment to the organization's mission, but also an insight into just how seriously she viewed wildlife crime in the global context.

Her career as an international criminal lawyer had seen her work at the UN International Criminal Tribunal for the former Yugoslavia, set up to prosecute war crimes committed during the Balkan Wars of the 1990s, the International Criminal Court in The Hague and the Dutch Ministry of Foreign Affairs, while she also somehow also found time to lecture at Harvard and Leiden universities.

Her personal beef was the issue of accountability. 'It's one thing to sign up to a treaty and commit yourself to accountability for massive crimes, and another thing to actually get governments to do that,' she told me. She gave it her best shot and worked on those issues for 25 years, but she wasn't seeing the impact she wanted. 'I wanted to do something a little bit different. I wanted to ensure accountability and I wanted to do it for really impactful crimes, but I wanted to see my impact,' she said. Olivia hoped to see faster progress here than tends to be made with stopping genocide, war crimes and crimes against humanity.

When she heard about the Wildlife Justice Commission she was impressed with what this nascent organization was setting out to achieve. 'It was really early days and seemed to me like a really phenomenal approach towards addressing a problem that is incredibly systemic and devastating,' she told me. 'You have individuals that are destroying our biodiversity for profit, and because of the approach of the international community towards that, they're getting away with it; [but] I thought that the problem was more solvable than other types of international crime issues that I've been addressed with.' Talking to Olivia, elegantly dressed and with her soft American accent, you would be forgiven for thinking this is simply a successful lawyer discussing some moderately complex legal issue – but only if you missed the quiet but steely determination in her voice.

In addition to building the team, one of Olivia's key areas of focus was to think ahead – to 'keep our nose above the pavement', as she puts it. 'How do we raise the profile of these types of crimes? I want my grandkids to be able to see a rhino and a helmeted hornbill, and if we don't do something different than what we had been doing, that won't be the case.'

The Environmental Investigation Agency (EIA) pioneered the field as one of the early organizations to stress the need to investigate environmental crime, and the WJC took this a step further by supporting governments and building the capability and political will to address wildlife crime as transnational organized crime.

The first thing Steve did when he started working in WJC's offices was to go through the case files. He found some undoubtedly interesting evidence, but perhaps more importantly for him it contained also his own particular catnip. There were 'some decent crooks', he told me. The task was to catch them.

Steve remembered Dave Andrews from his time at the UNODC and offered him a job as senior investigator. Between them, Steve and Dave had brought 50 years' worth of experience as ex-cops tackling global serious organized crime; experience that was invaluable to WJC's mission to investigate the criminal networks behind wildlife crime. It was time to get to work.

'We were doing a lot of work in Laos at the time, some work in Vietnam and a bit of work in Thailand, Cambodia and Malaysia as well,' Steve told me. 'So we started running all sorts of jobs in those different countries, basically following around targets that other people had worked on in the past. That was the idea of the WJC – to pick up failed investigations. But as we developed, we started to develop our own intelligence sources. I was doing all the sneaky stuff, running random human sources, surveillance work and running undercover jobs.'

But this was not a sustainable model, or a realistic one – not least because as Westerners it was rather hard to blend in to largely Asian criminal gangs. Dave's and Steve's role was to recruit and to provide on-the-job training to nascent undercover operatives – 'UCs', in police parlance – who came to their notice largely via word of mouth. These new UCs were put through an induction course where they learned basic surveillance skills. If that went well, the training got more interesting.

'If they've got the right aptitude and background, we'll put them through a basic covert operator's course, where we teach them techniques to infiltrate people online,' Steve told me. 'And if they're successful at that and show real aptitude, then we'll give them another course – an advanced course to teach them the trickier techniques, to actually attend undercover meetings and to deal with and infiltrate criminal groups.' To me, this sounded like the equivalent of a military 'live fire' exercise with one crucial difference – the enemy was real.

The trainers comprised very experienced former UCs. 'There's not a lot our trainers haven't seen,' Dave said. 'They've infiltrated crime groups at top level – and not just wildlife criminals, either. It's drugs, terrorism, that sort of thing.' Dave paused for a moment, recollecting his time as a detective in the UK. 'If only back then I had the team that I can call on now. We've got people of all races; males, females, we got young kids, we got older people. You know, a real diverse mix of appearances, backgrounds – everything you want as a surveillance commander.

'We're lucky to have the team that we've got. They're really motivated, a group of good people, almost without exception. They're really keen; they want to do the job because they want to do the right thing for wildlife, and that's what motivates them. They're keen to learn, but if they fuck up, they'll say, "Look, I fucked up," and then they'll get it right the next time. I think as a manager, you can't ask for more than that.'

If they make the grade, these new UCs can be deployed anywhere in the world, at any time. And as WJC's investigations cranked up in recent years, there was one thing for sure – they would never be bored.

The illegal wildlife trade is estimated to be the fourth-largest branch of global serious organized crime, just behind the drugs trade, weapons trafficking and the trade in human beings. According to the international organization TRAFFIC, which monitors the trade in wild species, wildlife trafficking is one of the most lucrative criminal activities worldwide, worth around US$23 billion a year. It has driven numerous species of plants and animals to the brink of extinction – including pangolins, whose scales are valued in traditional Chinese medicine, tigers, elephants and rhino.

Under the Convention on International Trade in Endangered Species (CITES), the trade in any of these species is banned under international law. Moreover, the wildlife trade has been linked to zoonotic diseases, the most famous of which is Covid, and is a massive contributor to the sixth mass-extinction event, with the World Economic Forum's 2023 'Global Risks' report citing biodiversity loss and ecosystem collapse as one of the fastest-deteriorating global risks over the next decade.

Those people watching Teo Boon Ching and Ah Nam in Hanoi were part of a movement critical to helping end that trade – the same movement I started my career in that day in 1990 when I walked off a north London street and volunteered at the Environmental Investigation Agency, where I met my fellow co-founders of Global Witness, Charmian Gooch and Simon Taylor. It was with the EIA, one of the foremost organizations campaigning for a ban on the ivory trade, that Charmian had cut her campaigning teeth in 1989.

'These are fairly young people with limited surveillance experience,' Dave told me about WJC's undercovers, remembering his early days as a detective. 'I remember when I first started doing covert surveillance I used to feel I was driving around in a police car with a blue light on the roof and everyone's looking at me, but they're not.'

This also chimed with my memories of Global Witness's first undercover investigations – you're convinced that the subjects know exactly what you're up to, that they must have spotted the secret camera you're carrying and you're about to be rumbled.

'Our team managed to get right on his [Teo Boon Ching's] shoulder, right on all their shoulders, with video and audio tape.' Dave spoke with pride as he described the operation in that lowly backpackers' hostel. 'There's an audio record of this whole mafia meeting. If you could liken it to drugs or something like that, the top agencies in the world would have given their right arm to have been at a meeting of minds like that. And our guys were right there.'

INFILTRATION

WJC had first come across Nguyen Van Nam, whose criminal alias was Ah Nam, in June 2016. Having infiltrated a particular trafficking network, a WJC undercover team were taken to view a 440-kg (970-lb) ivory stockpile in the village of Bai Uyen, northeast of Hanoi. Ah Nam and his sidekick, Ah Phong, happened to be there, but they weren't on WJC's radar at the time.

Six months later, another ivory trader who had been guiled by a WJC team mentioned that two associates of his were putting a 1-tonne ivory stockpile on the market. These turned out to be Ah Nam and Ah Phong. One tonne is a lot of ivory, and if they hadn't been on WJC's radar before, they certainly were now.

Given that these two crooks seemed to be rising stars in the echelons of wildlife traffickers, Steve and Dave had decided to make Ah Nam the key focus of their Operation Medusa and opened a case file on him – a method of structuring evidence that law enforcement could use to bring a prosecution. Ah Nam and Ah Phong were blissfully unaware of this newfound interest in their activities and the fact that for the next three years undercovers from WJC would stick to them like clay on the soles of their boots.

Ah Nam was definitely the boss, with Ah Phong keeping the show on the road and responsible for the smuggling of wildlife products from Vietnam into China.

'Ah Nam was dumb as shit,' Steve explained succinctly. 'He was very easy to get into, very quickly, because of his lack of tradecraft and his arrogance [. . .] These guys are not mental giants like if they were in real crime, I mean, serious organized crime. This is more like disorganized crime.'

Anyone who has seen *The Wire* knows about burner phones, but Ah Nam had obviously not seen *The Wire*. Eschewing the use of disposable phones, which is second nature to serious criminals, Ah Nam used the same phones throughout the period he was being investigated. He gave his Chinese bank account details to multiple surveillance teams and maintained those same accounts. Unlike 'serious' criminals or their fictional counterparts in books and films, who never meet in the same place twice, Ah Nam frequented the same coffee shops, often reserving the same seats for his meetings with suppliers or potential customers. Indeed, the only really noticeable fluctuations in his lifestyle were related to how much money he was making.

'When he had lots of product available, he was driving a nice flash car,' Steve recalled, and surveillance photos capture Ah Nam at the wheel of various high-end SUVs, or standing proudly next to a Jaguar saloon. 'But then when he had several seizures in a row, he dropped down to smaller cars. This is a guy that was not surveillance-conscious; he was not aware of his surroundings. But he was like a honeypot. People just kept coming to him and we were able to build cases off of him with little effort. He was a very easy target to work.'

I don't know whether it was this lack of tradecraft that resulted in the codenames WJC applied to Ah Nam and Ah Phong: Bert and Ernie.

'You know, from *Sesame Street*,' Dave told me enthusiastically. 'We had all the *Sesame Street* characters. Bert, Ernie, Elmo, Grover . . . I can't remember the others. But there were loads of them. When we ran out of *Sesame Street* names we started to use the Muppets. I think we've done all the *Sesame Street* characters and all the Muppets. At the end of it we had a cast of thousands that we were following, that would turn up in some way or other, but it was Bert that was directing operations.'

While Ah Nam's lack of tradecraft meant that he quite often behaved like a Muppet, he couldn't be treated like one. He was a serious criminal and security was a key concern for Steve, Dave and their investigation teams. 'For the guys on the ground, the thing we fired home to them all the time is safety, safety, safety. If something's not safe, we simply walk away from it,' Dave explained. 'There is a risk and it takes a certain kind of person to be able to do this. One of the qualities of the people we've got is bravery. That's the bottom line. They're brave to go into some of the situations they go into.' Dave was deadly serious now. 'We've had jobs in the middle of the night where the undercover operatives have been on their own in a car in the middle of nowhere, in a strange place they don't know, and it's a scary experience for them. A real nerve-racking experience, but they sort of swallow that and they do the job.'

These UC teams had confidence in Steve and Dave's direction because they knew that they had a safety net wrapped around them, with a back-up team shadowing their every move. But, as Dave stressed, it was these UCs who were stuck in a roomful of strangers. 'What we're doing is taking money from their pockets,' Dave emphasized. 'The higher up the chain we go against these criminals, the higher the stakes get; and when you start taking away people's livelihood, taking away their money, potentially taking them away from their family for a few years – putting them in jail – the stakes get really serious.'

This was no understatement. The seizure at Kuala Lumpur airport had cost the traffickers US $2 million, and the economic stakes don't get much more serious than that. That is why those kingpins of the wildlife trade had gathered that day in the backpackers' hostel in Hanoi. Among the subjects of the meetings they would hold over the next few days was the possibility of a 'buy back'.

'I think somewhere along the line, there had been a terrible fuck-up,' Dave recalled. 'They'd lost a load of money that they had promised to this client, the Chinese investor. Whoever had put the money into this must have lost an absolute fortune when this stuff got intercepted by law enforcement. So I think they were all panicking about, "How can we recoup this money? And how can we get it quickly? Now? What products have we got available that we can sell in a hurry? Or is there any chance we can get it back through any corrupt contacts?" That was, in essence, what the meeting was about. It was a reaction to events. It was someone calling all of their colonels together.'

Could they make well-directed entreaties in Kuala Lumpur, pay off the right officials and get those rhino horns back? It would add to their costs, of course, but perhaps that was a small price to pay compared to the total loss they were facing now.

Despite the occasional vagaries of his income, Ah Nam's business enabled him to enjoy a luxurious lifestyle. His wife owned a real-estate company, but it didn't operate at a level that would justify the two upmarket houses stuffed full of luxury rosewood furniture that they owned in Hanoi; or their spending habits, photos of which she posted on her Facebook account together with shots of her latest designer fashion buys and luxury holidays. In case anyone was in doubt about her family's success, one photo is completely taken up by an image of a US$10,000 stack of banknotes sitting on a table, and this goes straight to the heart of the business in which Ah Nam was becoming a king.

The trade in ivory and rhino horn or pangolin scales is all about wealth and status. Those tusks and horns, chainsawed off the faces of thousands of elephants and rhinos, are fantastically expensive. In January 2017, the price per kilogram (2.2lb) of rhino horn in Vietnam was just under US$15,000. It rose to a high of just over $20,000 in April the same year and then declined to US$12,700 by June 2019. It's this luxury status, plus the carving of the ivory and horns into intricate ornaments long beloved of the mainly Chinese market, that confers prestige upon the owners. There is a widespread misconception that the trade in rhino horn is due to its aphrodisiac qualities. It is not, although the display of a massive and hugely expensive horn might well quell some of the buyers' insecurities in that department. Much like owning a Ferrari.

Ah Nam and his wife craved this prestige and liked to bask in it, advertising their wealth for anyone to see. For a criminal, that is careless – and carelessness is never a good trait to have in the world of organized crime.

INSIDE THE NETWORK

Just like legitimate businesspeople, organized criminals depend on a supply chain; but for them it's a little more complicated because their supply chain needs to be hidden and designed to deflect unwelcome interest from prying eyes. It needs dead ends to prevent penetration further into the network. For wildlife criminals, the supply chain begins in the oceans, forests, savannahs and great plains that are host to some of the most iconic species on Earth.

In Africa, poaching gangs – usually poor villagers who are trying to earn a crust and who are the most expendable part of the operation – are supplied with high-powered weapons and ammunition by a local broker who will stockpile the ivory and rhino horn. This is then transferred to a shipper who ensures the goods reach Vietnam and into the hands of the new owners, the wholesalers of the tusk or horn.

'Teo Boon Ching is the transport guy,' Steve told me. 'He's the guy that could change a bill of lading; he's the guy that could move a container and not have it found. You take out a guy like that and that causes problems.'

Ah Nam and Ah Phong are the next link in the chain, responsible for negotiating the deal between these new product owners in Vietnam and the buyers. This way, the owners and buyers may never meet, may never know who each other are. Once the deal is done, it's then over to the packers and the transporters who take responsibility for the goods reaching their final destination.

The buyers, mainly Chinese, transfer the funds in Chinese renminbi (RMB) directly into the Chinese bank accounts of a network of currency converters, who then change the money into Vietnamese dong (VND), in cash. This cash is then smuggled back into Vietnam and into the hands of the sellers. People like Ah Nam and Ah Phong.

Ah Nam plays another role, one that he probably didn't think about enough. The three weakest links in this long chain are those that connect the African end of the network to the Vietnamese one; the money-laundering operation; and the role that Ah Nam plays – the link connecting the sellers to the buyers. If you want to catch the spider, you go to the centre of the web.

Among the billion or so monthly users of the Chinese messaging app WeChat are the UCs of WJC, although you won't see those credentials in their online profile. In August 2017, a tantalizing image came up on their feed – perhaps the most tempting they had seen yet. Wrapped in the plastic they were shipped in and illuminated by the flash of the camera, 76 rhino horns loomed out of surrounding darkness in Ah Nam's photograph. Like the soldiers of China's Terracotta Army, the horns were arranged in serried ranks, placed upright on a bare concrete floor and grouped together by size and type. This wasn't just a lot of horn; this was a whole new ballpark.

'Initially, we were thinking Ah Nam had positioned himself at a broker level, what we would call a Level 2 trader,' Dave told me. The drug-trafficking equivalent would be the people giving drugs to the street dealers. 'And then one day out of the blue, he sends us this picture of 76 rhino horns and it was just a complete eye-opener. You just don't see that amount of rhino horn all in one place,' Dave said. 'Just to see that volume of stuff elevated him in status [. . .] which is a massive, massive trader.'

This was the greatest number of horns the WJC team had ever seen assembled in one place. Given a rhino has a front and a back horn, Ah Nam's stash were the only reminders of 38 rhinos that had been slaughtered on the plains of Africa, a not insignificant proportion of the remaining global population.

Further posts by Ah Nam depicted the same horns, this time on scales, their weight in stark red figures on the illuminated display. Each horn bore a white-painted number, like lots in a deathly auction. Images of 27 horns for sale appeared on another WeChat site, operated by a subject of WJC's Operation Phoenix, depicting the same scales, the same painted numbers, the same floor and same background wall as in Ah Nam's images. The same consignment.

The undercovers met with this person in a cafe in Hanoi who told them that the horns he was selling had arrived in a shipment of 300kg (660lb) of horn and 10 tonnes of ivory. In Vietnam at that time, this equated to US$7.6 million for the horn and US$5.5 million for the ivory. The seller referred to the bigger fish in the trafficking chain, including someone he called his 'big brother', and showed the images he had in a WeChat exchange on his phone. The other end of that conversation was Ah Nam.

Examining the photos, the team judged that some of these horns were freshly poached; they were full horns, bloodstained, with flesh still hanging off them. Some of the other horns had evidently been farmed, because they came from rhinos that had previously been dehorned and the horn had grown back.

'It was an odd mix,' Dave remembered. This large consignment had come close on the heels of another significant seizure in South Africa, with the horns contained in similar packaging. 'So it probably came from the same source [. . .] all the intelligence points towards that. And now it was in Vietnam, ready to go, and Ah Nam had access to all of it.'

I have nothing but respect for WJC, especially for their undercovers. I know from my own experience how it feels to assume a false identity and be in constant fear of discovery, accidentally letting slip your colleague's real name for example. I know what it's like to engage with criminals, parlaying some crooked deal, always in the knowledge that your intention is to cost them a lot of money, which is the only thing they care about. The UCs of WJC have been deployed again and again and have been phenomenally successful – not many jobs can give you the same sense of pride. But there's something else to think about.

These undercovers are seeing, first hand, the sheer brutality of the wildlife trade. Other than a few farmed rhinos, every tusk and horn came off an animal shot down to feed this trade, many with the rotting flesh still attached. They had seen videos on the phones of people like Ah Nam that depict the butchery in action. And then there's the poachers, caught up in a shooting war brought about by their own desperation to feed their families.

'If they see stuff like this day after day it really wears them down,' Dave told me. 'It has an effect on them that I think can be too easily overlooked. And the traffickers trade this stuff like it's a bit of plastic; they don't think about anything other than the money.'

Steve shared these views completely. He found it hard to comprehend how the traffickers could close their eyes both to the suffering of the animals they traded and the impact on the local population in Africa, where people were literally losing their lives, violently, so that the traders could make a profit.

'Probably the biggest thing that sort of stood out for me throughout this whole operation was how little empathy there was [among the traffickers for the victims of the trade],' Steve said. 'It's just a commodity to them that can make money. They don't connect it to a dead animal that's connected to a dead poacher or a dead ranger. It's just a money-making opportunity. And when these commodities run out, they just move to another commodity. It's just a commodity-based business with these guys.'

As Steve had said, WJC are realistic in that as long as there's a demand for the products – and there will never be a shortage of poachers – the criminal gangs will keep plying their trade, always around the equation that balances profit against risk. At best that risk is a financial one; at worst, it's jail time – and tipping the balance of that equation to high risk, low profit is where WJC focus. Steve summed it up in one word: disruption. And to maximize disruption, the team need to understand every aspect of the trade. WJC also needed to look at the poaching operations in Africa and elsewhere, the frontline of the wildlife trade.

'You'll get poaching groups in, say, South Africa's Kruger National Park. They're probably being run by someone in Mozambique or South Africa,' Dave explained. 'These poaching bosses will control the actual poaching; they'll supply the weapons and the ammunition and send people into the park to go and poach rhino. What they pay these guys I'm not sure, but it won't be a lot of money; these guys are just doing it to make a living, I guess. And then they'll get the rhino horn. They'll sell it on locally if they can, but you'll also get groups of Asian buyers – they'll pop up in places like Mozambique, South Africa, Angola, DRC, Cameroon, places like that.'

Many of these people are Vietnamese. 'They will control the trade and source products from the local poaching bosses,' Dave continued. 'They might have three or four on their books. They'll get their stockpiles of horns as they come in and stockpile them in country until they've got enough to send back to Vietnam.'

One of the most notorious of these poaching bosses was 'Boss Navara'.

On 26 July 2022, Simon Ernesto Valoi and Paulo Zukula made their way into a hotel in Maputo, capital of Mozambique, the former Portuguese colony on Africa's southeastern coast. They were carrying eight rhino horns weighing a total of 7.5kg (16.5lb).

Valoi, known as 'Navara' after the Nissan car he favoured stealing when he was in the hijacking business, was one of southern Africa's most infamous wildlife traffickers, and one of its most ruthless. At the appointed time, he and Zukula went down to meet the prospective buyer, who left shortly afterwards, but Navara and Zukula wouldn't be left alone for long.

'He told us to go down. We went down, we entered the [hotel] reception. He [Valoi] is the one who knows him. They started talking. When he left, the police came in,' Zukula told a press conference three days later, telling the story of his own and Navara's arrest.

Navara had fallen foul of a well-orchestrated sting operation mounted by Mozambique's National Criminal Investigation Service (SERNIC). Posing as buyers, they'd supplied Navara with a mobile phone to communicate with his accomplices and the poachers themselves, so they not only bagged him but were also able to round up the gang.*

A photograph of Navara on the website of African investigative environmental journalism outfit Oxpeckers shows a fit-looking, shaven-headed man, a heavy gold chain around his neck, dressed in a white T-shirt and unzipped blue hoodie. His expression is one of defiance. His hands are handcuffed in front of him while Zukula, a smaller man with his back to the camera, has his hands handcuffed behind him.

Navara's luxury villa mingled with those of his fellow poachers in Mozambique's Massingir District and stood in stark contrast to the other dwellings in this otherwise rundown town bordering South Africa's Kruger National Park, the happy hunting ground for Navara's poaching teams. The Kruger's population of white rhinos collapsed by 75 per cent from 2011 to 2020 because of poaching, with around only 2,500 animals remaining, while the number of rarer black rhinos are down by 51 per cent

---

* https://clubofmozambique.com/news/mozambique-poaching-ringleader-detained-for-second-time-235937/

since 2013 to around 200.* Those numbers have doubtless declined further, given some of the horns Navara was carrying were from Massingir and Kruger, while the remainder were from Mozambique's Gaza Province.

Steve knew that the best strategy at the African end of the supply chain was to tackle these intermediaries, because there was little point in catching the traffickers and brokers in Vietnam without also trying to disrupt the poaching operations in Africa. Navara had long been in their sights, and they had provided some of their intelligence to the Mozambican authorities.

'Navara's notorious in Mozambique, and he's a bad guy,' Steve told me, describing how Navara was a suspect in three murders and several rapes and allegedly shot and killed his own brother over rhino horn. 'Poachers are like drug users; they're just a readily available resource because there's very few other ways to make money in the poor villages around protected areas,' Steve explained. 'They're never going to run out of poachers. You can't shoot your way out of it; you can't arrest your way out of it. You've got to figure out a way to divert these guys and give them another form of income. It's literally a hearts-and-minds thing.'

Steve was being pragmatic. The shooting of a poacher wasn't going to solve the problem – and would in fact create more problems. 'It's a waste, because all you're doing is losing a potential source of intelligence; you're alienating the family and the village,' he said. 'So, it does become a bit of a cycle. It's very easy to make that statement when you're not on the ground facing these guys with those high-powered weapons, so I understand how it gets to that; but I just think that we're not addressing

___

* https://africageographic.com/stories/kruger-rhino-poaching-update-75-population-reduction-in-10-years/

this holistically. For too long we've adopted a military approach rather than a police approach. At the end of the day, a dead suspect doesn't tell you anything.'

A key part of understanding the dynamics of the global wildlife trade is to document the seizures of wildlife products worldwide. 'We monitor all the seizures that are happening around the world,' Dave told me. 'The seizures reported, either by the media, or by the World Customs Organization, by our friends in other countries, our police and law enforcement friends . . . Whatever they're happy to share with us.'

In addition to this kind of solid research, WJC keep a handle on the going rates for the products and the weak points in the chain of enforcement, where corrupt customs might let contraband through for a price – as WJC found in Kuala Lumpur. It is an ever-changing map, with smugglers shifting methods and routes when law enforcement gets too close.

'They always go with the route that makes the most money and is the least risk, always, and they'll pay a premium to avoid seizures,' Dave explained. 'But news travels fast among the bad guys when seizures do take place. When, where, how – what's the flavour of the month for law enforcement?'

To nail Ah Nam, the Vietnamese police had to prove an offence; and to do that they needed to seize the horn – so the task now was to pinpoint where stockpiles were located, and then the well-oiled machine would crank into action. Dave's UCs would usually negotiate for a small amount of the horns or ivory; but the wildlife trade is not one built on trust, and an expression of interest is met with a demand to see the cash.

'There's always this game of cat and mouse – you show me yours and then I'll show you mine,' Dave told me. 'The difficulty is you don't often get shown a location without showing them that you've got the dollar.' But the WJC couldn't actually pay any money or they would be guilty of an offence themselves. 'If they can't take the money, they'll take people,' Dave explained, telling me how on one previous operation, when they'd wanted to view a 1-tonne ivory stockpile, Ah Nam had insisted on keeping one of the undercovers as a sort of light-touch hostage while the other one went to view the ivory.

'But as soon as it's done, they say, "Your mate here can pay the bill." It's all about negotiation after that,' Dave said. 'They will invariably bend and try and accommodate your wishes, because at the end of the day they want the money, and 90 per cent of the time greed wins.'

Between 2016 and 2019, Steve and Dave deployed multiple undercover teams to dog Ah Nam's and Ah Phong's footsteps, undertaking 35 field investigations into their operations. Each of these would involve approaches by different UC teams, often initially via Facebook and WeChat and all with the objective of sighting stockpiles of ivory and rhino horn. When the teams knew where these stockpiles were, the police would be notified and the seizures began to mount up.

Ah Nam's suppliers seemed to be getting a little more cautious. After all, they were the ones taking the hit, and they began refusing to let his customers sight the stockpiles of horn, ivory or pangolin scales. Ah Nam himself began to develop some basic tradecraft by adopting various anti-surveillance methods, but his arrogance and boastfulness still shone through.

'I have so much stuff, I'm just afraid you don't have enough money,' he told a WJC investigator in early 2017. He was no more modest in June 2019 when he told one UC, 'My reputation in Vietnam, you must know. Many people deal with me; they all can tell you how I am like, you know.'

In December 2017, WJC submitted a detailed case file to the Vietnamese and Chinese authorities. This, together with the intelligence supplied during the course of their operations, led to the seizure of just under 1.5 tonnes of ivory and 18 rhino horns in Vietnam. Perhaps more serious for the criminals was the arrest of 12 people in Ah Nam's Vietnamese network. In China, 34 more people were bagged, while 2.25 tonnes of ivory, 63kg (139lb) of rhino horn and 28.5kg (62.8lb) of pangolin scales were also seized. The net was closing in, although it had failed to ensnare Ah Nam and Ah Phong. On top of that, there was another complication for the traffickers – on 31 December 2017, after years of effort by numerous environmental groups and many governments, China announced a total ban on the import of ivory. As China was the main market, this was a gigantic moment.

Pete Knights – a former colleague of mine at EIA who we affectionately nicknamed 'Pet-shop Pete' and who went on to lead WildAid – described this event as 'the greatest single step toward reducing elephant poaching'. And undoubtedly the traffickers' lives had become a little more difficult. But, as with most crime, greed is a powerful motivator.

In February 2018, one of WJC's undercover teams learned that Ah Nam was selling a 600-kg (1,323-lb) stockpile of ivory that was secreted in Khanh Ha, a village not far from Nhi Khe. A meeting was arranged so that the UCs could inspect the ivory, but it was a meeting they didn't want to keep. Instead, they cut out the middleman and directly informed the Vietnamese Environmental Crime Police of the rendezvous details. Upon entering the gated house, the police seized what turned out to be a 971-kg (2,141-lb) stockpile. It was the largest seizure in Vietnam outside of a port at that time. Of the four suspects arrested, two were convicted and, in March 2019, were jailed for five years.

Ah Nam was not blind to the risks and had told WJC UCs on several occasions that he didn't leave Vietnam for fear of arrest. 'That man he looked for me many times,' he once told them. 'I am afraid, now I don't dare to meet him in South Africa, I don't dare to meet him.' It seemed the threat of arrest was getting closer to home, but Ah Nam couldn't stop working – his lifestyle depended on it. That same month, he let it be known that he had access to 10 tonnes of ivory.

At US$405 per kg, including delivery to Dongxing in China, this ivory was half the price it would have been in 2016 but was still worth just over US$4 million. Perhaps a better gauge of its real value was that this amount of ivory had resulted in the slaughter of around 1,000 elephants. To Ah Nam, though, it was just a commodity.

Half of these raw tusks were stockpiled near to the Cambodian border, but 1 tonne, he told them, was being stored at various secret locations in Hanoi. The UCs expressed their interest in purchasing 300kg (660lb) of this ivory and were told that 200kg (440lb) was stored at a single location. If they could find out where this was, then maybe they could get the Vietnamese Environmental Crime Police to make a seizure and perhaps net Ah Nam into the bargain. It wasn't going to be easy. The spate of recent seizures had rattled Ah Nam, who, despite his slow start in honing his woeful tradecraft skills, was becoming more cautious. He refused to let them get a sighting of the stockpile.

As the UCs were negotiating to try to inspect the goods, other members of the team were keeping him under constant surveillance. Video footage taken by WJC's undercover teams shows how closely they were dogging Ah Nam's footsteps over those few days. Wearing a blue polo shirt and in the company of a taller man, he leans into the boot of a gold hatchback car; in another video he meets various contacts on the side of a road. One close-up shot, taken from an adjacent table, shows him sitting in a cafe, glued to his phone – a stark indicator of how closely he was being watched. But Ah Nam utterly refused to take the UCs to see the ivory stockpile for themselves.

The team resorted to the next-best option, which was to persuade Ah Nam to take their own phone and at least film the ivory. That way they would at least know that the stockpile existed, and maybe a video would yield some other clues. It wasn't perfect, but it would have to do. Ah Nam agreed and that evening he took their phone, promising to return it, complete with a video of the ivory, the next day.

'He was smarter than he looks,' Dave told me, because Ah Nam immediately switched off the phone for fear of being tracked. That didn't stop the UC teams following him that evening, but luck wasn't on their side and they lost him in the crowded nighttime streets. There was no sign of him still for much of the following day. The team had no option but to sit and wait.

When Ah Nam called the next day to say he had the video, the UC team arranged to meet him in a restaurant in the old quarter. One UC team went ahead to the restaurant while another followed Ah Nam as he drove towards the meet. 'And then he takes this weird diversion,' Dave told me. Ah Nam drove into a network of narrow backstreets and stopped to make a phone call. A little while later, a woman dressed in red knee-length leggings and a distinctive black T-shirt with cutaways at the shoulder, her hair pulled back into a bun, rode up to Ah Nam's car. The UC team were close enough to see her hand Ah Nam a phone, and they were pretty sure it was their phone. As the woman left, weaving back into the traffic, the UCs made a spontaneous decision to follow her. They were led to a noodle bar. When the woman picked up her phone to make a call, they were sat at a table close enough to overhear.

'I just gave it to him,' she said. 'He said everything is almost done, the quantity, the payment. Now the guy just needs to come and meet and settle the deal.'

In addition to this conversation and the babble of other customers talking, the audio recorders also picked up the Vietnamese muzak going round in an endless loop. The UCs' secret cameras filmed everything around them, just in case something in this everyday-looking shop might have yielded a clue. It was one of their smarter moves.

Immediately after Ah Nam returned the UCs' phone and the meeting broke up, the two UC teams compared their video footage. The ivory stockpile certainly existed: the video showed stacks of yellowing tusks lying on the white and grey pebble-pattern floor tiles. 'You can see the feet of the guy that's filming the product. He's very careful not to show any faces, but it shows his own feet. And you can see the sandals. He's wearing flip-flops,' Dave told me. 'And the guy at this cafe was wearing exactly the same flip-flops; they were really distinctive.' Dave was right – in one shot, taken from inside the noodle shop through the decorative metal window grid onto the street, a man is wearing the same flip-flops.

'And then everything started to fall into place,' Dave continued. 'The floor tiles in the cafe were the same as the floor tiles where the ivory was; and there was a Vietnamese song playing in the background on the UC video, exactly the same soundtrack that was being played in this noodle shop. It was on a loop. The writing was on the wall.'

Wasting no time, Dave's team notified the Vietnamese Environmental Crime Police, who raided the shop. They found the 207kg (456lb) of ivory in a locked bathroom, the only remains of the 20 elephants that had been killed before their tusks were sawn off and began their long journey to Vietnam.

'That was a highlight. It was a real cracking bit of work,' Dave enthused. 'We finally got the evidence we needed to sink Bert. The cops got the ivory; they arrested people at the scene with loads of evidence against them.' But this high point was followed by a low one. 'They weren't able to follow it up and pin anything on Bert, so he wriggled away.'

However, in September 2019 a prospective Chinese buyer contacted Ah Phong and said they were interested in buying a significant quantity of ivory. The deal was sealed and Ah Nam and Ah Phong, driven by Ah Nam's cousin, loaded the ivory into a car and drove to the agreed rendezvous, where they were arrested. Ten months later, on 16 July 2020, the duo were sentenced to eleven years in prison, while their cousin got ten.

Meanwhile another of Dave's long-term UCs was after a bigger fish. He was getting ever closer to Teo Boon Ching, but there was one snag. His cover identity was wearing thin, and it was touch and go how long he could continue to engage with his target, with whom he had built a close relationship over many years. Dave and his team had heard on the grapevine that US law enforcement wanted to make an arrest in Bangkok, where they had a bilateral extradition treaty, so were working to keep Teo Boon Ching there as long as possible. They felt that they might lose their prey if he got on a plane back home to Malaysia.

The UC invited Teo Boon Ching for an expensive meal at an upmarket hotel in Bangkok, along with one of Boon Ching's contacts. Dave meanwhile remained close by, in case some extra support was needed. This turned out to be a wise precaution, because the UC realized he had a problem. He needed to pay the bill – the meal was due to be on him – but he didn't have any cash and he couldn't risk using his credit card, which was in his real name. He sent an urgent message to Dave, who rushed out of the hotel to get cash from an ATM. But how to get the cash to his man? They decided on a brush-past.

Dave waited in the gents' toilets and as the UC came in the pair brushed past each other as Dave left, pressing the wad of cash into his hands. At the same time, though, Boon Ching's colleague also came into the toilet and it was a close shave as he held the door open for Dave to leave. Thankfully, it went so smoothly that he didn't spot the exchange.

A few days later, on 29 June 2022, Teo Boon Ching was arrested by the Thai police for being in possession of 70kg (154lb) of rhino horn worth US$725,000. It was downhill from there. Just over three months after that, on 7 October 2022, the US Treasury's Office of Foreign Assets Control (OFAC) announced sanctions against him for being part of a

Wildlife Trafficking Transnational Criminal Organization (TCO), and for the cruel trafficking of endangered and threatened wildlife and the products of brutal poaching. Teo Boon Ching specializes in the transportation of rhino horn, ivory, and pangolins from Africa, generally utilizing routes through Malaysia and Laos and onward to consumers in Vietnam and China.

That same day, he was extradited to the US, where he was put on trial. Just under a year later, on 19 September 2023, Damian Williams, the United States Attorney for the Southern District of New York, issued a press release announcing that 'Teo Boon Ching, a/k/a "Zhang," a/k/a "Dato Sri," a/k/a "Godfather"' was sentenced to 18 months in prison for conspiring to traffic hundreds of kilograms of rhinoceros horns worth millions of dollars, which involved the illegal poaching of numerous rhinoceroses, an endangered wildlife species. The press release stated that

> Ching met with a confidential source to negotiate the sale of rhinoceros horns. For example, on July 17 and 18, 2019, the confidential source met with Ching in Malaysia. During those meetings, Ching stated that he served as a 'middleman' – one who acquires rhinoceros horns poached by co-conspirators in Africa and ships them to customers around the world for a per-kilogram fee. He also promised the confidential source 'as long as you have cash, I can give you the goods in 1–2 days.'

The sentence attracted widespread press attention. Olivia Swaak Goldman told CNN that Ching's conviction 'sends a strong message that wildlife crime will no longer be tolerated,' while EIA, which had also dug up intelligence on Teo Boon Ching's operations, said that his jailing was a 'body blow' to the illegal wildlife trade.

For the damage Teo Boon Ching inflicted on some of the most endangered species on Earth, 18 months doesn't seem like nearly long enough. On the plus side, though, in addition to the US sanctions and Boon Ching's involuntary sojourn in the US penal system, he and his partners in crime will never again be confident that the eager buyer in their illegal deal really is who he or she claims to be.

Looking back on a job well done, Steve Carmody's chief regret was that they didn't get access to Ah Nam's phones.

'These guys are not smart. They keep stuff on their phones for years and it's a great way to map these networks and get evidence of other crimes. We never got that,' Steve told me. 'I assumed that the Vietnamese cops got it [. . .] and shared it with someone else.' But overall, Steve was pleased. 'I would have liked to have seen Ah Nam go down for something bigger than just 200 kilos [440lb]; but in defence of the people that got him, that was probably all you were going to get him with at that time.' Steve's law-enforcement background, especially countering the drugs trade, also meant that he was an experienced pragmatist.

'With wildlife, once they're gone, they're gone. So it's not just about arrest; it's about disruption. It's about stopping the flow, taking out people that have the biggest impact on doing that. You don't have to sit and wait for the perfect case with these guys; you've just got to keep putting them before the courts, keep costing them money,' he continued. 'With drugs, you work up a job for two or three years and then take out 30 people. Unfortunately, I think with wildlife you don't have that luxury. We're just swimming against the tide.'

'Because I'm a lawyer, I think strongly about accountability,' Olivia Swaak-Goldman reflected. 'We've signed up to protect the weak in society, to protect those that cannot protect themselves. So whether that's children in armed conflict or whether it's a rhino or an elephant, we have decided that they're deserving of protection. Therefore, we need to be living up to those obligations to do so. That's the sort of legal side of it.

'But I really think it's about who we are as an international community. What do we think about our relationship with nature? I think we should treat nature as if it's valuable to us. And it is valuable to us not only in and of itself, but also for us. So if you look at wildlife crime and the impact it has, it has a huge impact on climate change, for example, because if you take the sharks out, for example – we have a huge problem with shark finning – you have a change in the ecosystem. The ocean can't absorb as much carbon as it normally would. The same with illegal logging. If you take out a lot of really valuable timber, it's not absorbing as much carbon as it should. It's also about the rule of law. If citizens can't count on their communities and their institutions to protect them and to enforce the law, then they don't have that kind of belief in their system.'

On 26 July 2022, South African wildlife ranger Anton Mzimba was gunned down at home, in front of his family. He was 42 years old. Despite numerous death threats against him he had continued to do what he felt was a critically important job. 'I'm doing this for the world, for my children's children, so that one day, when I hang my boots – when I retire, when I die—they are going to enjoy the wildlife.'

He is just one of the 565 park rangers in Africa alone who have died in the line of duty since 2011. Over 50 per cent of these deaths were caused by homicide.

'We saw that Vietnam was a hub for wildlife crime,' Olivia told me. 'Nhi Khe was a village where [wildlife products] were being sold openly. This is about accountability and rule of law. We knew – everybody knew – that it was illegal to do this. But you or I or anyone could go to this village and buy things that were clearly illegal, and people were losing their lives to protect these animals in Africa.'

During the three years that they were tracking Ah Nam, WJC documented that he had had access to 17.6 tonnes of ivory and 477kg (1,052lb) of rhino horn, between them worth just over US$17.25 million. This equates to around 1,760 elephants and 106 rhinos.

Ah Nam's and Ah Phong's arrests and subsequent convictions were undoubtedly a major blow against Vietnamese trafficking networks.

Together with China's ivory ban, the bringing down of Ah Nam perhaps gave elephants, rhinos and pangolins some breathing space, but organized crime abhors a vacuum. International law enforcement and organizations like the Wildlife Justice Commission, the Environmental Investigation Agency and many others will continue to be an essential frontline defence for some of the most emblematic species on Earth.

6

THE GATEKEEPER

'The Gertler Family Foundation is committed to improving the lives of the most vulnerable communities in the Democratic Republic of Congo, focusing on healthcare, education, infrastructure development, agriculture, emergency assistance and culture.'

—Gertler Family Foundation website, 21 October 2023

KINSHASA, DEMOCRATIC REPUBLIC OF CONGO, JANUARY 2018

Leaving the rain and clamour of Kinshasa's traffic-clogged Boulevard du 30 Juin, Shlomo Abihassira and his escort eschewed the main entrance of Afriland First Bank, instead making their way to the quieter rear entrance and up to the second floor. If his appearance didn't attract any attention – ultra-orthodox Jews are not a common sight on the streets of Kinshasa – the contents of his suitcase certainly did.

Shlomo was ushered into the office of the bank's assistant director general, Patrick Kafindo, who summoned one of the cashiers to join them and not to forget the cash-counting machine. When she was ready, Shlomo opened the suitcase. Inside, in neat stacks, lay US$1 million in cash. The cashier ran the bills through the machine, verified the total and duly recorded the deposit in favour of RDHADG, an obscurely named company Shlomo had formed only a few weeks earlier. It was 23 January 2018.

Over the next two days, Shlomo made two further cash deposits, one of US$875,000 and another for US$926,000, following the same procedure. If the cashier thought there was anything strange about this, she kept it to herself.

On 8 March, Shlomo returned to the bank and made three more deposits into the same account: one of US$2 million, another of US$3 million and a final one of US$1 million. By June that year, Shlomo had visited the bank 14 times, paying a total of US$19 million into the now very flush account of RDHADG. In addition, another two million had gone into an account under Shlomo's own name. It's not clear whether these multiple trips were governed by the availability of the cash, or simply by how much Shlomo could physically carry in one go: US$21 million weighs 210kg (463lb), enough to fill 21 airline carry-on bags.

The money lay snugly in these accounts until 14 August, when someone withdrew the entire sum and deposited it in the account of a company called Dorta Invest SAS, which had been opened at the same branch in February. Over the next eight months, a further US$28 million was deposited into Dorta's account while during the same period US$22 million was transferred out again to various accounts held abroad.

Shlomo Abihassira's banking spree and newfound interest in the Democratic Republic of Congo (DRC), together with the hatching of a gaggle of new companies, were merely the latest in a chain of events that had begun with a Global Witness exposé six years before. As with any bank, all transactions at Afriland First Bank are confidential and the institution's grandees had no reason to suppose that there was any outside knowledge of these multimillion-dollar deposits. They had not reckoned on inside knowledge.

KINSHASA, ZAIRE, 1997

Dan Gertler could probably have taken life quite easy, but he wasn't the type. The dust had barely settled on what became known as the First Congo War, and the hundreds of thousands of deaths and widespread destruction that came with it, when 23-year-old Gertler's plane took off from Tel Aviv and touched down in the capital of the country that would soon be renamed the Democratic Republic of Congo. The 32-year dictatorship of President Mobutu Sese Seko had just collapsed and a victorious new leader took to the stage, Laurent-Désiré Kabila.

Described as a 'beacon of hope' by US secretary of state Madeleine Albright, the fat and shaven-headed Kabila initially won hearts with his jovial demeanour and trademark Stetson hat, which was perhaps a deliberate snub to Mobutu's leopard-skin cap and thick tortoiseshell-framed spectacles. But Kabila's regime would soon become as brutal as Mobutu's and, although it was a low bar, even more corrupt. This was fertile ground for a young man on the make.

The scion of a leading Israeli diamond-trading dynasty and a former trader of conflict diamonds, one of Gertler's first deals with the country's brutal new leader was to secure an 18-month monopoly on the production and export of artisanal diamonds for his company, International Diamond Industries. In return he paid US$20 million, funds badly needed by Kabila as he embarked on the Second Congo War, which was to draw in nine African countries, a pantheon of rebel groups and militias, and result in around 5.4 million deaths – the highest death toll of any conflict since the Second World War. Against this backdrop, Dan Gertler struck up what was to be an enduring friendship with Laurent Kabila's son – a friendship that would set him on the path to becoming a billionaire.

Joseph Kabila, around the same age as Gertler, ran his father's army but didn't do a very good job of protecting him. Laurent-Désiré Kabila was assassinated by one of his own bodyguards in 2001 and the young Kabila became president. Part of Laurent Kabila's legacy to his son was Augustin Katumba Mwanke, a successful banker with HSBC in South Africa, who had been asked to return to DRC by Kabila senior to provide economic advice. Following Laurent-Désiré's death, Joseph appointed Katumba as his principal economic and political adviser.

Katumba became known as Dieu le Père' – 'God the Father' – of the DRC. 'He sort of ran the country,' Bloomberg journalist Michael Kavanagh told me. 'He was extremely intelligent and an amazing strategic thinker [. . .] He and Dan were thick as thieves [. . .] they just went around the country asking themselves the question, "What's valuable?" '

Gertler did well from these tours and secured the permits for three oil blocks on Lake Albert plus the DRC's western oil blocks – the most valuable in the country. Not yet satisfied with that, he acquired mining permits for iron ore and then the mother-lodes – copper and cobalt. On top of the diamond monopoly he already had, Dan Gertler was doing rather well, and he had only just begun.

ZUG, SWITZERLAND, MAY 2012

On 9 May 2012, Glencore, the world's largest commodity company, held its first AGM. The company's new shareholders gathered together on a cool day in the opulent Theater Casino Zug, a small building resembling a French chateau on the shores of Lake Zug in the prosperous Swiss town of Zug – whose wealth largely derived from the swathe of dodgy brass-plate companies registered there. Oblivious to the gentle wind ruffling the waters of the lake outside, the investors were impatient to hear CEO Ivan Glasenberg's ambitious plans for the newly floated corporate giant upon which their precious shareholdings depended. Much of these plans rested on Glencore's massive new investments in the DRC and the shareholders were looking forward to the event with anticipation. They were not the only ones.

Daniel Balint-Kurti and his colleague Dino Mahtani, two of Global Witness's key investigators, had been busy too, and on the day of the Glencore AGM, Global Witness released a ten-page memo entitled 'Secrecy surrounding Glencore's business deals in the Democratic Republic of Congo risks exposing shareholders to corrupt practices'. Not exactly a snappy title, but you shouldn't judge a book by its cover.

Dan has the quiet air of a scholar. Seemingly diffident, thoughtful and curious, he could easily be mistaken as someone consumed by study or as a harmless sort of chap. A few of the world's super-crooks – and that includes the inhabitants of the boardrooms of some of the world's most powerful companies – have made exactly that mistake.

Dan and Dino's memo was the first of two that we called the 'Secret Sales' scandal and was the result of many months' work exploring the dark labyrinths of corporate records, offshore companies and opaque business deals. It detailed how a series of anonymously owned companies based in secrecy jurisdictions like the British Virgin Islands had snapped up world-class mining assets sold by the DRC's state-owned mining company Gécamines for a fraction of their true value and then, within months, sold them on to Glencore at full commercial value. The difference between what these anonymous companies paid for these assets and the amount they sold them for just months later was a mouthwatering US$1.4 billion. That's a lot of money wherever you are – in this case, the loss to the Congolese state was twice the country's combined health and education budgets. All of these companies were connected to Dan Gertler, who had, through his influence building with Joseph Kabila and other influential figures in DRC, become the de facto gatekeeper of the country's mineral resources. If you wanted to mine in DRC, the chances were that Gertler would be involved somewhere along the line – and his services didn't come cheap.

Where did the US$1.4 billion go? Part of the answer was that the timing of these deals overlapped with DRC's 2011 presidential election – a time when Joseph Kabila needed funds to fight an election campaign. Gertler's old friend was returned to power in polls that were marred by violence and branded as flawed by international diplomats and election observers. It wasn't long before the dominos began to fall.

Following Global Witness's exposés, in 2013 the Africa Progress Panel, chaired by former UN secretary-general Kofi Annan, accused Congolese state-owned companies of 'systematically undervaluing assets', citing that the Congo had lost US$1.36 billion because of these deals – very close to the US$1.4 billion in Dan and Dino's memos.

The IMF halted its loan programme to the country while UK, Brazilian and US law enforcement began investigating Glencore for bribery and corruption. Not to be outdone, the US Securities and Exchange Commission (SEC) initiated an investigation into one of the world's largest hedge funds, Och-Ziff, under the Foreign Corrupt Practices Act. As Gertler's fingerprints were all over these deals, his lawyers were fighting rearguard actions left, right and centre, but it's difficult to ward off the inevitable.

On 21 December 2017, the US Treasury's Office of Foreign Assets Control (OFAC) imposed sanctions on 39 individuals under the US Global Magnitsky Human Rights Accountability Act. One of these was Dan Gertler plus a swathe of individuals and companies linked to him. The US designation didn't pull any punches, describing Gertler as

[. . .] an international businessman and billionaire who has amassed his fortune through hundreds of millions of dollars' worth of opaque and corrupt mining and oil deals in the Democratic Republic of the Congo (DRC). Gertler has used his close friendship with DRC President Joseph Kabila to act as a middleman for mining asset sales in the DRC, requiring some multinational companies to go through Gertler to do business with the Congolese state.

All in all, things had gone just as we had hoped. There was a lot at stake. The DRC is one of the most resource-rich countries in the world, a major source of copper and in possession of two-thirds of the world's cobalt – a strategic mineral critical to the energy transition away from fossil fuels, including the production of electric car batteries. However, the country's population see little of this wealth; two-thirds of the DRC's population of 91 million live below the poverty line in a country riven by corruption and conflict.

*

Any company or individual sanctioned under the Global Magnitsky Act is shut out of the US financial system. In plain language this means that they, and anyone doing business with them, cannot use US dollars. Given the global mining industry is based on US dollars, Dan Gertler and his business partners were faced with a gargantuan hangover. The secret network of companies they had built up over the years was now useless to them and they needed to find a creative solution. Quickly.

Gertler called in an old business associate, Congolese businessman Alain Mukonda, whose LinkedIn profile describes him as an 'Advisor, mining environment & geology at Denovo Congo' – a company connected to Gertler. Mukonda got to work and like a seasoned croupier began to shuffle a bunch of offshore companies like cards in a pack. BVI-registered Fleurette Mumi Holdings Ltd, for example, became Kinshasa-based Ventora Development SASU. Caprikat – a company that played a starring role in Global Witness's 'Secret Sales' exposés – was rechristened Albertine DRC SASU. By the time Mukonda had finished, the bones of a new corporate structure had been put in place. All it needed was flesh.

Meanwhile back in Kinshasa, in the first six months of 2018 Mukonda had joined Shlomo Abihassira as a prolific banker of large amounts of cash into accounts held at Afriland First Bank, depositing US$1 million in one of Shlomo's accounts and another €11 million into the accounts of some of Gertler's new companies. He was just warming up. In August 2018, in the space of a month, Mukonda created ten more companies.

AFRILAND FIRST BANK, KINSHASA, JANUARY 2018

That day in January 2018 had started like any other day for Gradi Koko, but it didn't end like the others. As he was returning to his office from the toilet he brushed past a bearded and burly ultra-orthodox Jew, accompanied by a security guard, leaving the office of the bank's assistant director general, Patrick Kafindo. Gradi didn't think anything of it until his colleague, Navy Malela, called him over.

'Did you see that person?' Navy said. 'That's Dan Gertler. We are going to have problems.' Navy had remembered seeing a newspaper photograph of Gertler at the wedding of the country's president, Joseph Kabila. Given Gertler's high-level connections, Navy was right to be worried.

The first problem for the two auditors at Afriland First Bank was that they knew Gertler had been placed under economic sanctions by the US just a few weeks before; and because Afriland banked US dollars, he shouldn't have been in there at all. There was also another reason for Gradi and Navy to be surprised. Afriland was a small bank, perhaps the eleventh or twelfth down the scale in the DRC. Most of its customers were small businesses and it didn't number any mining companies among its customers. Why would a tycoon like Gertler, one of the biggest figures in the country's mining sector, choose this bank?

Whatever his reasons, Gertler turned out to be good for business. Gradi was acutely aware that the bank had long suffered liquidity problems and never found itself in a position to lend money – in 2017 it had banked just US$31 million in corporate deposits. 'But from 2018 we had millions,' he told me. While this seemed like good news for the bank, as auditors, Gradi and Navy asked themselves where this money – and the prestige that came with it – could have come from.

Gradi began instituting a series of routine checks and quickly found that the registration records for a group of accounts weren't where they were supposed to be; in fact, they were in the hands of the bank's No. 2 – the assistant director general, Patrick Kafindo. Gradi thought that was odd; and given that his job was to ensure that the bank's compliance systems were in order, he asked Kafindo if he could see the account files. That was what Gradi calls 'the start of it'.

'Why?' Kafindo responded.

The atmosphere in the room changed and Gradi felt intimidated by his boss. *Why, if something is OK, would he ask why I wanted them?* he thought.

Kafindo told Gradi he could see the documents but imposed shackles on his ability to do the job he was paid to do. He refused to let Gradi take the files to his own office, where he had the tools to run the checks he needed to do. Instead, he was directed to examine them at the visitors' desk in Kafindo's office; for good measure, he was also refused access to the internet. However, despite the strictures imposed on him, Gradi found enough information to be seriously worried; all of the accounts he looked at were in some way connected to Dan Gertler.

'To open an account, you need the customer's name, address, phone number,' Gradi told me. 'But these details were not there [. . .] also, the assistant director general was listed as the manager of these accounts; but according to the rules he could only be the adviser for these accounts, not the manager.'

Kafindo's parting words left no doubt in Gradi's mind as to where he stood: 'Everything you see stays in your head,' he ordered.

Gradi returned to his office and he and Navy pondered their next move. Kafindo had shown Gradi enough for him to realize there was a serious problem in Afriland's main Kinshasa branch, but he had also been walked into a brick wall. Navy agreed. They tried to access the physical records from the archives but the files were not where they should have been. Accounts had been opened without a signature and there were no specimen signatures on file – the system was wide open to abuse. Gradi's next move would change his life.

He wrote a formal letter to Kafindo and cc'd the bank's headquarters in Cameroon. In it he warned that Gertler was not only under United Nations [*sic*] sanctions, but was also acting as a signatory to several accounts that he was not a signatory to and whose registration files did not include his name. These accounts were Ventora Development, Palatin SARL, Cosha Investment SARL and Shlomo Abihassira. None of them, Gradi noted, were involved in the mining sector, which was odd given that that was Gertler's business. Gradi's letter recommended that these accounts should be blocked. He also referenced another suspicious account in the name of Zoé Kabila, the brother of the country's president, and for good measure mentioned accounts linked to Hezbollah and North Korea. The summons to Kafindo's office was not long in coming.

'These people are not just anyone,' Kafindo warned him. 'It's dangerous; you could walk out of the bank and be shot – just like that.'

Gradi stumbled out of Kafindo's office, shaken to the core. In the space of just a few weeks he had gone from having a career he was proud of to being sandwiched between his personal ethics, his boss, one of the most powerful businessmen in DRC and talk of being shot. Gertler-connected companies alone were responsible for depositing US$77 million in Afriland during 2018, more than twice the total corporate deposits made in the previous year. It seemed inconceivable that the bank's head office in

Cameroon were unaware of where much of this money was coming from, but Kafindo had made it plain that the branch's auditors should keep a lid on the secrets behind the bank's soaring fortunes.

Gradi had done what he was required to do and the response had been a thinly veiled death threat. If he carried on doing what he was paid to do he could well be killed, but he couldn't turn a blind eye.

By luck, he had been planning a trip to Europe and was already in possession of a French visa, so in March 2018 he packed his suitcase, his laptop and a bundle of internal bank documents and flew to France, where he applied for political asylum. The process turned out to be frustrating and protracted, and after many months his application failed. Gradi, alone in a strange country, was pondering his limited options when he tuned into a two-minute piece on TV5Monde.

It told the story of Jean-Jacques Lumumba, who was working for the BGFIBank Group when he uncovered extensive evidence of suspicious transactions worth tens of millions of dollars involving Congo's presidential family and the state mining company Gécamines. After he had alerted the company's auditors to what he'd found, he received numerous death threats and then fled to France bearing a wealth of evidence of the corruption he had exposed. Once there, he contacted a small, newly formed organization based in Paris called La Plateforme de Protection des Lanceurs d'Alerte en Afrique – Platform to Protect Whistleblowers from Africa – (PPLAAF). The 'Lumumba Papers' resulted in an international scandal. For Gradi Koko, the next steps had become clear.

PARIS, FRANCE, FEBRUARY 2019

The first communication came through on Facebook Messenger in February 2019. The sender claimed he was Congolese, had recently arrived in Paris and needed help. PPLAAF's director, Henri Thulliez, had co-founded the organization only a year before; and although it was still a tiny and poorly resourced outfit, the highly successful collaboration with Lumumba had demonstrated their efficacy. Henri, just 31 years old at the time, had originally begun training to be a diplomat but quickly realized he had no appetite to represent French policies abroad. With a Master of Laws from London's School of Oriental and African Studies, he instead embarked on a career in human rights – working at the sharp end, taking testimonies from victims of torture in Senegal.

His colleague Gabriel Bourdon-Fattal, was also a lawyer. Half French, half Israeli, he had been brought up in Israel – a fact that, although he didn't yet know it, would prove invaluable in this case. Both Gabriel and Henri were sceptical about Gradi's message and automatically biased against approaches by Facebook Messenger. In their experience, many people claim to be whistleblowers but can sometimes just be spinning a yarn to help an asylum application. Still, they would hear the man out.

Gabriel and Henri's first meeting with Gradi Koko took place on a cold winter's day in PPLAAF's small office in République, Paris, and any doubts they had about the man's bona fides evaporated quickly. Gradi, a tall, slim, studious-looking man of around 30 with a neatly trimmed goatee beard and large, thick-rimmed spectacles, sat hunched forward, his crossed arms hugging his bag tightly to his chest. As he told Gabriel and Henri his story it was clear that he was extremely traumatized, very scared and very alone.

'What information do you have?' they asked him gently. In response, Gradi pulled a few documents out of his bag. Gabriel and Henri leafed through what looked like a number of bank records that started in 2017 and ended at the moment Gradi left the bank in March 2018. Some of the records were just a couple of lines: companies with names like Interactive Energy Russia, Ventora and Dorta Invest, which meant nothing to them. Only one name, Shlomo Abihassira, rang a bell with Gabriel; Shlomo's father is one of the most prominent rabbis in Israel, and one of the richest.

Other than the fact that these accounts had huge amounts of cash flowing through them – one account alone had US$19 million in it – neither Gabriel nor Henri could spot any links between them. However, one of the documents Gradi possessed was the letter he had written to his boss, Patrick Kafindo, warning of the links between some of Afriland's most lucrative accounts and Dan Gertler and highlighting the suspicious account of the president's brother, Zoé Kabila.

It was this letter that convinced Gabriel and Henri that Gradi was indeed a true whistleblower, because he had alerted his employer of his concerns before he left the Congo. PPLAAF decided to help him pursue his asylum claim in France, but they broke the news to him that, because of the dearth of information about the companies, Gradi's information may not be the revelation he clearly thought it was. It was an unrelated trip to Africa that would cause PPLAAF to reassess this opinion.

LONDON, ENGLAND, EARLY 2018

Light poured through the glass ceiling of Global Witness's bustling office on the top floor of a WeWork building in the slowly gentrifying district of

Shoreditch in London's East End. Margot Mollat, a young Global Witness staffer, sat hunched over her computer trying not very successfully to get to grips with an oil company she'd been asked to research. When Margot, half French and half American-British, arrived in the UK the year before, just 22 years old and freshly graduated from Canada's prestigious McGill University, there was little to suggest that within two years she would be giving some of the richest, most corrupt and most powerful men in Africa a very big headache. It began when her boss, a seasoned investigative journalist called Pete Jones, appeared at her desk and asked her to come into one of the glass-walled side offices. They could talk more securely there.

One of Pete's sources had come up with a bunch of information that Pete's gut told him was worth probing into. This source, an industry insider, had come across a series of newly established companies that had aroused his suspicions. Most of them had been established in the DRC, with a couple based out of Hong Kong, and there was a potential connection to another network of companies in Europe. Pete's contact also suspected that Dan Gertler was connected to someone behind a carbon-trading VAT carousel fraud in France.

Pete asked Margot to drop what she was doing and see if she could delve more deeply into the information they'd been given. It was a big ask. Margot was new to this world but she had taken to it like a duck to water, happily paddling in the murky ponds of corruption investigations, and she wasn't going to turn down the opportunity. Besides which, perhaps this vague reference to the carbon fraud would give her something to go on.

At first sight, many of these companies appeared to be unconnected, but to truffle hunters like Margot, who like scraping away the surface soil to find the treasures that lie underground, the scent of something not quite right was pervasive. Pete's source had examined various website domain names, the use of the same pages on different websites, patterns of company incorporation, coinciding timelines – the bones on which the flesh of a company hang – and had come up with a theory based on a date, 21 December 2017. The date that the US had imposed sanctions on Dan Gertler.

Like the regrown heads of a hydra, the companies that Pete Jones's source had given him had started popping up in different countries just a week after sanctions were imposed. It was possible this may have turned out to be nothing, of course – just a coincidence – but it was worth a look.

Genius, thought Margot as she took the information in. Whoever it was that orchestrated the establishment of these companies had contrived an incredibly complex structure. While some of the companies were obviously connected, many were seemingly random and there were a thousand dead ends to confuse anyone curious enough to look. However, what possessed them to give one of the new companies the name they did was perplexing.

Fleurette Mumi Holdings Ltd was incorporated in Hong Kong on 28 December 2017. This was surprising. Dan Gertler owned a company of exactly the same name in Gibraltar. The new Fleurette Mumi Holdings Ltd's director was a French national, Elie-Yohann Berros, who on the face of it had no links to Gertler. The company had no website and a trawl of social media had drawn a blank. But surely this couldn't be just a coincidence?

A month and a half after she first began her research, Margot took the Eurostar to Paris, where she met a French journalist who had covered what the French authorities called the 'heist of the century', a carbon-trading VAT scam in around 2006 that cost the French taxpayer €1.6 billion and lost the EU a further €5 billion. Could this be the fraud Pete's source had mentioned? One of the perpetrators was a French-Israeli citizen called Avi Ben Ezra; he had been convicted and sentenced to four years in prison for the scam but had instead fled to Israel. *What was this guy up to now?* Margot mused.

Using OSINT methodology,* Margot discovered that since the carbon fraud Avi Ben Ezra's next commercial foray – outwardly, at least – had been into the world of tech, founding a new messaging platform called SnatchApp, based out of Israel. Margot took a look at the app.

'I tried to download it; I tried to use it. But there was no product – it was fake,' she told me. 'There was nothing there. The website was just text that could have been copied from anywhere.' Undeterred, she kept digging and did find something else about SnatchApp: the company's corporate records. These were in Hebrew but, despite the quirks of Google Translate, something leaped out of the page. She read it again and felt a tingle of excitement, which is not a common reaction to trawling through corporate records.

One of Avi Ben Ezra's fellow shareholders in SnatchApp was Elie-Yohann Berros, the man behind Fleurette Mumi Holdings Ltd, together with another character called Johan Shimon Lamant. So, in piecing together the puzzle so far, Margot had Avi Ben Ezra, on the run from the French authorities and holed up in Israel, and Elie-Yohann Berros as the frontman of a Hong Kong-based company with exactly the same name as one of Gertler's Gibraltar-based companies. *There is no way Berros, a random middle-aged Jewish French guy, would suddenly crop up in DRC and at the same time be connected to Avi Ben Ezra,* she mused. But who

---

* Open-source intelligence.

was Lamant, and what else was Elie-Yohann Berros up to? Margot was beginning to enjoy herself.

ENTEBBE, UGANDA, APRIL 2019

It was the end of a long day for the people gathered under the auspices of the anti-corruption coalition Le Congo n'est pas à vendre – The Congo is Not for Sale – (CNPAV). Margot was there, as were Gabriel and Henri from PPLAAF, together with Elisabeth Caesens, the highly respected founder of a small organization called Resource Matters. Returning to their hotel, Margot and her fellow delegates made their way across the lawn to a cluster of wooden tables and benches arranged along the shores of Lake Victoria. As they sat there looking out across the water, an expanse so vast it looked like a sea, their thoughts dwelled on a virtually landlocked country some 350km (217 miles) to the west, the DRC.

The four of them, for different reasons of confidentiality, were cautious about disclosing their hands, so they played one card at a time. Gabriel said they had been approached by a whistleblower from a Congolese bank who had shown them internal bank records documenting tens of millions of dollars of suspicious transactions. Margot watched as Gabriel jotted down some names on a piece of paper: Dorta Invest, Ventora, Interactive Energy . . . 'Whoa,' Margot exclaimed. These names matched many of the names given by Pete's source. PPLAAF and Global Witness were investigating the same network.

Margot dived in and told the group about the companies she had been digging into and how they were connected to each other. In response, Gabriel began listing the companies he had bank records for. Together this information began to fill some of the gaps in what was a super-complex jigsaw puzzle, further complicated because some of the key pieces were missing. Gabriel opened his computer to show some examples of the account activity detailed in the bank documents PPLAAF had received.

'We had the smoking gun,' Henri told me, but he knew that PPLAAF were too small to embark on this investigation on their own. 'And you guys already had a lot of information that we wouldn't be able to get ourselves.' He also knew that the legal risks resulting from investigating Dan Gertler were about as high as they come and that Global Witness had not just the investigative experience but also a long record of facing off highly litigious very bad people. All true, but none of us realized how dirty this fight would become.

In late spring 2019, Margot swapped her desk in Shoreditch for the seat of a Eurostar train as she crossed the Channel to join Gabriel and Henri in their small office in Paris. She met Gradi and listened intently as he walked her through the bank records. As evidence mounted, Margot started to spend more and more time in Paris. They sat around a table going through the banking transactions, mapping things out and looking at leads to try to understand what was going on. They didn't know it then, but they were passing into a shadow network where the normal laws didn't apply. It was fraught with danger.

Gradi knew that the story he had to tell was so fantastic and complex that it was going to take time to get both PPLAAF and Global Witness up to speed. He started by showing them screenshots of PDF documents he had on his computer. To Margot, these internal bank documents looked essentially like standard bank statements but with additional information from the bank branch, including details such as the official responsible for approving the transaction and the transaction type.

As Margot's investigations took her deeper into the Gertler network, she asked if Gradi had information on particular companies – the ones identified to Global Witness by our source. And she was able to watch the movement of money, almost in real time, as accounts like Shlomo Abihassira's grew fat with huge cash deposits. Then, on some seemingly random day, the money would be withdrawn – in cash – and deposited into another account. She knew that a straightforward wire transfer from account to account would have been easier, but not so convenient if you had something to hide.

The hours were mad, but the feeling that they were getting somewhere was energizing. A key focus seemed to be forming around Elie-Yohann Berros – the team were pretty sure that he was the financial front for Gertler.

Berros had incorporated Fleurette Mumi Holdings Ltd in Hong Kong in late December 2017, just one week after Gertler had been hit by the sanctions. Using a stringer, Margot and PPLAAF established that Berros was also behind Dorta Invest SAS, the company that had been set up in February 2018 and had received US$1 million from Shlomo Abihassira during his spree in the early months of 2018.

Using OSINT methodology, Margot found another company called Dorta Invest, which had been registered in the Czech Republic in 2013. This too was owned by Berros. Margot decided to check this company's history and tuned in to the Wayback Machine, a vast repository of archived websites. A 2017 version of its website redirected her to a company called Interactive FX, which apparently provided currency-exchange services.

By 2019, however, Dorta Invest had been repurposed to become a commodity trader with a focus on copper and cobalt, two minerals central to Dan Gertler's mining empire in the DRC. The timing of this change coincided with the establishment of Dorta Invest SAS in February 2018.

Margot knew that it was just possible that these sister companies were legitimate. If they were, that would mean that large money transfers between their European and DRC entities wouldn't be unusual, and quite likely wouldn't raise any eyebrows from the compliance officers of banks on the lookout for money laundering. But if they were not legitimate, the lack of any eyebrow raising over such transfers would be very convenient for someone who wanted to move serious money around the world on the QT. Margot was convinced that Berros was now Gertler's frontman in the DRC.

As far as the team could discern, many if not all the dodgy bank accounts they were interested in were managed by Afriland's Patrick Kafindo; so, rather than search all of the documents for suspicious transactions, they decided it would be easier just to look at accounts managed by him, and to narrow down the search to look at transactions that took place between certain dates. It was worth a try.

Margot's eyes scanned her computer screen as she searched for Kafindo's name in Afriland's internal records. Sure enough, the names appeared in the neat computer-printed columns: Anat Gertler and Keren Dobrovitski, Dan Gertler's wife and mother; Shlomo Abihassira, Dorta Invest SAS, Elie-Yohann Berros, Interactive Energy DRC and a bunch of other companies and individuals connected to Gertler. What was becoming apparent to Margot and the wider team was that in the main it didn't look like the big money was going through the accounts of companies that were obviously linked to Gertler, but rather through different 'layers' like those of Elie Berros and Shlomo Abihassira. Why, the team asked themselves, had someone gone to such lengths to create such a complicated system? On this they had a working theory and one document in particular bore this theory out. It showed that on 14 August 2018 someone withdrew US$19 million from the account of Shlomo Abihassira's company RDHADG – the money Shlomo had deposited in cash over the first few months of that year, plus US$2 million from his personal account – and deposited the whole lot into Dorta Invest SAS's account in the same Afriland branch. A straightforward transfer would have been far easier than withdrawing cash, but that would have created a paper trail. What was happening was that with the newly deposited cash safe in its account, Dorta could now transfer that money abroad to be picked up by someone else. *If you wanted to dodge sanctions this was a pretty good way of doing it*, thought Margot, and then Margot had what she called 'my eureka moment'.

She looked at the Czech Dorta's website and realized that the company's 'people' were just photographs randomly copied from the internet. It looked like it was simply a front. However, the website was hosted by Interactive Energy AG, a Swiss-registered company established in 2015 and one of whose directors was Johan Shimon Lamant. He was also the third shareholder of the Israeli 'dodgy tech' company SnatchApp that Margot had unearthed before. Alongside Elie-Yohann Berros and Avi Ben Ezra, SnatchApp brought together all three of the main protagonists she was looking at.

The scent was getting stronger and Margot began digging deeper. SnatchApp was owned by a company called Nobi Tech, an anonymously owned Gibraltar-based company established by Gibraltar's biggest law firm, Hassans International – who we knew to have acted for Gertler in the past.

But who was behind Interactive Energy AG, the firm that hosted Dorta Invest's website?

According to Wikipedia, admittedly not the most reliable source of information, the owner of Interactive Energy was a Russian billionaire called Ruben Katsobashvili. His Wikipedia page shows a grainy photograph of an elderly man, smartly dressed in a dark suit and silk tie and sporting a neatly trimmed white moustache, staring out of the screen into the middle distance.

Born in Georgia in 1933, the page said, Ruben now lived in Moscow. His academic and business achievements were, on the face of it, considerable, including founding a multibillion-dollar oil and gas company. But even Wikipedia smelled a rat – Ruben's Wikipedia page carried a warning: 'This section of a biography of a living person does not include any references or sources.'

Despite trawling through various corporate records, Margot could find no record of the companies mentioned on the Wikipedia page, but she did find an address for Ruben. She checked it out on Google Earth and found 'a crappy old apartment building' in Moscow. It didn't look like the property of a billionaire oil and mining magnate. Other than that, she could find virtually no trace of Ruben online.

He doesn't exist, she thought. *He's a fake*. What she did find was that the author of the Wikipedia page was a SnatchApp employee. Margot sensed that this really was one coincidence too many. Then she had a bright idea.

If you want to dig deep into public records in Russia, there are few better places to go than to Bellingcat: the investigative-journalism organization that famously identified the members of the Russian FSB hit squad that carried out the botched assassination attempt of former Russian military intelligence officer Sergei Skripal and his daughter Yulia in the usually quiet English cathedral city of Salisbury in March 2018.

Margot got in touch with one of Bellingcat's leading journalists. One of the few positive outcomes of the incredible corruption in Putin's Russia is that most official records are for sale – a resource that Bellingcat makes good use of. Within a few weeks, the journalist had turned out a bunch of information for Margot.

'Your guy exists,' he told her. 'He has a second-hand Peugeot and a flat in his name, worth US$360,000, and that's all he owns.' It also seemed that Ruben had been visited by a bailiff in 2018. Finally, the team managed to get Ruben on the phone, but the old man pretended he couldn't hear them and hung up. It turned out he wasn't as deaf as he pretended. Following the call, Margot received a letter from Ruben's lawyer instructing us not to contact his client directly again. This lawyer, based in France, also represented Elie-Yohann Berros.

'What we didn't expect was for Katsobashvili to actually be involved,' Margot remembered, and she didn't think it likely that this 87-year-old Russian with his second-hand car was the billionaire bankroller he was claimed to be. Margot was in little doubt that Katsobashvili had been paid to give his identity to a key part of the company network.

In June 2018, Interactive Energy DRC – the company Ruben purportedly owned – was the recipient of one of Shlomo Abihassira's millions. Later that month, another US$8.5 million flowed into its account, deposited by a Gertler-connected company known as Rulco. This money was in turn wired to Interactive Energy AG in Switzerland. This time it did raise eyebrows.

'I was trying to understand whether these people perhaps recycled an existing network in order to launder cash for [Gertler], and I'm pretty sure that's what they did,' Margot told me. The story the team were unearthing grew bigger and more complex with the wealth of information they were uncovering. This labyrinthine company network – ranging from Hong Kong, the DRC, Gibraltar, the British Virgin Islands, Switzerland, Israel and France, many of them linked by the shareholders of SnatchApp in Israel – looked like a multimillion-dollar scam enabling Dan Gertler to continue to profit from the Congo's mining sector despite being subject to US sanctions.

If we were right, this shadowy network that Margot and PPLAAF had unearthed had immense political and economic ramifications, not least in showing that the people of DRC – who number among the poorest people in the world, despite living in one of its most resource-rich countries – continued to be robbed blind by unseen corrupt networks. This was a story worth telling well and in summer and autumn of 2019 we and PPLAAF signed memorandums of understanding with key media organizations: Bloomberg in the US, *Haaretz* in Israel and *Le Monde* in France. It was in the hectic spring of 2020, as Margot, Gabriele and Henri were working on a joint report, that Gabriel made a discovery that sent a jolt through his system.

He noticed that the dates of the most recent transactions on the bank records we were seeing were really close to the date when we asked Gradi for the information. This meant that Gradi could not have possessed these documents when he arrived in Paris over a year before. There must be a second whistleblower – and whoever they were was still working at the bank. Gradi confirmed the team's fears. 'I have someone at the bank who believes in what I'm doing,' Gradi told Gabriel. 'He's giving me the information. He wants this to come out; I want this to come out.'

'I freaked out because we didn't realize the level of risk that Gradi was taking, let alone his colleague who was still at the bank,' Margot told me. Of their own volition, Gradi and Navy had established a secure way to communicate. Using a web-based email account, they would save messages as drafts but never send them. Only people who knew of the account's existence and who possessed the passwords could access these communications. But given the not-very-veiled death threats that Gradi had received, the inside man was undoubtedly in extreme danger. Gabriel decided that the team should not ask for any more information like this. They felt that the only safe way to engage with the second whistleblower was to meet in person in Kinshasa. Now they just needed someone to do the job.

Michael Kavanagh has been a journalist ever since he left university. He first reported the Congo around 2004 and fell in love with the place. After some years reporting on the war tearing apart eastern DRC, in 2009 he was offered a job at Bloomberg and inherited the Kinshasa beat from Bloomberg veteran Franz Wild. Since then, Michael has become one of the gurus of all things Congo – a fact which he is very modest about. His understanding was critical to the investigation into the dark secrets emanating from Afriland.

'You cannot write the history of modern Congo from 1997 onwards without Dan Gertler,' Michael told me. 'He is one of the top-five key players in Congolese history of the last twenty-five years.'

Michael was the obvious candidate to meet the second whistleblower. He called the number he'd been given. A man answered and Michael called him by an agreed codename. There was a long pause before Navy Malela acknowledged who he was – he was entering uncharted territory. They arranged to meet where Michael was staying.

Navy told Michael that he had read various articles of his about the vast business interests of the Kabila family, especially those based on the testimony of Jean-Jacques Lumumba, the Congolese whistleblower whose story had prompted Gradi to contact PPLAAF in the first place.

'He was amazing,' Michael said of Navy. 'He is a typical Kinois – someone who loves the ambiance and creative chaos of Kinshasa. He was in a T-shirt and jeans [. . .] not in a banker's uniform – and we laughed and laughed. He was a great storyteller [. . .] One of the hardest things about the work that we do is trying to make documents come to life, and he was really good at making that happen.'

Over the course of two very long meetings, Michael probed into what was going on at Afriland: who was involved, what Navy had seen and what documents he had pulled. At the second meeting they went through the documents themselves. With these, Michael gained a better understanding of the story and he relayed the information back to Gabriel and Henri in Paris, to Margot in London and to Gur Megiddo, a journalist at *Haaretz* in Israel.

Navy talked Michael through the requirements to make a bank transfer; the names of both the sender and receiver, their addresses, dates of birth and all the information to ensure the transaction was legitimate. Then Navy showed Michael what was actually happening. 'It would be like a single name, not a full name, just a first name. And that would be without an address, without a reason for why the transfer was made – and it would be for a $5 million cash transaction. It was hilarious,' Michael told me.

As they began to better understand the documents, so they understood too the enormity of what they were dealing with – and this rammed home, if it needed to, the danger that Navy and Gradi faced. The assistant deputy director general of the bank, Patrick Kafindo, was linked to a lot of very powerful people in the Congolese security forces.

Michael knew that this wasn't just another example of random corruption. In his conversations with figures in Congo's banking sector, Michael learned that they knew something fishy was going on at Afriland. 'They knew that Afriland was Gertler's bank and they knew that the US government was monitoring the situation closely. The US didn't necessarily know about Afriland in particular,' Michael mused. 'But they certainly knew that the Congo is a great place to launder money. It's a dollar economy and billions and billions of dollars in cash, physical dollar bills, come into Congo every year. In the Congo you still have access to the global financial system while also being on the outside of it. It's a good place to do dirty business.

'The US had warned the sector and they were very explicit about it. The Congo could lose all its access to correspondent banks, and without that you don't have access to the global financial sector. The economic fallout from that would be monumental.'

While Dan Gertler had undoubtedly brought millions of dollars into the country, the sanctions-evading scheme centred around Afriland threatened its entire economy. The stakes could hardly be higher, and certainly not for Navy. The net was closing in.

PPLAAF was the brainchild of Gabriel's uncle, William Bourdon, who still serves as its president. William is a renowned and flamboyant French human-rights lawyer whose organization, Sherpa, Global Witness has worked with over many years. As the new report was coming together, the team were getting ready to send out the 'opportunity to comment' letters (OTCs) when Eric Moutet, a former Sherpa board member, called William. Out of the blue he told him that he was now representing Gertler, that Gertler knew PPLAAF were writing a report in collaboration with Global Witness, Bloomberg and *Le Monde* and, more worryingly, that they knew there was another source and that he was still at the bank. This was a real shock. How Gertler knew we did not know, but the team immediately put a hold on sending the OTCs until the situation became clearer.

Gabriel was on holiday in Italy with his girlfriend when Henri called him. 'This is way too much information for them to have,' Henri told him. 'We need to get Navy out.' The publication of the report was put on hold and PPLAAF went into overdrive to secure visas for Navy and his family from the French embassy in Kinshasa. It was only when Navy was safe in France that Henri and Gabriel told him the extent of the threats they felt he faced in Kinshasa.

'We didn't feel we could tell him before he reached France that we really felt that he could die, or that something else very bad could happen to him,' Henri said. Navy, the ultimate Kinois who loved his life in Kinshasa, understood that he was never going back and would need to apply for political asylum. And then the Covid lockdowns hit.

On 12 March 2020, as Covid lockdowns were coming into force and with Navy and his family safely in France, the team sent the OTCs. As these letters were opened, from Israel to Kinshasa, from Washington, DC to Paris and London, they began to spoil a lot of people's breakfasts.

Meanwhile, this standard due-diligence process turned up some unexpected titbits. Using ContactMonkey, an easily downloadable app, Margot checked to see whether the OTC emails had been opened and if so how many times and when and where. The email addressed to Ruben Katsobashvili, the would-be 'billionaire' director of Interactive Energy, was not opened in Moscow, where we believed he was at the time, but in Israel. Given that these emails were sent during the height of the Covid pandemic it seemed unlikely that the elderly Russian was on the road. The smell of kippers was palpable but got even smellier. The OTC letters emailed to Elie-Yohann Berros and Avi Ben Ezra were opened at the same Israeli IP address as Ruben's. The significance of this was not lost on Margot. All these emails were being opened on the same device or on the same shared Wi-Fi network in Israel. That network belonged to Avi Ben Ezra.

Eric Moutet, evidently not one to give up easily, contacted William and asked him to meet for lunch. In a rather surprising turnabout, he now presented himself as Afriland's lawyer and was accompanied by one of Gertler's lawyers, Marc Bonnant, a former president of the Geneva Bar Association, who coincidentally acts for another Israeli mining tycoon trying to ward off accusations of corruption, Beny Steinmetz (a big presence in my previous book, *Very Bad People*). The civilized atmosphere of the bar belied the nature of the conversation between the three men and was a portent of how dirty and desperate Gertler's fightback would be.

Moutet and Bonnant showed William a criminal complaint they had prepared against PPLAAF and Global Witness, which they said they would file in Paris if publication took place. They also said they had a secretly recorded conversation between William and a man called Noël Dubus that, so the lawyers suggested, showed that William had secretly taken money from the United Arab Emirates and had also shown interest in working for Libyan warlord General Khalifa Haftar. They threatened to expose this information if publication went ahead. William was undeterred by this attempted blackmail; the accusations were false and Noël Dubus was a convicted fraudster.

More worrying was the 12 pages of A4 they showed William. These pages represented the results of a covert surveillance operation and contained grainy photos of Gradi, Navy, their wives and various contacts from their private lives. One photograph was of the apartment building in France that Gradi and his family lived in. The document included brief biographies of the whistleblowers, their children and their phone numbers. Their social-media accounts had been analysed, even recording that Navy was a fan of Real Madrid. It was clear that Gradi could be in danger – even in Paris. PPLAAF wasted no time and relocated Gradi and his family.

THE FIGHTBACK, LONDON, MARCH 2020

Judging by what happened next, Dan Gertler was seething and hellbent on shutting down any publication that threatened to expose the connections between him and this parallel company network. Even our seasoned in-house media lawyer Nicola Namdjou was taken aback by the letter she received from Gertler's lawyers, Carter-Ruck – known as Carter-Fuck by satirical magazine *Private Eye* – one of the great white sharks of the legal profession, although sadly not so endangered.

Their letter started mildly enough: 'Both Global Witness and PPLAAF hold themselves out to be responsible and ethical organizations seeking to serve the public interest. In this case matters appear to have gone very seriously wrong.'

b) Notarized evidence has been provided to our client, copies of which we have in our possession, that in 2016 Global Witness journalist XXXXX and researcher XXXXXX* tried to engage the NGOs, CNDHJ and FIHJ to obtain confidential information about him, in return for funding for the NGOs and other payments to interested parties to act against the law;

c) Notarized evidence has been provided to our client, a copy of which we have in our possession, that Global Witness journalist XXXXX, and colleagues who replaced [them], approached multiple NGOs in the DRC to try to obtain confidential information about the tax and banking affairs of companies in the DRC, in return for bribes to those providing the information and scholarships for training abroad to NGO members who provide such information;

It was complete bollocks from beginning to end. None of our expert DRC staff nor any of our colleagues in other organizations had heard of these NGOs. Moreover, the Global Witness staff Carter-Ruck referred to hadn't worked for the organization for years. What really shocked Nicola was that Carter Ruck were accusing us of offering bribes in return for confidential information. 'These are serious allegations of criminality and impropriety,' she told me. 'The moment they start naming and threatening individual staff, it gets really ugly. Especially when they were relying on patently false [. . .] fake information.'

With Gertler's limitless pockets to cover Carter-Ruck's huge fees, both we and PPLAAF faced a barrage of accusations, including blackmail,

---

* Names removed for reasons of security and confidentiality.

document theft and fabrication of information, which is a bit of a conundrum: why bother to steal a document if you can fake one? This was the beginning of a long, dirty and expensive fight. Their letter concluded on a distinctly sour note:

> Global Witness and PPLAAF are requested to respond to this letter by 18 June. Thereafter, our client will decide whether or not to refer the whole or any part of the above conduct to the Police in England or lodge a criminal complaint in France and/or make a complaint to such other appropriate authority such as the Charity Commission, and in which country or countries.

This was highly irregular. 'If you are concerned that there's criminal activity you should make a complaint, but this was a conditional complaint – i.e., Carter-Ruck would make the complaint unless we didn't publish,' Nicola explained.

'It's bullshit,' Margot said when she called Nicola. 'We have to go ahead.'

This, after all, is exactly the purpose of a SLAPP suit. A SLAPP – strategic litigation against public participation – suit is an increasingly popular legal avenue open to you if you are very, very rich indeed and want to shut somebody up. The point about a SLAPP is not necessarily whether the litigant has a strong legal case; it's about silencing unwelcome critics and drowning often poorly resourced organizations in lawyers. Nicola had absolutely no intention of bowing to Gertler's tactics. She engaged Rupert Cowper-Coles, a top defamation lawyer with London law firm RPC who had been on the Global Witness team in numerous legal fights. He was to become a vital partner to Nicola and Margot.

*

As Nicola and Rupert were dealing with the unwelcome attentions of Carter-Ruck, Margot and a fellow Global Witness campaigner, Jon Noronha-Gant, were working late into the evening before publication, amending text and double-, triple- and quadruple-checking the facts. For months now a flurry of correspondence from Gertler's lawyers had alleged that we and PPLAAF had got our facts wrong. We had responded by asking them to send us proof, but had received nothing. Then, on the eve of publication, in what looked a lot like another desperate delay strategy, a bundle of documents arrived.

'These documents seemed to materially contradict what we had,' Margot told me. 'One of them was a redacted bank statement which, on face value, showed that neither Abihassira nor Mukonda had deposited a million dollars into Abihassira's account.' So whose information was correct? Given Gertler's vast financial resources and his effectively unlimited financial capacity to throw expensive lawyers at us, there was a lot riding on this question.

We, PPLAAF and the whistleblowers examined the bank statements and sensed something was up. In addition to the fact that the documents were redacted, there was no metadata – the information that would identify the documents' history. These documents had been wiped clean and we didn't trust them. Thanks to Gradi and Navy, over the course of the investigation we had had access to reams of documents and the information in them had been cross-referenced, not least with some of the subjects of our report. 'We are confident in our source material,' Margot told Nicola.

In the end it was up to the lawyers. Would the results of this epic investigation be consigned to the dustbin – or rather, a super-shredder – or would the launch button be pressed? The more Nicola and Rupert read, the more they felt that there was nothing to suggest we hadn't got our facts straight. Meanwhile, Gertler's evidence, delivered months after we had asked for it, was redacted and lacked veracity. Moreover, there was the issue of public interest.

'Go for it,' Nicola said.

The report was launched automatically at a minute past midnight US Eastern Standard Time on 2 July 2020, around 5am UK time. Bleary-eyed, Margot woke up just before the launch to see the fruits of so many long months of hard work go out into the world. What she actually saw was a portent of the most aggressive response to a publication that Global Witness has ever experienced, and indeed has few parallels anywhere that I have ever heard about. Global Witness, PPLAAF and *Haaretz* came under not only an unprecedented legal attack but also a dirty-tricks campaign the Kremlin would have been proud of. It was much, much worse for Gradi Koko and Navy Malela: it was clear that their lives really were at risk.

Global Witness's data-investigations team dived into the fray with relish and found evidence that this was no random outpouring from offended citizens but instead what looked like a coordinated campaign, with links to a Congolese communications agency that in turn had links to Joseph Kabila and state mining company Gécamines.

Jossard Munima's tweet on 5 July, for example, accused Global Witness and Bloomberg of being criminal organizations that falsified documents. However, it seemed likely that Munima may have actually falsified himself. His profile picture appears to be a stock photo from an Australian digital-assets agency called Envato, of a male fashion model advertising the RAM fashion brand.

In addition to Jossard, the data team identified two other accounts, supposedly belonging to young Congolese men, posting similar content, that were all set up within twenty minutes of each other on 20 June 2020. Such a coincidence is possible, of course; but given that the OTC letters had gone out in March, a smear campaign would have had plenty of time to prepare.

Meanwhile highly defamatory videos were being posted on YouTube, one of them on a site purporting to be that of fellow anti-corruption organization Transparency International, but it was a fake. Numerous Congolese media sites sided with Eric Moutet's version of events and, despite Covid travel restrictions, he appeared at a press conference in Kinshasa. Gertler filed a complaint against our Israeli media partner, *TheMarker*, the business magazine of *Haaretz*, while one of the protagonists unsuccessfully tried to obtain an injunction on *Haaretz* itself. But the real danger began unfolding during August 2020.

Afriland issued a summons requiring Gradi and Navy to appear in court in Kinshasa. It was served at PPLAAF's office in Paris and under French law a summons cannot be served on a law firm or organization, so it didn't hold up legally. More than that, PPLAAF were in possession of the surveillance material shown to William Bourdon, which showed that Eric Moutet knew Gradi's address very well – so they had no excuse not to serve the documents on him directly had they wanted to.

Nevertheless, Henri and Gabriel took the decision to appoint a lawyer to attend court in Kinshasa on the appointed day, 7 September 2020. Mr Jean-Marie Kabangela Ilunga duly turned up to inform the court that the summons was irregular – but when Afriland's representative didn't show up, the hearing was immediately postponed and Kabangela left.

Unknown to Gradi, Navy and PPLAAF, however, a second summons from Afriland had been served, and although it noted that the whistleblowers were now living in Europe, it was served on their former neighbours in Kinshasa. A second hearing was held in the same court that same afternoon, in the absence of the defendants and their lawyer. This second hearing found Gradi and Navy guilty of theft, private corruption, breach of professional secrecy, slanderous denunciation, breach of trust and concealment. The two whistleblowers were sentenced to death.

As Henri told the press in response: 'When one unmasks the world's largest corruption networks, the response can be extremely violent.' The judgement was condemned by the United Nations OHCHR in the DRC and by the embassies of Belgium, France and the United States.

On 21 May 2021, William Bourdon and Global Witness CEO Mike Davis also received a summons from Kinshasa, requiring them to appear at a public audience on 19 July 2021. They did not go.

CONCLUSION

On 6 December 2021, this new Gertler network was sanctioned by the US treasury. Alain Mukonda and 12 entities connected to him were described as providing 'A Financial Lifeline for Dan Gertler'. Bruised and battered, the mining heavyweight was down, but not out – he and Congo's president Félix Tshisekedi settled on a backroom deal.

Gertler, via Ventora, would return around US$2 billion of oil and mining rights to the DRC, but there was a catch. The contract stipulated that the government of the DRC would intervene with the US to get sanctions against Gertler removed. Accordingly, on 5 May 2022, President Tshisekedi wrote to US president Joe Biden outlining Dan Gertler's long contribution to the Congo and the recent handover of the US$2 billion.

Stating that 'the Democratic Republic of Congo no longer has any grievances' against Dan Gertler, Tshisekedi made a plea for sanctions against him to be dropped.

In turn, a group of Congolese and international civil-rights organizations wrote to the US secretary of state Antony Blinken and secretary of the Treasury Janet Yellen, pointing out that under the Magnitsky rules sanctions could not be dropped, and highlighting that, under the deal between Ventora and the DRC, Gertler would continue receiving royalties of around $200,000 per day for the next decade – around three-quarters of a billion dollars, which is a bit like giving amnesty to a bank robber but allowing him to collect interest payments on the loot stashed in the same bank that he robbed.

Meanwhile, those individuals and groups who had challenged Gertler continued to face his ire. In addition to the legal cases launched against Global Witness, PPLAAF and *Haaretz*, Gertler's lawyers launched a blizzard of lawsuits against a number of Congolese civil-society organizations who had neither the legal nor financial capacity to defend themselves. Their directors faced ruin. But then something really unexpected happened. Out of the blue, on 13 April 2023, Gertler offered an olive branch.

> The Jewish holiday of Passover, which we have just celebrated, honours the concept of freedom. I believe in freedom – the freedom to work, the freedom to prosper, the freedom to express oneself, the freedom to disagree and the freedom to make mistakes.

In this letter, he called off all the legal cases he had brought against its addressees. The letter failed to mention the freedom to corrupt politicians or asset strip a country, but maybe these fell under the category of 'mistakes'. He remembered to outline his contribution to the economy in DRC, omitting the inconvenient exposure of the US$1.4 billion he had cost the economy by buying up state-owned mining assets on the cheap and flogging them to Glencore for a vast profit. He did manage to remember how his reputation had suffered from 'groundless and defamation [*sic*] reports'.

Nevertheless, he had done something that was genuinely significant in handing over US$2 billion in cash and assets to the DRC government; what he described as 'the largest ever consensual transfer to an African state in the history of the region'. Which is possibly true. Like most corrupt tycoons, Gertler presides over a charitable foundation that is 'committed to improving the lives of the most vulnerable communities in the Democratic Republic of Congo'. However, his latest move may not have been a pure act of philanthropy.

On 11 October 2023, the *Wall Street Journal* carried an article headlined 'U.S. Considers Dropping Sanctions Against Israeli Billionaire in Push for EV Metals'. The article described how, according to insiders, sanctions against Gertler would be dropped, thereby allowing him to do deals with Saudi Arabia. The US would get some of the proceeds and access to some of the DRC's vast reserves of cobalt, essential to electric-vehicle production.

Gertler's amnesty did not stretch to Global Witness. Gradi and Navy are still in exile and remain under sentence of death. It seems unlikely they will be able to go home any time soon – it would be too big a gamble to test whether the leopard really had changed its spots.

7

THE SPY INSIDE

'That's their goal: to make you paranoid, isolate you from people and lock you in a prison.'

—Hicham Mansouri, Moroccan journalist

QUEBEC, CANADA, JUNE 2018

Omar Abdulaziz looked up from his computer and glanced at the text message. He grunted in satisfaction:

'Dear Customer, DHL shipment No, #1751455027 is scheduled for delivery on 28/06/2018, Manage delivery at https://sunday-deals.com/xxxxxxx, DHL*

He had ordered something from Amazon just the day before. He clicked on the link and then returned to his work. That click was a mistake.

---

* I have changed some characters in the link in case it is still active.

As Omar continued with his work, an infection – known in the trade as an exploit – began to pry open his phone, probing its operating system and apps for vulnerabilities that the phone's manufacturers were themselves unaware of. Once an exploit finds a vulnerability then the operator – the person or organization that had sent the link – can do anything with the phone that the phone's owner can do. And more. Whoever sent this exploit to Omar could turn on his phone's microphone and camera, and could monitor everything that was going on with the device. They could intercept communications sent or received by Omar before they were encrypted or after they had been decrypted. They could alter the phone's security settings. In fact, they had full control. In Omar's line of work, that meant that he and anyone he was communicating with were severely compromised. The consequence of Omar clicking on the DHL link was the creation of one more link in a chain of events that, through no fault of his own, would prove catastrophic.

HERZLIYA, ISRAEL, 2010

Fresh from two failed tech startups, three Israeli schoolfriends – Niv Karmi, a veteran of military intelligence and Mossad; Shalev Hulio; and Omri Lavie – finally got a break. It was one that would make them rich beyond their dreams and see them become the darlings of their own government as well as some of the most authoritarian regimes on Earth. Conversely, they would be both reviled and feared by anyone furthering the interests of democracy and freedom of speech. Their invention was a superweapon.

The second of their ventures, CommuniTake, was innocent enough and a good idea. It would enable a cellphone company's customer-support staff to take control of their clients' smartphones – with their permission, of course – to help them sort out problems. The idea didn't take off but it did attract the attention of a European spy agency, because they had a problem. Governments and others had been able to intercept phone and other communications for decades, but new, commercially available encryption – one of the key components of WhatsApp, Signal and other instant-messaging services, for example – was so strong that government agencies couldn't penetrate them. The only way they could intercept their targets' messages was to read them before they were encrypted or after they had been decrypted, which meant they needed to take over their phones and intercept the messages before they were even sent. Alive to this new use of their benign creation, the three Israelis formed a spyware company. They named it using the first letters of their forenames: NSO. They called their main product Pegasus.

Ron Deibert is quick to explain that he is an academic and that Citizen Lab, which he founded in 2001, is a university laboratory. Indeed, his academic credentials and the pioneering research carried out by Citizen Lab are breathtaking. However, I cannot help but think of him as a modern version of a warrior philosopher, because he is a leading combatant in the battle against the misuse of cyber espionage and can count some of the world's most brutal authoritarian governments among his enemies. That's what makes his calmness all the more surprising.

For his PhD in the early 1990s he decided to focus on information technology. As a conventional scholar, he was hired at the University of Toronto on the basis of his first book. Working mostly alone, he carried out traditional academic work, researching and publishing articles, and then he got the germ of an idea. The internet was in its infancy and the telecommunications revolution was only just beginning. Something inside Ron's head told him that all of this would likely involve some big impacts on global security.

Things began to change for Ron when he was seconded to the Canadian government for a couple of studies looking into how the emerging market for commercial satellite imagery could be used for arms control. He noticed how most commercial satellite imagery then was pretty low resolution – around 30m (98.4ft) – which is OK for spotting large-scale construction and deforestation but nothing like the highly sophisticated high-resolution spy satellites operated by governments. Then everything changed for him.

'I was introduced to the world of signals intelligence and the spooks who were doing stuff with very high-resolution imagery. I saw a lot of the KH-11 imagery that the Americans had around the period of the first Gulf War,' he told me, referring to the US spy satellites. 'That experience really stuck with me and I had this vision of a distributed net of sensors that would hold governments accountable, using technology.'

Ron wrote internal reports for the Canadian Foreign Affairs Ministry on how they might employ commercial satellite imagery to hold governments accountable for their commitments to arms-control agreements. It wasn't long before his restless curiosity started focusing on the nascent internet.

'It dawned on me that the internet was a repository of data on what everyone was doing,' he explained. 'As computers were connecting to each other, they were a means by which you could navigate through the internet to find things that are going on, that should be exposed in the public interest.' A particular inspiration was one of Ron's students, Nart

Villeneuve, who was working on a paper for which he connected to computers in mainland China to manually check for internet censorship.

'He would, from Canada, connect to a proxy computer in Beijing, and then run automated queries for websites to see if he could access them. And then he would run trace routes, and he would see exactly where the "filtering" – the censoring – was taking place along the network path. He even discovered that he could see the type of routers that were being used – in this case, Cisco routers.' Ron was impressed, and then happenstance took a punt.

Anthony Romero, a young program officer at the Ford Foundation, contacted Ron out of the blue and invited him to New York. Anthony also realized the importance of Ron's field of interest and offered him a job. Ron declined, so instead Anthony asked him to put together a funding application to do more research. He had caught Ron at a good moment: Nart's work was still fresh in his mind.

'I realized that what Nart had found was a technical means of mapping the internet; similar to the work I had done with satellites, but in a completely subterranean realm,' Ron explained. 'For example, mapping the internet using evidence-based research to identify that there's an American company, Cisco, supplying the technology to filter the internet in China.'

With that in mind, he wrote the proposal for the Ford Foundation. 'I described our aspirations to provide an evidence-based counter-intelligence service for global civil society, using forensic evidence or technical information that can't be disputed,' Ron said. The Ford Foundation liked the idea and Ron's proposal formed the basis of the Citizen Lab, part of the Munk School of Global Affairs and Public Policy at the University of Toronto. Ron's first hire was Nart Villeneuve. Over the next 12 years, Nart and Ron expanded what Nart had done in China and collaborated with Harvard in the US and Cambridge University in the UK, testing internet censorship in more than 70 countries annually. 'We had people running network-interrogation tests, often at great danger to themselves, in places like Uzbekistan, Africa, the Middle East and Southeast Asia. With MIT we wrote country reports detailing how nations were trying to implement information controls and how they were tracking them,' Ron told me.

Then Nart started focusing on information warfare. In 2008, he ran experiments on the Chinese version of Skype to show that there was a backdoor, and that the Chinese government were using it to monitor text and chat messages. Then Citizen Lab began to hear from Tibetans worried that they too were under surveillance. Not everything can be done remotely, so over the next few years – right up until the Covid pandemic – Ron dispatched a series of research teams to the base of the Dalai Lama and the Tibetan government in exile at McLeod Ganj in India, a small town nestling in the foothills of the Himalayas a stone's throw from Tibet. A key member of the team was Greg Walton, who was working with Nart Villeneuve.

'We collected network traffic from the computers in Dharamsala and other Tibetan offices worldwide – Brussels, New York and London,' Ron told me. 'We mapped all the connections made by the computers back and forth over the internet, and in scouring through that, Nart observed I think it was 22 or 26 characters that kept coming up.'

Nart took that string and cut and pasted it into Google and just one result came back: a web server in mainland China. Nart clicked on the link and it took him to a portal, which the Chinese had not password protected. 'I think it was hubris; they thought that no one would ever notice it,' Ron told me.

The portal turned out to be the entry point to all of the Chinese operator's very carefully documented victims; effectively a control panel. Columns listed the name of the computer and sometimes included the target organization's identity, for example, Indian Embassy, Washington, DC. Commands could be sent by the Chinese operator to those computers that were under their control, and then the data would be exfiltrated from those computers. Ron and Nart decided to play guinea pig.

'We captured a copy of GhostDraft, which was the malware they were using, and infected one of our own computers,' Ron explained. 'And we could see our own computer checking in to the Chinese server. So we had verified that this was indeed the control panel. We could see the Dalai Lama's computers, the Tibetan computers, but also all of these other ones as well.

'The hackers – the China-based operators – made a mistake in their infrastructure that allowed us to observe what they were doing for eight months. We watched them hack ministries of foreign affairs, governments, international organizations and a mail server at Associated Press,' Ron told me.

Their resulting report, published by the Munk School's Information Warfare Monitor in March 2009, focused on China as an example of a global problem. It exposed a malware-based cyber-espionage network they called the GhostNet. They documented that the Chinese – whether through a state or non-state operation they couldn't tell – had penetrated 1,295 computers in 103 countries. The fact that the Dalai Llama's computers were being hacked helped propel the report to be one of the top news stories that day, including an exclusive in *The New York Times*.

'It was massive,' Ron told me. 'This type of hacking happens all the time now, but back then, outside of the classified realm, very few people knew that this was going on and certainly didn't have evidence for it.'

Citizen Lab's teams continued to work with the Tibetans at McLeod Ganj over the next decade and a half and helped build up a strong local capacity to deal with the threats. When Ron visited years later he was really impressed by the Tibetans. Looking out from the balcony of his hotel room, he could see the home of the Dalai Lama, the spiritual leader of Tibet, just over the next mountain, and he ended up having a brief meeting with him. 'It was perfunctory, but he thanked me and said how much they appreciated our team,' Ron recalled. 'And I said back to him how much I appreciate the people that we were working with, who are just excellent – which they are.'

Ron was also impressed by the public-education campaign via videos and cartoons that was developed under the banner of 'Detach from Attachments', a play on Buddhist philosophy, which advised Tibetan activists not to click on attachments.

One of the next key targets for Citizen Lab was the commercial market for spyware, private companies selling super-sophisticated software to government agencies. There was very big money to be made and, of course, any companies involved would be on the side of the angels, because they would be helping governments catch crooks, intercept terrorists and keep their citizens safe. Or so the theory went.

The home page of the Italian company Hacking Team sounded perfectly reasonable: 'We believe that fighting crime should be easy: we provide effective, easy-to-use offensive technology to the worldwide law enforcement and intelligence communities.' Germany's FinFisher advertised itself as 'The Global Trusted Advisor for Law Enforcement and Intelligence Agencies'.

Trumpeting their credentials as companies that could help

governments tackle organized crime and terrorism, their dirty secret was that their software was more famously used to target various governments' political opponents and human-rights campaigners, and that comes with risks. Both Hacking Team and FinFisher went out of business amid scandals relating to the use of their software by oppressive regimes to target journalists and human-rights activists – scandals exposed by organizations like Citizen Lab. However, another spyware company didn't just survive, it thrived – this was the Israel-based NSO Group.

CITIZEN LAB, TORONTO, CANADA, AUGUST 2016

Ahmed Mansoor was understandably cautious. In 2011 he had been sentenced to three years in prison. He and several others in the United Arab Emirates were being silenced for their peaceful campaigns defending press freedoms and calling for democratic reforms. Although reviled by his own government, Mansoor was celebrated by leading human-rights organizations; and, following an international outcry, he was pardoned by the country's president, Sheikh Khalifa bin Zayed Al Nahyan. He was well aware that from that point on the government were watching his every move, so when he received a suspicious-looking text message promising 'new secrets' relating to the torture of people imprisoned in the UAE, he knew exactly what to do.

He forwarded the message to Citizen Lab and asked them to take a look. Citizen Lab clicked on the link and obtained three 'zero-day' exploits – so-called because of the timeframe in which a software developer must fix the problem – on Mansoor's iPhone, as well as a copy of Pegasus spyware. Microsoft defines a zero-day vulnerability 'as a flaw in software programming that has been discovered before a vendor or programmer has been made aware of it. Because the programmers don't know this vulnerability exists, there are no patches or fixes, making an attack more likely to be successful.'

In other words, zero-day exploits were something that companies like Apple or WhatsApp didn't know about. Citizen Lab immediately notified Apple, who created a patch to block the spyware.

Between 2016 and 2018, Citizen Lab 'fingerprinted' the exploit link and the behaviour of the command-and-control servers connected to the attack on Mansoor. They discovered 237 servers, but within a week the NSO Group – Pegasus's creators – took down the servers Citizen Lab had detected. When a few of these came back online, they no longer matched the fingerprint Citizen Lab had created. Not to be deterred, Ron's data scientists developed new fingerprints – which they named ξ1, ξ2 and ξ3 – and a technique they christened Athena because, according to Greek myth, Athena had tamed Pegasus.

As Citizen Lab scanned the internet for the Pegasus fingerprints, Athena clustered the resulting IP addresses into 36 groups. These, Citizen Lab believed, represented 36 operators – distinct NSO clients – in Bahrain, Kazakhstan, Mexico, Morocco, Saudi Arabia and the United Arab Emirates. Between them, they had infected mobile phones in 45 different countries. Citizen Lab's interest was piqued when they looked at the data, because one of these operators, in Saudi Arabia – which they had codenamed KINGDOM – was spying on someone in Canada, Citizen Lab's home turf.

'This was in the summer of 2018. At that time, the Canadian government was in the midst of a big diplomatic dispute with Saudi Arabia,' Ron Deibert told me. 'Our foreign affairs minister had criticized the regime publicly for its women's-rights record. The Saudis retaliated; they kicked out our ambassador – it was a big brouhaha – so we're like, "Oh, geez, I wonder who they're spying on in Canada? Let's see if we can figure this out." '

The only data Citizen Lab had was the IP address from which the hacked phone was checking in and the internet service providers that it was logging in to. What they could see was that this was coming from Montreal. Through its contacts Citizen Lab put together a shortlist of people in Montreal that they thought the Saudi government would be interested in. They also narrowed the search area because they could see that the infected phone routinely connected to two internet service providers. One of these was hosted by the University of Quebec and the other was a commercial ISP called Vidéotron. Judging by when the owner of the phone logged into these ISPs, the researchers knew they were looking for someone who lived no more than 20 minutes from the university.

OMAR ABDULAZIZ, MONTREAL, CANADA

As the anti-government protest movement that became known as the Arab Spring spread across the Middle East in the early 2010s, Omar Abdulaziz took to Twitter in his own country, Saudi Arabia, challenging the country's autocratic regime. If annoying people can be judged as a mark of success, as I think it can, he was doing well, and the authorities were concerned enough to ask that his father bring him to a particular government office in Riyadh. Smelling a rat, Omar went to the airport instead and in 2014 applied for political asylum in Canada. There he burgeoned into a very prominent human-rights activist and became a major thorn in the side of his country's authoritarian government. He started a satirical YouTube channel targeting the regime and its ruler Crown Prince Mohammed bin Salman in particular, and he built a 340,000 following on Twitter. His influence was such that another dissident, a prominent Saudi Arabian journalist, approached him to suggest they combine forces.

They realized that their government had deployed an army of trolls to dominate Saudi social media so they could quickly obliterate any sign of dissent and hunt down the perpetrators. Omar and his friend called these propagandists 'the flies', and together they decided to build an anti-regime social-media-based youth movement in Saudi Arabia. They referred to their own nascent Twitter army as the 'cyber bees'. These cyber bees would use social media to broadcast the truth about human-rights abuses in their country. Given that 80 per cent of the Saudi population use Twitter, this was a significant problem for the regime. Part of Omar and his new friend's plan was to raise money and import foreign – and therefore untraceable – SIM cards into the kingdom that could be used by the activists there. This was a challenge that the state-propaganda machine would go to any lengths to thwart.

Around this time, Omar was called by someone saying they represented Saudi Arabia's ruler and extended an invitation for him to return home – with royal protection, of course. Omar politely declined. His countrymen were persistent and in the early summer of 2018 two envoys flew to meet him in Montreal. His fellow campaigner warned Omar to meet these people only in public places. When they met, the two men offered Omar the chance of hosting a TV chat show back home, where he could become the voice of the youth. Omar didn't think this was very likely. 'You have just arrested many people who said nothing really. And you're telling me that you want me back in Saudi and nothing is going to happen to me?' he recalled to the interviewer in Bryan Fogel's acclaimed documentary *The Dissident*.

The two envoys fell back on their last option, which was to invite Omar to come to the Saudi embassy to renew his passport, but, with his friend's warning fresh in his mind, he refused. Within a few months, the memory of this decision would freeze his blood.

A month or so later, Omar knew that something had gone badly wrong. 'It was then,' he told the interviewer, 'at the beginning of August 2018, that they started to arrest my friends, my brothers, my relatives. Every two, three hours I was receiving a new phone call from someone in Saudi telling me that someone was getting arrested. I was in shock. I made a YouTube broadcast and I said: "Guys, this behaviour shows me that something bigger than just arresting my brothers and friends is going to happen. I do believe MBS is going to do something huge."'

Omar knew the risks he was facing, telling the *Guardian*:

The [Canadian authorities] received some information regarding my situation that I might be a potential target. MBS and his group or – I don't know – his team, they want to harm me. They want to do something, but I don't know whether it's assassination, kidnapping, I don't know – but something not OK for sure.

They asked me, 'What do you think about it?' I said, 'I'm happy,' Abdulaziz said, laughing. 'I feel that I'm doing something.' You know, if you're not doing anything that bothers MBS, that means you're not working very well.

These risks were all too real, and one of Omar's contacts also told him that the Saudi authorities knew all about the cyber bees. As soon as he could, he told his fellow conspirator.

'How did they know?' asked Omar's friend.

'There must have been a gap,' Omar responded.

There was a long pause before his friend replied, 'God help us.' His name was Jamal Khashoggi.

Citizen Lab's Bill Marczak, a senior technical researcher, arrived in Montreal and literally went door to door, contacting members of the Saudi diaspora on his list to see if he could track down the needle in the haystack, the one person he knew had been targeted by Pegasus. Eventually, he found a match. Omar Abdulaziz attended Quebec University and the timing of his phone connecting to his home and the university's internet service providers corresponded with the information Citizen Lab had found in the Pegasus infection.

Omar was understandably wary but a mutual connection vouched for Citizen Lab's bona fides and he agreed to meet Bill in a cafe. Bill asked Omar if he could check his phone. He looked for suspicious links that may have been sent in emails and texts and they came across the one from DHL.

Their opinion was clear. On 1 October 2018, Citizen Lab published 'The Kingdom Came to Canada', a report detailing their investigation into the spyware attack on Omar Abdulaziz. In it they stated:

We conclude with high confidence that a government customer of NSO Group targeted and infected Omar Abdulaziz, a Canadian permanent resident, with Pegasus spyware. The infection took place while he was on Canadian soil, after seeking and receiving asylum from the Canadian government. We further believe that this operator, which we named KINGDOM, is linked to the [*sic*] Saudi Arabia's government and security services.

Citizen Lab's researchers had found the needle in the haystack. Omar was not surprised but now he had something else to worry about. Since he'd clicked on that fateful DHL link, Omar's phone would likely have been checking in with the Saudi Pegasus operator, who could not have missed the 400 or so WhatsApp messages between Omar and his interlocutor, which included their plans to send both money and foreign SIM cards to the cyber bees, their fellow activists in Saudi Arabia.

The timing of the report was uncanny. Ron was at a security conference in the Netherlands when he and Bill both received a WhatsApp message from Omar: 'I'm really worried, Jamal has gone missing.'

'Who's Jamal?' asked Ron.

SAUDI ARABIAN CONSULATE, ISTANBUL, TURKEY, 2 OCTOBER 2018

Jamal Khashoggi, a Saudi Arabian *Washington Post* journalist, vocal critic of his country's regime and, with Omar Abdulaziz, co-creator of the cyber bees, walked into the Saudi consulate in Istanbul, Turkey to pick up some documents confirming his divorce, which would enable him to marry his fiancée, Hatice Cengiz, who was waiting for him outside. She didn't notice the man dressed in the same clothes as Jamal who left the embassy less than an hour later and would probably have put it down to coincidence if she had. She waited outside the consulate for ten hours for Jamal to reappear but gave up and returned the next day to once more wait in vain.

Omar was looking at events unfolding in Istanbul with alarm. As he followed the news coverage, he came across a photo in which Hatice is pictured holding what appeared to be Jamal's phones. Omar had circled these in red, saying, 'You guys should check these phones.' And WhatsApped the photo to Ron and Bill. 'That was how I first heard about Khashoggi; it was right on that day,' Ron told me.

Media attention on Khashoggi's disappearance was becoming global and three days after he had entered the consulate the *Washington Post* wrote:

> JAMAL KHASHOGGI, a journalist who has turned a trenchant and questioning eye on the leadership of his country, Saudi Arabia, entered the kingdom's consulate in Istanbul on Tuesday to take care of what should have been routine paperwork. Saudi Arabia says he then left. His fiancée, waiting for him, says he did not, and he cannot be found. Turkey says it has seen no sign that he left the building. Mr. Khashoggi, a contributor to *The Post*'s Global Opinions section, appears to have disappeared, and we are worried.

The Saudi authorities stuck to the line that he had left the embassy within an hour of arriving, releasing CCTV footage of someone wearing similar clothes – the man Jamal's fiancée had not noticed as he passed her in the street – leaving the embassy. His fiancée vigorously rejected that explanation. The Turkish authorities turned out to be peculiarly well informed; they had been illegally bugging the embassy. The tapes of what went on inside the consulate that day documented the grisly chain of events once the door closed behind Jamal Khashoggi. He had been met by a 15-person assassination squad. After a struggle, Khashoggi was injected with a lethal drug. A Saudi surgeon, flown over for the purpose, took out his bone saw and dismembered the dissident's body, which was then disposed of. No trace of it has been found.

There was little doubt internationally that the murder had been ordered by Saudi Arabia's crown prince, Mohammed bin Salman, although the Saudi government issued various denials. When their ruse about Jamal leaving the embassy fell flat, they finally blamed a Saudi intelligence team for exceeding their brief to bring Jamal back to Saudi Arabia. Presumably to appease world criticism, five members of the assassination team were subsequently sentenced to death and others to long periods of imprisonment. The architect of the crime remains free but the US director of National Intelligence was in little doubt as to who it was: 'We assess that Saudi Arabia's Crown Prince Mohammed bin Salman approved an operation in Istanbul, Turkey to capture or kill Saudi journalist Jamal Khashoggi.'

Jamal Khashoggi's disappearance and murder captured global headlines for weeks and the spotlight of international attention blazed down on Mohammed bin Salman's corrupt and brutal regime. Citizen Lab meanwhile checked the phone of Khashoggi's fiancée Hatice Cengiz and found that it too was infected with Pegasus. They couldn't check Khashoggi's phones – the ones Omar had ringed in red on the news photo – because Cengiz had handed them over to the Turkish police. The use of this spyware had proved that even in exile no one is safe. If a government wanted to keep tabs on its enemies, Pegasus was undoubtedly a good buy – and someone wanted to buy it.

OFFICE OF THE STATE TREASURER, OREGON, UNITED STATES, 1 NOVEMBER 2017

On 1 November 2017, the Oregon Investment Council (OIC) met to approve a series of proposed investments of the State of Oregon's trust funds, including the Oregon Public Employees Retirement Fund, the Common School Fund and the State Accident Insurance Fund. It was their job to grow these funds as much as possible. Item III on the agenda was a pitch by a company called Novalpina Capital.

Stephen Peel, Stefan Kowski and Bastian Lueken had all worked together at TPG – one of the biggest private-equity buyout companies in the world – and had created Novalpina as an investment vehicle to buy 'mid-size' companies. Their first target was the Israeli-owned NSO Group, maker of Pegasus spyware, and they had embarked on a US$1 billion fundraising round. This meeting in Oregon was an important one: they were pitching for US$232.9 million.

Their slot began at 9.53am. Peel and Kowski were presenting for Novalpina and they faced the five members of the investment council who were seated behind the long, pale wooden desk at the head of the room. Perhaps aware of the potential controversy of this investment, and maybe also injecting a sense of intrigue to attract the usually staid investors, Peel said, 'As investors, we assume we have to be contrarian. We have to find deals that other people don't see or don't want to do for various reasons.'

He found one. Within 30 minutes, the OIC unanimously decided to commit US$232.9 million to Novalpina's debut funding round, becoming the single biggest investor. The Alaska Permanent Fund Corporation came in with US$59 million while the UK's South Yorkshire Pension fund coughed up another US$33 million. There was no doubt that Stephen Peel and his colleagues were very good at their job, and within the next few months Novalpina's debut fund had reached US$1 billion – including US$75 million invested by the three founders.

LONDON, ENGLAND, 15 FEBRUARY 2019

The first thing I saw when I picked up my phone on that Friday morning was a Signal message from my colleague at Global Witness, Daniel Balint-Kurti. 'Have you seen what Stephen Peel has done?' Dan had been called by a contact of his, John Scott-Railton, a senior researcher at Citizen Lab, who had told him that the NSO Group had just been bought by a private-equity firm called Novalpina Capital. The founder of Novalpina was Stephen Peel, an Olympic gold-medal rower and a veteran investor. He was also a board member of Global Witness.

We were not Citizen Lab but we knew enough to know that spyware companies were very bad news, anathema to everything we stood for. I sat back in my chair and thought, *What the fuck?* I could not believe that a board member of ours thought it was OK to combine a leading role in an international human-rights organization with being the owner of an Israeli weapons-grade spyware company.

Simon, Charmian and I convened our leadership team, led by our CEO, Gillian Caldwell, to work out how to deal with this. The first thing to do was to find out Stephen's side of the story. When I called him that morning, he seemed genuinely surprised that we were surprised and apologized for inadvertently dragging Global Witness into this. He told me he'd spoken to Mark Stephens, our chair, about the purchase of

NSO; Mark, he said, didn't think it was a problem. I told him there was a problem.

Stephen, I think sincerely, outlined how NSO's main mission was to aid law enforcement in tackling criminals and terrorists and therefore this was a good thing. To avoid the risks of a state targeting human-rights groups using Pegasus software he said he would ensure that NSO would operate to the best human-rights standards. He explained how he intended to create an independent advisory panel – the Business Ethics Committee (BEC) – consisting of various luminaries – he cited (an unnamed) former head of the US Joint Chiefs of Staff – and which would also include a civil-society representative. I asked him if he meant 'like a Global Witness-type organization?'

'Or a Mark Stephens-type lawyer,' he responded.

However, Global Witness's operational leadership was unanimous in that we could not have a board member who was a major investor in a spyware company with an already egregious reputation for its products being used to target journalists and pro-democracy and human-rights activists. Stephen resigned from the board that day. His woes were only just beginning.

The following Monday, some of the world's most respected human-rights organizations – including Amnesty International, Privacy International, Human Rights Watch and Reporters Without Borders – wrote an open letter to Novalpina Capital, as the new owner of NSO, to voice their concerns about its human-rights record, noting that:

Research has documented the use of NSO Group's Pegasus spyware to target a wide swath of civil society, including at least 24 human-rights defenders, journalists and parliamentarians in

Mexico, an Amnesty International employee, Omar Abdulaziz, Yahya Assiri, Ghanem Al-Masarir, award-winning human-rights campaigner Ahmed Mansoor, and allegedly, the targeting of Jamal Khashoggi.

The letter went on to make a number of demands and requested reassurances from NSO that they would not sell Pegasus to governments with a history of spying on civil-society activists, would provide information about who NSO licences were being sold to and would address various other human-rights concerns. The letter also expressed regret that NSO had not sought the advice of any human-rights organizations ahead of the sale. I sympathized with that – Stephen was on our board and hadn't even asked us.

Stephen responded on 1 March 2019 with an 11-page open letter. He stressed, as he would do repeatedly over the coming months, that Pegasus was a critical tool to help law enforcement tackle criminality and terrorism. Central among his reassurances was that:

> Any form of marketing engagement or proposed contract that is assessed to be compliant with export control rules under the regulatory regime summarized above must then be reviewed by the NSO Business Ethics Committee (the 'BEC') before proceeding.
>
> We are determined to do whatever is necessary to ensure that NSO technology is used for the purpose for which it is intended— the prevention of harm to fundamental human rights arising from terrorism and serious crime.
>
> The BEC is a key Committee of the NSO Board and comprises seven members: three NSO executives, and four external

independent members. The external independent members are individuals of international standing in the fields of law, technology, security and international relations that are relevant to NSO's business activities.

Whatever controls NSO had in place, it was soon terribly obvious that they weren't working. A joint investigation by the *Guardian* and Spanish newspaper *El País* discovered that between April and May 2019, WhatsApp messages connected to Roger Torrent, the speaker of the Catalan regional parliament, had been targeted by Pegasus. Torrent blamed the Spanish state for the attack.

'The Catalan case was just phenomenal,' Ron Deibert recalled. 'There were four Catalans who we notified [. . .] and we realized that this was probably the tip of the iceberg.' Citizen Lab and WhatsApp embarked on a months'-long investigation. 'We uncovered a massive domestic espionage operation in scope and scale.' Ron paused. 'As a Canadian I think about Quebec, and imagine that if the Royal Canadian Mounted Police had hacked the phones of the sitting Quebec premier and every other premier of the last ten years, their entire cabinet and all of Quebec civil society, I'm pretty sure the Canadian government would fall. But somehow in Spain, it's like, "Oh, well, it's, you know, Catalonia, whatever." '

Ron remains genuinely shocked by the magnitude of this. 'Then we were subjected to a low-level disinformation and smear campaign that continues really to the present day, like, oh, the Citizen Lab's report is full of errors [. . .] I take money from Apple, we're part of a Russian clandestine operation, all of this nonsense coming from pro-Spanish right-wing tabloids? It's been kind of interesting to deal with,' he said laconically.

OSLO FREEDOM FORUM, NORWAY, MAY 2022

Dubbed the 'Davos for Human Rights' by the *Economist*, the Oslo Freedom Forum is a magnet for dissidents and activists across the world to meet each other, to get their messages broadcast to a wider audience and to garner both moral and actual support. John Scott-Railton (JSR) was manning a booth for Citizen Lab that among other things offered to test delegates' phones to see if they were infected with spyware. JSR recognized the distinctive African woman with braided hair who approached the booth one day: Carine Kanimba wanted Citizen Lab to test her iPhone.

Carine's father, Paul Rusesabagina, was an unlikely hero. He had held a good job in his native Rwanda as the manager of the Belgian-owned Hôtel des Mille Collines in the country's capital, Kigali. Caught up in the 1994 Rwandan genocide, the hotel had been flooded with refugees and, at extreme risk to himself and his family, Rusesabagina had managed to take in 1,268 of them, all of whom survived the war. For this he was awarded the Presidential Medal of Freedom by US president George W. Bush, and the episode was made famous in the Hollywood film *Hotel Rwanda*, with Don Cheadle playing Rusesabagina. Rusesabagina went on to become an in-demand public speaker and a vocal critic of the repressive regime of Rwanda's new president, Paul Kagame. He was about to find out, if he didn't know already, that Kagame was a man who would go to any lengths to silence his critics.

Rusesabagina, a Belgian national and US permanent resident who had lived in Texas since an assassination attempt in the 1990s, accepted an invitation from a Burundian pastor, Constantin Niyomwungere, to talk at various churches in Burundi about the Rwandan genocide. He would be collected by a private jet in Dubai for the onward journey. As he took his seat in the plane the pastor had laid on, he did not know that his host was an informant for the Rwanda Investigation Bureau.

In the early hours of 28 August 2020, the plane touched down not in Burundi, as scheduled, but in Kigali. Rusesabagina screamed and struggled but, 'They tied my arms and legs, eyes and nose, mouth and ears,' he subsequently said in an affidavit.

Rusesabagina had been kidnapped, although the pastor used the word 'tricked'. 'Myself, the pilot and cabin crew knew we were coming to Kigali,' Niyomwungere told Rwanda's High Court in Kigali in March 2021. 'The only person who didn't know where we were headed was Paul.'

Just a month later, Rusesabagina appeared in court, accused by the government of supporting a rebel group – a charge he denied. He was found guilty and sentenced to 25 years in prison.

Ron Deibert smelled a rat. Both Citizen Lab and Amnesty International, which had its own independent digital team, checked the phones of several of Rusesabagina's family members. Their findings matched – the phones had been infected by Pegasus spyware. Right there, in the Citizen Lab booth at the Oslo Freedom Forum, almost two years after her father's kidnap, JSR checked Carine's phone.

First he talked her through how to generate a crash log from her phone. 'These "bug reports" should look a certain way; there should be certain processes and so on, and we look through it for anomalies,' Ron explained to me. 'Sometimes we get a crash report and we can tell right away that it's been hacked with Pegasus because we can see process names that only we know, that we don't give out and that NSO doesn't know we have, which tells us with 100 per cent confidence that this is part of their spyware.'

Carine's phone was infected by Pegasus.

Following her father's kidnap, the US-educated Carine had embarked on a campaign to get her father released and had toured the corridors of power in Europe and the US. She had met MPs, MEPs, prominent US politicians and senior US officials, including the US special envoy for hostage affairs, Roger Carstens, and during all this time her phone may well have been infected with Pegasus. If the Rwandans were spying on her communications, then they were, by default, also potentially spying on the officials she was in touch with. A major breakdown in Rwanda–US relations ensued. The EU Parliament and the US Congress called for Rusesabagina's release and the US State Department said he had been 'wrongly detained'.

Rusesabagina's family launched a civil court case in the US District Court in the District of Columbia, accusing Rwanda of having 'engaged in a wide-ranging conspiracy to surveil, kidnap, and ultimately imprison plaintiff'.

In his Memorandum Opinion released on 16 March 2023, Judge Richard J. Leon noted that:

Plaintiffs allege that two critical elements of the scheme were carried out while Rusesabagina, a United States lawful permanent resident living in San Antonio, Texas, was physically present in the United States [. . .] First, plaintiffs allege that agents of the Rwandan government illegally surveilled Rusesabagina and his daughter while in the United States using spyware illegally planted on their telephones. No later than 2018, Rwandan intelligence agents acting in furtherance of the conspiracy allegedly infected Rusesabagina's Belgian cell phone with Pegasus, a form of spyware, while he was in Belgium. Rusesabagina continued to use that cell phone when he returned to the United States to communicate by voice and text message.

THE PEGASUS PROJECT

Coordinated by French media nonprofit Forbidden Stories and with technical support from Amnesty International's Security Lab, 17 major global news outlets – including *Le Monde*, *Süddeutsche Zeitung*, the *Guardian*, the *Washington Post* and PBS – began collaborating on a major investigation into the use of Pegasus spyware. They called it the Pegasus Project.

On 20 July 2021, two days after the Pegasus Project was launched, the world's headlines were dominated by the news that Forbidden Stories and Amnesty International had unearthed a leaked list of 50,000 unattributed phone numbers they suspected to have been selected by NSO's government customers as belonging to people of interest.

Although Ron Deibert doesn't know the provenance of this list, his insights into it are sobering. 'If you think about it from a user's perspective of the spyware, like a government spy, you don't want to just fire this very precious exploit at any old device and hope it sticks. So you want to do some reconnaissance ahead of time. And there are all sorts of services to look up the location and details of a phone number affiliated with or associated with a particular person,' Ron explained.

'Say I wanted to infect your phone with Pegasus, I may want to see where you are right now. If Patrick's in Washington, DC, probably not a smart thing for me to try to hack your device there. So I'll wait till you're in a better location; maybe you'll be travelling in Angola or something and I can hack you there. Plus, I want to know what make and model of Android you're using so I can make sure I'm not just throwing something blindly into the wind. So NSO Group will set up for its clients a portal, where they would do what are called HTML area lookups. These are home-locator rent-record lookups; they are protocols that are used by telecommunications firms to exchange roaming information. You know how when you travel and you land and you boot up your phone, it says "Welcome to Germany, you're now on blah, blah, blah." Well, behind the scenes, what's happening is Deutsche Telekom is pinging British Telecom saying, "Can you tell me, is this your subscriber?" And they say, "Yes." It's all done automatically. Well, there are now these insidious firms that have managed to get inside this system and exploit it for geolocation or surveillance purposes.'

Amnesty Tech asked Citizen Lab to peer review their analysis of the 50,000 numbers and Ron noticed one thing in particular. 'Amnesty could see from the forensic logs that the hacks occurred mere seconds after the lookup on the phone-number list.' To him, that was pretty good proof of the legitimacy of the source of the 50,000 numbers. In his opinion, it was evidence of the surveillance of potential Pegasus victims.

Armed only with the numbers themselves, Pegasus Project members trawled through public records and known contact lists to try to put names to the numbers. They managed to identify 1,000 of them. The list included a swathe of top-level politicians, including several heads of state – France's Emmanuel Macron and South Africa's Cyril Ramaphosa among them. Iraq's Barham Salih was on the list too, as were the prime minsters of Egypt, Morocco and Pakistan. The list also included Morocco's King Mohammed VI, 189 journalists, 85 human-rights activists and 600 politicians. As the *Washington Post* headline on 20 July 2021 put it: 'On the list: Ten prime ministers, three presidents and a king'.

The political leaders didn't offer up their smartphones for analysis but 60 or so of the other targets did. Thirty-seven of those were infected with Pegasus. The news outlets were quick to say that infection with Pegasus didn't mean these people had been spied on, but that they could have been. NSO was vehement in its denials, but they had taken a big hit and fell back on the ropes. They were down but not yet out.

Meanwhile, Citizen Lab notified the UK government that they had detected suspected Pegasus spyware infections that had occurred in the prime minister's office at 10 Downing Street and the Foreign, Commonwealth and Development Office during 2020 and 2021. They linked these infections to the UAE, India, Cyprus and Jordan. Citizen Lab delivered another gut punch in April 2022.

Following the 2020 exposé by *The Guardian* and *El País*, Citizen Lab and WhatsApp probed deeper into what was going on in Catalonia. They exposed the shocking revelation that 65 people connected to the Catalan independence movement had been targeted with Pegasus, and within a fortnight they also found that the phones of no less than the Spanish prime minister Pedro Sánchez and the defence minister Margarita Robles had also been infected. As similar exposés took place around the world, NSO came under investigation in France, India, Mexico, Poland and Spain while the European Parliament established a special committee, PEGA, to investigate the use of Pegasus and other spyware in Europe.

On 3 November 2021, the US government placed NSO Group on its Entity List, for 'engaging in activities that are contrary to the national security or foreign policy interests'. The Biden administration placed another Israeli firm, Candiru, on the same trade blacklist – essentially,

Biden banned American companies from engaging in business with hacking firms. Since October 2023, the Biden administration has been conducting an investigation into the countries that have used Pegasus and other spyware tools against American officials.

Following Novalpina's purchase of NSO in 2019, Stephen Peel was publicly adamant that the company would align with top-level human-rights standards, in particular the UN Guiding Principles on Business and Human Rights. NSO's reputation prior to the Novalpina acquisition was already egregious, but during the following four years it got worse as a succession of cases of activists, journalists and politicians being targeted by NSO spyware continued to grab the headlines.

Meanwhile Citizen Lab were getting increasingly frustrated by their long correspondence with Novalpina, whose letters talked of open debate and discussion but stressed that because the company couldn't reveal the names of its clients, it couldn't comment on specific allegations. Citizen Lab were expected to rely on Stephen Peel's assurances that: 'The lawful, appropriate and responsible deployment of surveillance technologies such as NSO's by government intelligence and law enforcement agencies is essential to address the serious consequences of what would otherwise be untraceable crime, terrorism, paedophile rings, human trafficking, drug cartels and the like.'

An extract from one of Citizen Lab's letters illustrates their frustration.

Based on what we have read to date, we can only conclude that Novalpina Capital LLP and NSO Group remain intent on preventing access to sufficient information that would allow a meaningful evaluation of the company's response to the human-rights impacts of its business operations. You appear intent on keeping private details of how past abuses and wrongs will be remediated, despite the requirements of the UN Guiding Principles on Business and Human Rights and your own acknowledgment that there have been at least some cases of misuse of NSO Group's technology.

Ron and John Scott-Railton had become thorns, if not giant spikes, in Novalpina's and NSO's sides and were curious about what was being said about them behind the scenes. Using the UK's Data Protection Act, they filed Subject Access Requests (SARs) on Novalpina, which oblige any UK company to divulge what information they hold on individuals. Designed more to tackle the evils of direct marketing, the law nevertheless also applies to companies like Novalpina, and the SARs provided a rich trove. Ron and John sat down to go through the 473 emails that mentioned Ron's name and the 223 that mentioned John's.

They read that in February 2019, around the time Novalpina bought NSO, the company together with NSO had retained the US law firm Foley Hoag and in particular a lawyer called Vivek Krishnamurthy as a 'specialist external adviser'. His expertise was corporate social-responsibility practice and his job was ostensibly to advise Novalpina on how to ensure that NSO's operations were in line with the UN Guiding Principles on Business and Human Rights. On the face of it, this looked like a serious commitment on the part of NSO. However, it seemed there were other considerations.

Vivek Krishnamurthy was a former research assistant of Ron's and had secured a Rhodes Scholarship with Ron's help. Maybe this was a coincidence, but Foley Hoag's recommendation to NSO was that Vivek was 'in a unique position to conduct outreach to Citizen Lab should the NSO Group find it desirable to do so'. Accordingly, on 1 March 2019, Stephen Peel emailed Krishnamurthy telling him to 'reach out to Deibert to find out what is going on'. Krishna agreed, but warned that: 'He can be prickly, and he's clearly worked up about NSO.'

Ron was in no doubt about the strategy that was playing out – and if he wasn't prickly before, he certainly was now. Vivek told his former boss that he had thought deeply about whether to take on this work but had been convinced by his friend, the famous human-rights lawyer Mark Stephens, who had vouched for Peel's commitments to human rights. At that time Mark was still chair of the Global Witness board.

In an article published on 28 April 2022, the *Guardian* stated that Mark Stephens had confirmed that he had recommended Krishnamurthy to Stephen Peel. He also told the paper that he had previously worked for Peel, but not for Novalpina or NSO. According to the *Guardian*,

> Stephens praised Peel and criticized Citizen Lab for disproportionately focusing on NSO. 'The practical result of what they [Citizen Lab] have done is to ignore and effectively divert attention from the other players in this marketplace and they have given them a completely free pass and I think that's reprehensible,' he said.

When I spoke to Mark Stephens in January 2024, he said that the *Guardian*'s quote was inaccurate. 'What [Citizen Lab] did was a huge disservice to NGOs and others because the technology is widely used by states, like the UK, US, China and Russia . . . [while] . . . Israel outsourced theirs to this more commercial enterprise,' he said. 'The publicity that

NSO attracted led to the worst possible outcome.' He told me that states dropped NSO in favour of spyware marketed by totalitarian regimes, giving as examples the UAE dropping Pegasus in favour of using Russian spyware, while Zimbabwe opted for Chinese technology. 'Would you prefer to be monitored by something with some oversight [like NSO], or by the Russians?' Mark asked. However, a quick look at Citizen Lab's website demonstrates that they have long investigated numerous state actors, not least their 2009 exposé of China's GhostNet hacking of the Dalai Lama.

In any event, Ron turned down the meeting with Krishnamurthy. 'This guy [. . .] was my former research assistant, who took this job on the basis of him being close to me and then misled me to try to get meetings, which I turned down because I was aware that Peel and others at the NSO Group had been trying to co-opt us to have meetings with them, which we knew would be disingenuous and unproductive, but for them would be a big payoff, because they could tell everybody, "Oh, we've met with the Citizen Lab." We didn't want to give them that.'

Vivek tried again a few months later.

'Vivek sends me an email saying, "Look, I'm gonna be in Toronto; can we just have a beer, nothing work related," when clearly it was work related,' Ron told me. 'He was reaching out to me under false pretences. I was his mentor, so that's a horrible backstabbing thing to do. What people will do for money . . .' Vivek Krishnamurthy also came to regret his decision to take on the Novalpina brief. In a statement to the *Guardian*, he wrote that he had believed that Novalpina were intent on making 'real changes at NSO [. . .] However, the NSO Group's subsequent record of complicity in gross human-rights violations shows how wrong we were. I regret my brief time advising Novalpina in 2019.' He went on to wish

Citizen Lab success 'in bringing NSO's extremely harmful activities to an end'.

The *Guardian* reported that NSO paid Foley Hoag around US$220,000.

In May 2019, Stephen Peel had dinner with George Soros, whose Open Society Foundations funded Citizen Lab, as they do Global Witness. Whatever the two may have discussed, Soros has continued to fund both Global Witness and Citizen Lab.

Among Peel's emails obtained by Citizen Lab and quoted in the *Guardian* was one saying that it was 'an organization unknown except for its attack on NSO'.

Soros did not stop funding Citizen Lab but, according to the *Guardian*, subsequently advised Peel he should probably extricate himself from the NSO investment.

DENOUEMENT, JULY 2021

Since its purchase of the NSO Group, Novalpina Capital had come under increasing pressure as scandal after scandal involving the use of Pegasus spyware was exposed. Stephen Peel engaged with many of these critics, including Citizen Lab, Amnesty International, Global Witness and many media outlets, making assurances that under his watch the use of Pegasus would be strictly controlled. He was being either insincere or naive. At best, he evidently had little to no influence on who Pegasus was sold to or how it would be used.

As the storm grew following the findings of the Pegasus Project, so the fortunes of both Novalpina and NSO began to avalanche. Pressure on

NSO began mounting as lawsuit followed lawsuit from the likes of Google, Apple and Meta. WhatsApp alleged that NSO had hacked 1,400 of their users and in papers filed in April 2020 stated that 'NSO used a network of computers to monitor and update Pegasus after it was implanted on users' devices. These NSO-controlled computers served as the nerve centre through which NSO controlled its customers' operation and use of Pegasus.'

On 5 August 2021, Novalpina's first and largest investor added to their woes. The Oregon State Treasury's spokeswoman, Rachel Wray, told the press that the Oregon State treasurer, Tobias Read, 'is following and [is] concerned about the reporting surrounding Novalpina and the NSO Group.' Later that same month, Oregon's Senator Ron Wyden, a Democrat, called on the state employee pension fund to pull its investment in NSO because it 'enabled authoritarian regimes to target journalists and human-rights advocates'.

On 3 November 2021, the US Department of Commerce added NSO Group to its trade blacklist

> based on evidence that these entities developed and supplied spyware to foreign governments that used these tools to maliciously target government officials, journalists, businesspeople, activists, academics, and embassy workers. These tools have also enabled foreign governments to conduct transnational repression, which is the practice of authoritarian governments targeting dissidents, journalists and activists outside of their sovereign borders to silence dissent.

A week after the revelations exposed by the Pegasus Project in July 2021, rumours first started to hit the City that Novalpina would be removed as the manager of its fund. It was indeed the end of the road for them. Novalpina was wound up and the fund taken over by the Berkeley Research Group at the behest of Novalpina's biggest investor, the Oregon State Treasury.

Whether manufacturing swords, guns, warplanes, missiles or spy satellites, the arms industry has played an instrumental role in supplying their government customers, in both the cause of national defence and wars of aggression. In the age of super-high-tech, the involvement of companies like NSO marks a new stage whereby they are actually participating in operating these new weapons of war, for money. In this they are simply mercenaries and in the same company as organizations like the Wagner Group, their wares every bit as cruel and destructive. Their owners may aspire to ensure their products are only deployed according to a strict set of rules, but they are not the ones on the battlefield.

As *Guardian* journalist Stephanie Kirchgaessner put it, 'If you're in this business, you are kind of a villain character, and you just need to get on with your business. You're a weapons dealer. It's just what you are.'

By February 2022, Novalpina's three founders – Stephen Peel, Bastian Lueken and Stefan Kowski – were in the middle of a massive internecine bust-up over how to invest the fund's remaining capital. Although unconnected in investment terms, NSO loomed large in their discussions. Stephen Peel wanted to invest in a landmine-clearance company called SafeLane and thought that this would improve their reputation. Kowski and Lueken did not. In an email quoted in the *Financial Times*, Lueken said he felt that SafeLane could be criticized for 'making money in war zones' and 'putting locals in harms [sic] way'. That 'may be a harsh way of articulating the story but given the flak were [sic] already getting this may well be how this comes out in the media.'

In an email to Kowski, Stephen Peel said that he was 'quite upset that you somehow believe your investment judgment trumps mine'.

Peel lost the battle and was ousted from the company he co-founded.

In September 2022, Hanan Elatr, Jamal Khashoggi's wife, announced her plans to launch legal proceedings in the US against NSO and the governments of Saudi Arabia and the United Arab Emirates for their roles in Pegasus spyware being installed on her phone. In January that same year, Israel's attorney general had ordered an investigation into the Israeli police's use of Pegasus against journalists, human-rights activists and politicians within Israel.

Novalpina Capital's takeover of NSO is a parable of our time. Novalpina rode high towards the sun as NSO's value went from US$250 million to US$1 billion, but the heat their spyware created melted the wax that held the feathers onto their wings. Nonetheless, NSO itself is too valuable a tool for the governments that use it to let it die.

While the belief of Stephen Peel and other investors that the use of spyware as a key tool to tackle organized crime and terrorism may be justified, their faith in its use being denied to those regimes who want to stifle democracy at home and abroad is naive and dangerous.* As Danna

---

* I asked Stephen Peel for an interview for this chapter but he declined to talk to me on the record and didn't follow up my offer to talk off the record. In the absence of any information to the contrary, and knowing Stephen a little during his time as a member of Global Witness's board of directors,

Ingleton, deputy director of Amnesty Tech, told the *Financial Times* in 2021, 'Novalpina Capital's promises of openness and transparency ring hollow when the return on their investment entirely depends on the spyware giant staying in the shadows.'

Mark Stephens had asked the rhetorical question whether the smidgeon of accountability that a company like NSO might bring was better than having no accountability at all from state-sanctioned hacking. I imagine the victims of Pegasus spyware, at least those that survived the experience, wonder where that accountability was. 'As we speak, there are live infections of Pegasus victims,' Ron Deibert told me in September 2023. 'They're definitely supplying government clients with spyware and they are actively hacking. Their government clients come and go, but their spyware, their exploits, are constantly changing, taking advantage of some new toehold to get onto a device to install spyware.'

Over the past few years, democracy and basic human rights have increasingly come under threat from state-level institutions. In September 2023, Citizen Lab and digital-rights group Access Now found that Russian investigative journalist Galina Timchenko's iPhone was infected with a zero-click Pegasus exploit – very likely when she was in Berlin meeting other exiled Russian independent-media heads.

In the same month, Citizen Lab reported that Egyptian MP Ahmed Eltantawy's phone was infected with Cytrox's Predator spyware following

---

I can believe that he was sincere in his wish to improve NSO's practices, but events should have told him that the company's owners – of which Novalpina Capital were the majority shareholders – simply didn't know how to tame the beast they were riding. He would have been doing the cause of human rights and democracy a favour by telling his story and admitting that he and his colleagues had tried and failed.

his announcement that he would run for president in Egypt's 2024 elections. Citizen Lab had little doubt that the Egyptian government was the author of the attack.

As political movements and human-rights and environmental activists campaign to obtain or defend basic rights, they increasingly coordinate via social media – sometimes the only free media available to them in an increasingly repressive world – and are increasingly vulnerable to aggressive surveillance and worse. We daily see news reports of protestors being attacked, arrested and worse. Whether it's women suffering at the hands of the morality police in Iran as they campaign for gender rights, pro-democracy campaigners suffering under Chinese government repression in Hong Kong or environmental activists in the UK, EU and the US seeing their basic rights closed down, you can be pretty sure that state-level use of spyware is playing a role. Or perhaps, more disturbingly, you can't be sure that it isn't.

> 'The telescreen received and transmitted simultaneously. Any sound that Winston made, above the level of a very low whisper, would be picked up by it; moreover, so long as he remained within the field of vision which the metal plaque commanded, he could be seen as well as heard. There was of course no way of knowing whether you were being watched at any given moment.'
>
> —George Orwell, *1984*

8

AMAZON PALM

'Our government belongs to you.'
—Brazilian president Jair Bolsonaro's reassurance to the Pensar
Agro Institute (IPA), a Brazilian think tank financed by 48
agrobusiness companies and affiliated with major international
companies including Bayer, Nestlé, Cargill and Syngenta

ATALAIA DO NORTE, AMAZONAS STATE, BRAZIL, 15 JUNE 2022

The riverbank was thronged with people, their backs illuminated by the lights of town as they stared out over the river and the darkness beyond. Night had fallen but the humidity had not and people wiped the sweat from their eyes, not wanting to miss the moment they knew was coming.

For days, journalists from across Brazil had arrived at the remote town of Atalaia do Norte on the banks of the Javari River in Amazonas state, not far from the border with Peru. They were waiting for information about the fate of indigenous expert Bruno Pereira and British *Guardian* journalist Dom Phillips, who had gone missing just over two weeks earlier. Among these waiting journalists was Daniel Camargos from a dynamic investigative outfit called Repórter Brasil. He had been sent to cover the story by his boss, Ana Aranha, because he had travelled with Dom in the past, memorably covering the Fire Day in Pará state in 2019. The air was alive with rumours and conflicting reports about what might have happened to Pereira and Phillips, but the overriding sense was that their investigation up the Itaquai River had been their last.

Daniel learned what turned out to be the truth from a journalist colleague. 'They've found them,' the man said. He in turn had heard it from Valteno de Oliveira, a reporter with TV network Rede Bandeirantes who had sources within the Federal Police. Two suspects had been arrested and had confessed to shooting Bruno and Dom and then butchering and burning their bodies. The Military Police had found the bodies and were due to arrive at the port that day, although the word 'port' bestowed a sense of scale belied by the slippery mud riverbank that sloped into the water.

As darkness fell, a black Federal Police pickup, siren wailing and its blue and red lights flashing, hastened towards the river. Daniel joined the others on the bank, straining for the first sight of the Military Police boat. Finally, the staccato throbbing of the motor emanated from the darkness and people crowded closer to the shore. Then the boat loomed out of the blackness. The faces of the Military Police were hidden by the shadows cast by the soft brims of their jungle hats and their camouflage uniforms were muted in the gloom. As the boat's bows nudged the soft mud of the riverbank, several troops leaped to the ground and, along with their police colleagues on land, began to push people back, creating a pathway to the waiting pickup truck.

The crowd fell silent as the soldiers on the boat came forward with the first of two black plastic body-bags, its contents limp and the plastic cast with the oily reflections of streetlights off its slick surface. The soldiers carried the bag up to the police pickup and carefully placed it in the open back and then returned with the second one. With lights flashing, the pickup moved slowly through the crowd, which parted like the Red Sea to let it pass, then closed in again behind the throng of journalists who followed it to the police station, hungry for news.

The disappearance of British journalist Dom Phillips and Brazilian indigenous expert Bruno Pereira had grabbed world headlines for 13 days. The events that led up to their murders would not only tell a story about this remote area of Brazil, but also demonstrate the extraordinary lengths people will go to to hide inconvenient truths.

BELÉM, PARÁ STATE, BRAZIL, JUNE 2022

The sun was poking through the clouds as the two Jeep Renegades navigated the busy streets of Belém. The air conditioning was turned up as high as it could go, providing at least some defence against the 82 per cent humidity. As arranged, the team picked up the journalist, Cícero Pedrosa, and then crossed over the almost 2-km (1-mile) length Governador Almir Gabriel bridge spanning the Guamá River and headed south. They had a 200-km (124-mile) journey ahead of them; a pinprick in a country the size of Brazil, but it was a very, very bad road and they'd be lucky if they managed it in under five hours. The two Global Witness investigators Gabriella Bianchini and Marco Mantovani had notified the team in London when they started out and would check in again when they arrived, as they would every day.

The team's nerves were raw with the breaking news that Pereira's and Phillips's bodies had been found in an area of flooded forest near Atalaia do Norte. Their savage murders were a cruel reminder of how high the stakes could be in an investigation like this. Gabriella had considered postponing it, but the team were keenly aware that once you schedule a meeting with an indigenous leader – a logistical challenge at the best of times – then they are waiting for you to arrive. They felt they had to go; so, rather than calling the investigation off, they took enhanced precautions.

In addition to the satellite phone, they took a GPS locator with a panic button and agreed even more stringent security protocols with their fellow team members at Global Witness's London office. They also notified several journalists and the public prosecutor in Pará of their intentions. There are never any guarantees in situations like this, but at least people would know where they were.

Karina Iliescu and Rafael Mellim, the photographer and videographer, were with Cícero in the other vehicle. They were on their way to bandit country.

THE OFFICES OF POGUST GOODHEAD, LONDON, ENGLAND, 2021

Gabriella Bianchini, a young Brazilian lawyer, co-founded her boutique law firm in London to focus on human-rights and environmental cases – she felt it was the best way to use her legal training to make a difference.

The firm's first case sought compensation from Australian mining giant BHP for the 200,000 victims of Brazil's worst environmental disaster. The 2015 collapse of the Mariana dam in Minas Gerais state unleashed a flood of toxic mining waste into the Doce River, burying countless villages, killing 19 people and making thousands more homeless. If the case was successful, the victims could be in line for US$5 billion in damages. The law firm would receive what is known as a contingency fee, based on a percentage of the final damages. A win would be good news for the victims but something didn't sit right with Gabriella. An Australian mining giant with offices across the world in a variety of legal jurisdictions was a relatively easy target, but what about people whose lives and livelihoods were equally threatened yet there was no possibility of a neat legal case?

These thoughts were on Gabriella's mind when she was contacted by a lawyer from Belém, Pará, an Amazonian state bigger than France, Spain and Portugal combined and a whole lot more dangerous. She listened intently as the lawyer recounted allegations made by a group of indigenous peoples and Quilombolas against two of the biggest palm-oil companies in Latin America: Brasil BioFuels (BBF) and Agropalma. It was a tale of violence and land-grabbing, shocking even by the low standards of Pará, a state with a bloodier record than most. These were politically connected Brazilian companies in a country that had elected Jair Bolsonaro as president, a man who had openly declared war on indigenous peoples and the Amazon. These companies would make no easy legal target.

Gabriella walked away from the firm she helped create and from the good living it could potentially provide and in August 2021 joined Global Witness as a campaigner in our Land & Environmental Defenders (LEDs) team. It was a fresh start, but she had not forgotten the case she had left behind.

Later that same year, Shruti Suresh joined Global Witness and took over the leadership of the LED team – not an easy job in the midst of the Covid lockdowns. Meeting her team members for the first time via Zoom, Shruti sat down with Gabriella and fellow campaigner Jago Wadley to discuss their campaign strategy: what events should they investigate, and where? From her home in São Paulo, Gabriella told them what she'd heard about the remote community in Pará and pressed hard to be allowed to go into the field and investigate it first hand.

Shruti asked Gabriella to find out more, so she contacted the lawyer who had originally told her about the case. She told him she had left Pogust Goodhead and was no longer litigating, but that Global Witness might be able to shine a spotlight on what was going on in Pará. She emphasized that there were no guarantees of success and asked him if he could help. He thought it was worth a try and put her in touch with a journalist from Pará called Cícero Pedrosa. Of indigenous descent himself, Cícero knew the Amazon and was very well connected with and trusted by indigenous peoples and traditional communities. More than that, he knew the danger inherent in tackling Big Agribusiness. His knowledge and field experience would turn out to be crucial.

'Cícero was really key for me to understand what I was doing, who I should be speaking with and, mainly, where I could and could not go,' Gabriella told me. Sure enough, he began putting Gabriella in touch with numerous indigenous and Quilombola leaders and arranged meetings with them. It was not straightforward, but it was a start.

According to Brazil's constitution, everyone has the right to a lawyer. In recognition that many people, especially indigenous peoples, cannot afford one, there are public defenders in every state. Gabriella decided this could be a rich vein of research. Trawling through legal proceedings filed either against or by the two main companies they were honing in on – Agropalma and BBF – she downloaded thousands of pages of legal documents and spent long hours at her desk, scanning the reams of information.

She noted down the names of the public defenders presenting motions in favour of indigenous communities. These told her which lawyers possessed key information. Conversely, when she examined legal cases filed by the companies against indigenous peoples and Quilombolas she saw a clear strategy emerging. The companies' lawyers were criminalizing the communities on whose lands they operated – tying them up with expensive and impenetrable legal cases. But this was only part of the problem.

COUNCIL OF MINISTERS, BRAZIL, 22 APRIL 2020

As he prepared to speak, Ricardo Salles, Brazil's urbane and youthful-looking minister of the environment, looked around the expectant faces of his fellow cabinet members, including the boss, Brazil's extreme right-wing president, Jair Bolsonaro.

'Now that we are in a quiet time because the media is focused on Covid-19, we have to take the opportunity to pass the bill and simplify the rules,' Salles said. As ordinary Brazilian citizens were diverted because they were dying in their droves from Covid, Salles was taking the opportunity to accelerate his plans to gut the country's laws against socio-environmental crimes. One of the clear targets was the vast Amazonian state of Pará.

Pará stretches from the shores of the Atlantic to the heart of the

Amazon. It is home to numerous indigenous tribes, is vastly biodiverse and rich in timber, land and minerals – factors that have put it in the frontline of Bolsonaro's war against the Amazon. On one side, the indigenous peoples, the Quilombolas, the rural poor and the environment; on the other, the big landowners. Illegal logging, cattle ranching and mining are eating the heart out of the Amazon rainforest. Renowned Brazilian scientist Carlos Nobre has warned that if the Amazon loses 40 per cent of its original area, it will reach a tipping point and become dry savannah. When this happens – which at the current rate of deforestation could be in the next decade or two – then the battle against climate change cannot be won.

Of Pará's land area of 1.2 million km² (463,300 square miles), 228,834 (88,396) have been given over to palm-oil plantations, almost the size of Luxembourg. Much of this land is controlled by Agropalma and BBF. In many cases these vast plantations completely surround traditional communities and subsume the land they have been living on for centuries; their villages have become islands in a sea of palm. Like a boa constrictor, the new landowners have been squeezing the life out of these communities, and the landowners' best allies have also been the government's best allies. The Agricultural Parliamentary Front (FPA) is the most powerful lobby group in Brazil and better known as the Ruralistas.

The antics of the Ruralistas would stretch the credulity of fans of some of the wilder offerings of TV, but they are scarily real – as demonstrated when, in May 2023, a Cessna light aircraft landed at Belém International Airport with all its seats, bar the pilot's, removed. The Federal Police found that the plane was stuffed to the gunwales with 290kg (639lb) of skunk, a type of concentrated marijuana. Just another drug bust? The plane belonged to the evangelical International Church of the Foursquare

Gospel, the pastor of whose Brazilian division is Josué Bengtson. This was not Bengtson's first brush with controversy. A former member of the Chamber of Deputies, he lost his mandate for his involvement in corruption – diverting BRL R$ 110 million from the health service in what became known as the Ambulance Mafia. His son Paolo took over his political role while his brother Marcus was arrested following the torture and murder of a man over a land dispute. Marcus remains free while the legal process unfurls. Sadly, stories like these are not rarities among the Bancada Ruralista.

The big landowners of the FPA control around 75 per cent of Brazil's arable land, but their thirst for more is unquenchable. In mid-2022, politicians linked to the FPA controlled almost half the seats in the Chamber of Deputies and the Federal Senate; with Lula's election win in October 2022, these proportions increased to 58 per cent and 52 per cent respectively. The FPA hold the reins of power.

Meanwhile, in their report 'The Financiers of Destruction', the Brazilian organization De Olho nos Ruralistas – Eyes on the Ruralistas – delved deep into the Ruralistas' pet think tank, the Pensar Agro Institute (IPA). They found that between January 2019 and June 2022, representatives from IPA met the Ministry of Agriculture and Livestock at least 160 times. During the same period, the ministry held considerably fewer meetings with, for example, indigenous organizations. None in fact. Despite the Ruralistas' strident nationalism, the IPA is financed by 48 agrobusiness companies and is affiliated with some of the biggest commodity companies in the world, including US giant Cargill, Nestlé, Syngenta and Bayer. The vast gulf between the financial and political power of the agricultural lobby and the disenfranchisement of Brazil's traditional communities underlines the major causes of conflict and environmental destruction in Brazil.

So, by the time Bolsonaro assumed the presidency, the Ruralistas had prepared the ground meticulously and immediately embarked on a real and legislative chainsaw massacre. Laws that protected indigenous lands or the ability to demarcate new lands were swept away. The result was a de facto amnesty for illegal land seizure and an opening up of protected areas for mining and commercial agriculture. On top of this, laws banning the use of dangerous pesticides and restricting gun ownership were weakened. Between 2018 and August 2022, the number of privately owned guns doubled to around 2 million.

This toxic combination resulted in Brazil's natural environment – and the traditional communities that depend on it – facing a lethal mix of lawlessness, violence and impunity, a shocking parallel to the extermination of the Native Americans in what is now the United States of America.

At home in São Paulo, Gabriella's eyes scanned page after page of claims made by communities – claims that had been supported by Pará's Public Prosecutor's Office (MPPA) and Brazil's Federal Prosecutor's Office (MPF). She read that in March 2022, the latter had stated that BBF's plantations overlapped with territories demarcated by Brazil's Indigenous affairs agency (FUNAI) as belonging to the Tembé people. Was this a landgrab? The MPF also said that BBF had breached agreements requiring a 10-km (6-mile) buffer zone between their plantations and the communities. Without that, the communities would have nowhere to grow crops, to fish or to hunt – the only livelihoods they had. Worse still, while the law in these cases was on the side of the indigenous communities, this was of little comfort to the Quilombolas, whose land had not been demarcated at all. In April 2022 it became clear that things were getting worse and these communities began to realize that they were the victims of a lethal political timetable.

National elections were due to take place in October 2022 and the Ruralistas were terrified that Bolsonaro, their chief ally – the man who had delivered the riches of the Amazon to them on a plate – might lose. If he did, his successor would assume office on 1 January 2023. The indigenous and Quilombola leaders Gabriella talked to were in no doubt about the existence of a pre-election message from deputies and government officials. 'If Bolsonaro loses, you have three months in which to execute those who are protesting and creating problems, before Lula takes over.'

Bolsonaro did lose, and in the dying months of his presidency, before his successor Luiz Inácio Lula da Silva – known simply as Lula – took power in January 2023, the Ruralistas got busy. Their general direction is well illustrated by Delegado Caveira, a deputy in Pará's state legislature. A former policeman and Bolsonaro ally, Delegado was also known as 'Skull' after the Marvel-comic vigilante. He didn't beat about the bush. To rapturous applause, he told a rally of BBF employees outside the legislature that whatever 'is not solved through legal means, will be solved with gunpowder'.

At another meeting of BBF workers on one of the company's plantations, the heavily bearded Caveira, wearing a black T-shirt emblazoned with a white skull, his eyes hidden behind his ubiquitous sunglasses, told his enthusiastic audience: 'If this farm were mine, I would have solved it a long time ago [. . .] with fire and bullets.' At least he was consistent.

Gabriella needed to identify who the customers of BBF and Agropalma were so she could hold them to account. She switched her attention to major international trade databases such as Panjiva and China's Sinoimex to find out as much about BBF and Agropalma as possible before setting foot in their plantations. She needed to know how they operated, how large they were, how much palm oil they produced, what their daily records of imports and exports were and, critically, who their key buyers were. That could be their Achilles heel.

Another potential weapon was to understand the allegations of land-grabbing, so she homed in on disputed land areas; she needed to know the original boundaries of the traditional communities' land and whether these were being encroached upon. The key to this was satellite imagery. Gabriella pored over the PRODES database, compiled by Brazil's renowned National Institute for Space Research (INPE) to monitor environmental, social and economic impacts on the Amazon region, such as deforestation and forest fires. This would enable her to see when and where palm-oil plantations had replaced forests and therefore compare land boundaries over different time periods. She also looked at the Brazilian Rural Environmental Register (CAR) database, which had been created to allow companies, farmers and landowners to certify their claim over specific areas of land. But there was a catch.

'It is official, but it basically says, "The land within these boundaries is mine,"' Gabriella explained. 'You don't have to prove it; you don't have to prove you're not encroaching into other people's areas or into indigenous territory.' This was just one example of how the power of the agribusiness lobby had rigged the system in its favour. The companies could demarcate land however they wished. This research also highlighted one of the major hurdles the team faced: there were too many maps and most of them disagreed with each other.

'You might get maps available showing a specific Quilombola community, or a BBF farm, but there were no large maps showing how the farms overlapped traditional communities' land,' Gabriella told me. This led her to make a breakthrough.

Gabriella hired a consultant who overlaid the different maps available to clearly show the intersections of the boundaries recorded by the companies and those occupied by traditional communities. But these were just based on the satellite information. A key question was where the communities thought their land was. The only way to find that out was to go there and ask them.

Gabriella got the go-ahead to put an investigative team together. Their task would be to mount a field investigation to gather hard evidence of the land-grabbing, criminalization and violence carried out by two massive Brazilian palm-oil giants, Agropalma and BBF, and to find out who was buying the oil and therefore financing the de facto war in traditional communities. This was a task that would daunt many people, but not the team Gabriella was assembling.

The first choice was obvious. Fellow São Paulo resident Marco Mantovani had been on Global Witness's forest team for years, an experienced investigator and an expert in the impact of cattle ranching on the Amazon. Next she brought on Cícero Pedrosa, whose knowledge of the region and its peoples would be essential. Gabriella also wanted to document this investigation by including a professional photographer and filmmaker on the team and Gabriella really wanted one of these people to be a woman. She settled on Karina Iliescu, who introduced her to Rafael Mellim, a professional film-maker and teacher.

Gabriella was very happy with the team she had put together.

Finally, when all the preparations were complete, and not without a sense of trepidation, Gabriella, Marco, Karina and Rafael flew to Belém. There,

Gabriella met the lawyer who had first notified her about the case they were investigating when she was still with Pogust Goodhead. She also met with Cícero for the first time. Young, dark-haired and with a goatee beard, he exuded calm; he was already a veteran of the land wars taking place across the Amazon. If there had been any doubts that the team would get on with Cícero, they were soon dispelled.

'He is an extremely kind person,' Gabriella remembered, and she liked the indigenous artifacts he wore. 'He is very sweet, very careful and very brave.' He must have been. Cícero had known Bruno and Dom and had only just returned from a trip retracing their final journey. With their preparations complete, the team climbed into the two Jeep Renegades that they had hired and nosed their way through Belém's congested traffic to begin their journey south.

BELÉM TO TAILÂNDIA, JUNE 2022

Gabriella and Marco were in the lead vehicle while Cícero and the filmographers followed in the second. As she drove, Gabriella felt both tense and excited; she knew they were heading for a dangerous and virtually lawless area, but she was very happy that the long period of research and planning was over and the active field investigation had begun. It felt good to be on the road and Marco helped calm her nerves – if the worst came to the worst, they could simply turn round and go back.

As the road unrolled in front of them, Gabriella and Marco were the first to see a BBF truck loaded with palm fruit heading towards them. Excitedly, Gabriella called Karina and Rafael in the car behind and asked them to film and photograph it. It was the investigation's first physical contact with their target, always an exciting moment. She did the same again for the next truck that passed and then another, until there were so many it ceased to be remarkable – a clear indication of the scale of the problem they had come to investigate. As evening drew near, they began to notice other cargoes, trucks loaded with the trunks of rainforest trees, making the overnight drive north.

Cícero suspected that these nighttime journeys were because many of these cargoes were illegal, taking advantage of the darkness – which is one of the reasons the Global Witness team would not drive at night. They didn't want to be stopped and questioned by either criminals or the cops; the professional film cameras and the drone in the boots of their cars would likely generate some very awkward questions.

The going was slow. Stuck behind heavily laden, slow-moving trucks, there were no opportunities to overtake; and even if there were, the two-lane road was pitted with deep and treacherous potholes.

Once they had crossed the Acará River on the Acará–Tailândia ferry, the countryside changed. Everywhere the vista was of virtually uninterrupted palm-oil plantations, kilometre after kilometre of them. It was early evening before they finally drew into the rural town of Tailândia, where the first interviews with local communities would take place. The main asphalt highway bisected the town and formed its spine; either side of it the red-brown dirt roads of the side streets emanated outwards like ribs and the motorbikes, which vastly outnumbered cars, raised waves of gritty red dust. It was poor, noisy, chaotic and dirty. The town's central attraction was the communal food court, built at the behest of the town's mayor – who was evidently so proud of it that it was bedecked with huge photos of him, 'like in a dictatorship,' Gabriella told me. More photos showed him hugging the town's citizens. To top it off, there was a small stage with a microphone and a picture of him in sunglasses on either side. Gabriella's overarching thought was that it was really weird.

The food court was evidently as popular as the mayor hoped he was. In any event, the team had dinner there and it held the distinct advantage that it wasn't as weird as their hotel. The first impression had been good – it was spotlessly clean and neat, and the white and blue of the walls and tiled floors was in complete contrast to the chaos outside. That was the good part; the conversation was less favourable.

The woman at reception, who turned out to be the hotel's owner, was curious about why they were there. Her questioning was quite aggressive; not, in Gabriella's opinion, because she suspected anything – it was just her way. The team knew that Tailândia was a stronghold of the extreme right; and if they needed any confirmation of this, the woman swore at any journalist who appeared on the rolling news being broadcast on the TV in the hotel reception. Her husband appeared and joined in the lambasting of any Bolsonaro critic.

The team glanced at each other and Gabriella fobbed her off by saying they were doing some research into grains and palm – a lie with elements of the truth, as all the best ones have.

Then Gabriella took Cícero to one side. 'We need to talk,' she whispered. 'We can't tell them who we are or what we're here for.' He agreed and they beckoned the rest of the team down the hallway that led to the lifts, where there were a few sofas. Out of earshot of their hosts with the blaring TV, they nevertheless spoke softly about what they could and could not say.

They took the lift together and Gabriella checked that everyone's rooms were OK. They all felt tense – they knew that in Tailândia they were in the lion's den and they could never relax.

VILA PALMARES, TAILÂNDIA

Early the next morning, the two Jeeps headed northwest out of Tailândia for the 50-km (31-mile) drive to the small town of Vila Palmares. After the first 30km (18.6 miles) they hit palm country. The regimented rows of oil-palm trees turned the road into a monotonous green corridor, part of Agropalma's empire. Vila Palmares itself turned out to be a small town occupying a rectangular island of land just under 2km (1.2 miles) long and 0.5km (0.3 miles) wide, completely surrounded by the sea of palm-oil plantations. The Quilombola community lay just outside the main town and was achingly poor – the rough houses, some of timber, some of bare rough brick, reminded Gabriella of the favellas in her hometown of São Paulo.

They were met by two Quilombola leaders, Raimundo Serrão and José Joaquim dos Santos Pimenta, the president of ARQVA (the Quilombola community association that encompassed the communities of Balsa, Turiaçu, Vila do Gonçalves and Vila dos Palmares do Vale Acará) at the only space available to them, a *sítio* – a small ranch – on the outskirts of the town, owned by a man who lived in Tailândia. He was one of the few who believed in the community's struggle and allowed them to use this land to hold meetings like this. Surrounding them, on land that in the recent past had been part of the magnificent Amazon rainforest, were Agropalma's plantations.

It was intensely hot in the still air as they waited for other community members to show up. The team sat on logs in the dusty yard and the ubiquitous village hounds lay prone on the ground, lazily scratching themselves, giving off little puffs of dust. Meanwhile chickens roamed between them, pecking at any scraps they could find. Eventually, around 25 to 30 people had gathered.

'It took us four or five hours to get to a point in which they would actually speak with us because they were very concerned about who we were and that we would get information from them and sell it to Agropalma,' Gabriella remembered. 'They had trust issues.' But then Raimundo began to talk.

A wiry careworn man dressed in tracksuit trousers and a thin grey cotton check shirt that had seen better days leaned forward on one of the few plastic chairs the community possessed. As the team sat on logs under the fruit trees that dotted the yard, he began to tell them his life story. His grandparents had been slaves who had escaped and found a job on another farm but had been enslaved again, this time by debt. They moved again in the early 1900s and arrived in the Acará's river bay, as it was known then. They began to carve out a new life, a life that would not have been possible without the support of the local indigenous people, the Tembé. The team listened raptly, scribbling in their notebooks as Raimundo described how their community only survived because the leaders of the Tembé had come to their aid. They had allowed the Quilombolas to build houses and to plant their crops, and the communities had helped to protect each other. Raimundo stressed to the team how thankful he was for this and why there was a strong sense of community between the Quilombolas and the indigenous peoples in these areas. But from the 1950s onwards the land-grabbers began to arrive and forced people off their land. By the late 1970s, it was the turn of Raimundo's parents.

'After years of a happy life by the river bay,' Raimundo recalled, 'a land-grabber who was planning to sell our land to Agropalma entered our house with three other armed men offering a small amount to my father in exchange for the land [. . .] This happened in the late 1970s. If we hadn't accepted the deal and left, land-grabbers and their henchmen would have killed us all.' Raimundo had been 20 years old at the time. The future for a farmer without land was bleak and Raimundo's heartfelt testimony was imbued with a powerlessness in the shadow of an immense, faceless corporate power. This scenario was playing out all around them.

It was a shock to Gabriella to be listening to someone with living memories of his grandparents having been slaves. Joaquim, the president of ARQVA, told of the constant threats he received. 'Cars belonging to the company often stop in front of my house to monitor me. Armed security men that work for Agropalma told me many times I need to speak less, otherwise they will have to shut me up. They employ armed security to intimidate us.'

These two leaders did most of the talking – the team had to ask their permission for others to speak. Gabriella wanted to hear the women's perspective, and from them she got a picture of how all these people had been forced from their homes over the years and were now the unwilling residents of what she saw as a shanty town.

'The women remembered things their mothers told them about land-grabbers and rape,' Gabriella told me. Something, she noted, that the men had not talked about. 'The men talked about property and getting expelled from the land. The women gave us a different perspective – like how the land-grabbers would speak to their mothers and their fathers, how they threatened to rape their sisters.'

The oldest person there was a woman who told the team that she couldn't remember how many times her family had had to move from one house to another, and as their lands were stolen the territory controlled by the land-grabbers grew larger and larger until they were corralled in Vila Palmares.

'It is not a nice place to live in and they don't want to be there,' Gabriella told me. 'They want to go back to the forest. They want to go back to their houses in the river bay. They want to go back to where their families started as Quilombolas. They don't want to stay in Vila Palmares because it's like a small-town favela.' Gabriella felt that if we could do justice to the stories of these communities, then we would also be able to tell the story of what's been happening in Brazil for 500 years.

These representatives from the 206 Quilombola families of Vila Gonçalves and Balsa told the team they felt strangled by the forests of palm that surrounded them. Industrial-scale farms in Brazil must, by law, set aside 20 per cent of their land area to preserve natural vegetation. It seems like a good idea on paper, but Agropalma appears to follow a common Brazilian agribusiness tactic, ironically known as 'green' land-grabbing. The idea for the agribusiness companies is to farm as near to 100 per cent of your land holding as you can, plus find an additional area of land with natural vegetation on it, grab that and claim it as your 20 per cent 'legal reserve' even though you don't own it. These areas often happen to be the last bit of land where indigenous peoples and traditional communities live because it can support their traditional farming, hunting and fishing. The sting in the tail is that these 'legal reserves' must be free from human habitation, so these communities ultimately lose the land they've lived on for generations. From the Cerrado to the Amazon, the story remains the same – with these peoples harassed, intimidated and sometimes murdered. They have few choices left. It often boils down to a choice between leave and starve or stay and face constant harassment from the private security guards whose job it is to corral the people and further isolate settlements. They do this by digging trenches to render many roads impassable, thereby funnelling the villagers through controlled entry and exit points of plantation-owned land where they have to present ID to get through. To resist all this takes courage. Thankfully, there's plenty of that around.

Raimundo held up a framed photograph of his grandmother as he talked bitterly about how not just their farms but their cemeteries now too were just memories, the graves obscured by the shadows of the endless palms. 'My grandmother was buried there. I went to light a candle because it is our tradition. But I do not know where her grave is. From the moment I get there I feel sad because this is disrespectful,' he said.

Another Quilombola, Ana Maria Pimento de Silva from the Balsa community, also spoke up. 'This is a humiliation. If Agropalma has this legal right why don't we have ours?' She had a point. The public prosecutor had filed various complaints against Agropalma's landgrabs and in 2020 a court found that the company's land-acquisition documents were false and cancelled the farm registrations. However, rather than hand back the land to the communities it had been stolen from, the court allowed the company to try to 'regularize' the illegal registrations. The company said that it had acquired the lands in good faith and blamed legal technicalities. The communities were caught in the twists and turns of the well-resourced company's lawyers. They lived in a nightmarish limbo.

Manoel Barbosa dos Santos, who had also lost his land, summed up the situation nicely: 'It is absurd to see how the courts allow this company to continue to remain here even though the court said their land titles are fake. Agropalma is the law here.'

Gabriella was keen to complete her map-making project, so one of the team's first jobs when they visited a community was to ask them to draw sketches of where the original boundaries of their original territory lay. The indigenous people didn't possess surveying equipment and had no access to satellites, but they knew where the river was, they knew how long it took them on foot or by boat to reach a particular location and they knew the key landmarks in their area. They sketched them in Gabriella's notebook and she began to amass a map of the land that the community had recognized as their territory long before the industrial farmers showed up or satellites existed. The results were striking. 'It was incredible to see how aware they are of their own territory,' she recalled. 'They would say it's two or three days' walking or two or three days by boat from this place to that place. And if you do your basic math on how long a boat trip would take from one place to the other, you'd get the approximate location, the approximate distance between one point to another in the map.' Local knowledge matched satellite imagery.

When the team had learned as much as they could, they said farewell. They needed to cover the 80km (49.7 miles) to the town of Tomé-Açu before dark.

TOMÉ-AÇU

Nestling in a bend of the Acará-Mirim River, the Amazonian town of Tomé-Açu is situated in the midst of various indigenous territories; but the thing that immediately struck Gabriella was that all the road signs were in both Portuguese and Japanese and there was a profusion of Japanese restaurants. The large Japanese population had arrived as refugees fleeing their shattered country after the Second World War, but while Brazil had given them a good home it was also creating refugees of its own all around them. The irony was palpable.

They booked into the Green Hotel, a simple but clean brick-built hotel with no obvious right-wing fanatics in evidence and good air conditioning, which was the most important criterion for Gabriella. 'It's so humid and everything is so wet that you don't feel that you're sweating, but you are, so you're rapidly dehydrating.' She was drinking water nonstop. There was a plus side: the team took the opportunity of getting a good Japanese meal.

The next day, resplendent in their traditional feather headdresses with elaborate necklaces of beads partly covering the painted geometric designs on their skin, members of the indigenous, Quilombola and riverine communities gathered in front of Tomé-Açu's courthouse. A central small group revolved around an invisible axis, surrounded by a larger circle rhythmically clapping. They were protesting once more against systematic violence, torture, death threats, land-grabbing and forced evictions.

The Global Witness team filmed and photographed the protest and Gabriella talked to the community's lawyer, Jorde Tembé Araújo, himself indigenous. He told her that BBF, the palm-oil company that dominated this area, had filed over 550 police reports against the community: 'attempts to criminalize the protests of the indigenous and Quilombola peoples.' These were accusations that Felipe Moura Palha, the federal prosecutor, confirmed.

NOVA BETEL QUILOMBOLA COMMUNITY

The next day, the team had a date with another Quilombola community, Nova Betel. Because the community was totally surrounded by BBF's oil-palm plantations and neither the community nor the team wanted to create unnecessary risk, they had arranged to meet their contact at a remote farmhouse. It was one of the most difficult meetings they had to do. Without electricity and surrounded by palms, the community was achingly poor; and as descendants of former slaves, the Quilombolas faced horrific racism – greater even than the indigenous people.

'One of the leaders described the constant stress brought on by the armed private security guards,' Gabriella told me. 'People are very scared of leaving the territory and going to the city, especially during the evening, because the company security men are constantly driving around their territories and around the plantations. It can be very dangerous.' The team aborted their next planned meeting in Tomé-Açu for this reason. They didn't want the Quilombola leader to have to brave these dangers on the way to an interview. The disturbing accounts of racism, intimidation, criminalization and hardship were distressing enough but the team had to be very careful not to further endanger people by the sheer fact of their presence.

DAY 9, TURÉ-MARIQUITA

On Day 9 Tomé-Açu receded into the distance behind them as the two Jeeps took the road towards the Turé-Mariquita indigenous lands. After 15–20km (9.3–12.4 miles) they turned left down a dirt road, their tyres kicking up clouds of red dust as they drove along a track hemmed in by the BBF's palm-oil plantations on both sides. Finally, they came to a sign announcing that they were entering Turé-Mariquita indigenous land. Unlike Quilombola communities, by Brazilian law no one can enter demarcated indigenous land unless they've been invited by the community and possess an authorization from FUNAI – permissions the team possessed.

The community prepared fish as they sat together answering questions from Gabriella, Marco and Cícero, and Karina and Rafael photographed and filmed everything that was going on. When they were done, and the team were back on the road, Cícero decided to launch his drone to capture how the community was stranded in the midst of BBF land. As he stood on the side of the road guiding the drone, he glanced in surprise at the screen: community members were looking up, shouting and throwing stones and pieces of wood up at the drone. Some were aiming crude catapults in their attempts to bring it down. At first he couldn't understand this reaction, but then he realized that this was not the first drone they had seen. The team found out from Cícero that the company flew drones low over the communities on a daily basis – yet another form of intrusion and intimidation they were subjected to.

The team got out just in time. Shortly after they had left, they saw a convoy of three or four new black double-cabin pickups coming towards them, heading in the direction of the community they had just left.

'We had to stop so these cars could pass by us. It was really tense; it was hard to see who was inside – they had very black windows, all closed,' Gabriella recalled. But she did manage to see the driver of one of them through the windscreen. He was dressed in black and was wearing a bulletproof vest. In retrospect, Gabriella feels sure they were driven by one of the private militias that they knew existed. The team would never know for sure, but a close encounter with an armed and unaccountable militia in such a remote place was chilling and rammed home that the violence most people only ever read about was an imminent and ever-present danger in Pará.

DAYS 10 AND 11, VILA GONÇALVES

The next two days were to be given over to visiting the Quilombola community at Vila Gonçalves, north of Tailândia and about halfway to Acará. Vila Gonçalves was completely isolated within Agropalma's land and there were only two ways to get there, one of which was highly undesirable. If they wanted to travel by road they would need authorization to pass through the one and only gate that controlled access to the territory – and that gate was manned by Agropalma's security guards. That would be a risk point for the team and would advertise that the community were talking to outsiders, which would in turn expose them to further intimidation and potential retribution. The other route was by river.

A riverine community offered to provide the Quilombolas with a small boat as a favour, which would enable the team to reach Vila Gonçalves by the back door. The team would need to be up early the next morning to get to Vila Palmares's tiny river port, where the boat would pick them up.

But before they set off, the team got a call from the Turiuara indigenous community they had visited two days before. The previous evening, they were told, a group of Turiuara were on the way home to their territory, along the same dirt road the team had travelled, when they were stopped by a group of armed men alleged to be working on behalf of BBF. Paratê Tembé told the team what happened next.

'They were caught by surprise by the company's security guards. About 20 security guards set fire to their camp and shot at some people. There was a lot of torture. They threw people to the ground,' he told them. Then they ordered the Turiuara to lie face down on the road. Paratê described how the guards stood over the prone bodies, burning plastic and dripping the molten drops onto the bare backs of the community members. 'It was not the first time,' Paratê continued. 'In that same camp they threw a group of 10 men next to each other on the ground and started shooting near their heads.'

The team were stunned. Were those the black pickup trucks they had passed on that remote road as they left? Gabriella called Shruti and Marina Comandulli, a fellow Brazilian, in Global Witness's London office to let them know the situation. Her first impulse was to return to Tomé-Açu and go to the area where this happened, but London forbade it. Though Gabriella was persistent, Marina won the day. She reminded Gabriella that if something happened to her then she, and not the people whose stories they were there to document, would become the story. Gabriella knew that Marina was right.

The team were in a sombre mood for the journey upriver to Vila Gonçalves. They settled into a typical wooden Amazon riverboat, thankfully sheltering under a small roof that shielded them from the rain that beat down for most of the day. Given the attacks on the Turiuara, Gabriella was less than thrilled that they were out of reach of any mobile signal and internet connectivity.

As they passed the remnants of rainforest that cloaked the banks of the meandering river, they almost forgot that these were just a buffer between them and the vast swathes of palm-oil plantations a few hundred metres beyond. They passed by the remains of the cemeteries where Raimundo's ancestors had been buried and that were now just another part of Agropalma's plantations, but they didn't stop. They didn't want to attract any attention or cause any kind of conflict. Finally, they arrived at Vila Gonçalves without incident.

Sitting on the benches that lined the half-height timber-slatted walls of the community's small church, the rain beating down on exposed terracotta tiles, they spent the day interviewing the community members. They explored the borders between the community and Agropalma's plantations and at one point they saw an Agropalma pickup truck 500m (1,640ft) away through the trees, a reminder of the all-pervasive presence of the company. Discretion being the better part of valour, the team made their way back to the river port and on to Tailândia.

As they checked in, it seemed to them that the hotel owner's aggression had stepped up a level. She cheerfully informed them that she would happily shoot Lula voters in the face. Gabriella still flinches at the memory. 'She was saying many aggressive things that she was not saying so openly when we were there a few days before and we were extremely disturbed by that.'

The team took their stuff to their rooms and when they reassembled downstairs the woman was walking around their Jeeps – two of only five vehicles in the hotel's parking garage – and peering into the windows. 'That was the breaking point for me,' Gabriella told me. 'I asked her, "What's going on?"'

The woman mumbled something about looking for rats or cockroaches. Perhaps she was thinking of what were, for her, the human type. Karina and Rafael were particularly nervous as it would take only 30 seconds for the hotel owner to do a Google search for their names. If she did, she would find out that one of them was actively campaigning for Lula, and that Marco and Gabriella worked for Global Witness. They could only hope that the woman wasn't too curious. They judged that the risks of leaving in a hurry and driving in the dark were probably greater than staying – but it was to be an uneasy night. At 6am the next day, they grabbed a quick coffee and got out of there as quickly as they could. As they settled back in their seats and left, they breathed a collective sigh of relief.

'There are people on the extreme right everywhere in Brazil at the moment,' Gabriella explained to me. 'It's different when you are in São Paulo, where you can just leave and where there are so many other people around. But in Tailândia we knew that if something happened, or if there was a fight or an argument, people would be on her side and there wouldn't be anyone to support us if there was a conflict of any kind.'

Fifteen days after the team had first arrived in Pará, they climbed back into the Jeep Renegades and headed north, for home. Gabriella's first memory of arriving back at Belém was exhaustion – the whole team were emotionally drained by what they had seen and heard. 'We were just shocked,' she recalled. 'It was like going into a tunnel and then coming out the other side. But these feelings have stuck with me. When I'm having a coffee in São Paulo or London or wherever, I'm thinking of those people who are still there. They are living this conflict every single day. It's really crazy to think that all the traditional communities that were once living freely in the forest, accessing the river and everything they had, have ended up in this small-town favela in the suburbs of Tailândia. How is it possible in such a huge country that these people from different traditional communities with such rich cultures are now just marginalized and living in these tiny houses?

'When we arrived back in Belém that evening, I was thinking, "I'm having a beer and I'm calm and there is music here and I feel very safe. But those people are still there, and three days ago a violent attack happened, and these families are having to deal with it. They have family members in the hospital."' She paused. 'I'm clearly an outsider. I will never be able to understand what it is to be a defender.'

The 21 pages of 'Amazon Palm' laid out the devastating evidence of the impact of agribusiness on some of the most vulnerable people in Brazil, and provided yet another damning indictment of the ecocidal policies of the Bolsonaro regime and the power of the Ruralistas. The report also contained the results of Gabriella's scouring of the trade databases – the names of BBF's and Agropalma's customers were a veritable roll call of some of the world's biggest commodity traders. Now it was their turn to have their moment in the limelight.

Luiz Inácio Lula da Silva assumed the presidency of Brazil on 1 January 2023. He was vocal in his concern for the Amazon, and early indications gave some cause for optimism. 'If there is no future for the Amazon and its people, there will be no future for the planet either,' he told the press; and by April his government had recognized six new indigenous territories with more in the pipeline. By August, deforestation in the Brazilian Amazon was down by 66 per cent compared to the same period in 2021.

That same month, Amazonian heads of state gathered for the Amazon Summit in Belém. The leaders recognized that within a decade the destruction of the Amazon rainforest could reach a tipping point and the Belém Declaration stated that 'we must act now to prevent the biome from reaching the point of no return'. Both Brazil and Colombia vowed to end Amazonian deforestation by 2030 – an aspiration the other leaders unfortunately did not agree to.

If you're sitting down to breakfast eating your Kellogg's cereal or your Danone yoghurt, or perhaps less healthily chomping your way through a Mars bar washed down with a can of Pepsi, followed by a chocolate from Ferrero, Hershey's or Nestlé, then you could be eating palm oil from Tomé-Açu, Tailândia or Acará.

Before they had left for Pará, Gabriella had checked the mill lists of Agropalma and BBF together with various trade databases and has a pretty good idea where their palm oil goes. The largest agribusiness company in the world is also the US's biggest privately held company. Cargill's revenues in 2022 were US$165 billion. It is 88 per cent owned by around 20 members of the Cargill/MacMillan family that founded it, making them the fourth-richest family in America. It employs over 150,000 people and operates in around 70 countries.

Which is why it's strange that virtually no one has heard of it. Perhaps that's how they tend to get away with the many human-rights and environmental abuses they are responsible for.

To put this in context, Cargill, together with other commodities giants ADM, Bunge and Louis Dreyfus, control between 70 and 90 per cent of the world grain market; and all of these companies, except Louis Dreyfus, bought palm oil from BBF and Agropalma. Without their custom, these Brazilian palm-oil companies would be in serious trouble – which is, of course, exactly where they should be.

As a result of the 'Amazon Palm' report, Cargill suspended purchases from BBF and Agropalma. Major brands Hershey, General Mills and the Kellogg Company all bought their palm oil from Cargill so BBF oil was, de facto, no longer in their supply chain either.

In December 2022, the environmental-journalism organization Mongabay reported that around half of the 106,837 hectares (264,000 acres) of land registered by Agropalma was based on fraudulent land titles. The state prosecutor told Mongabay: 'It's so elaborate that they created a fictitious notary's office [. . .] It's many areas, it's a mosaic [. . .] What unites them all is an intervention of a *cartório*, which is a notary's office that never existed that produced documents that were apparently very reliable.'

In February 2023, the Roundtable on Sustainable Palm Oil (RSPO) suspended Agropalma, the only Brazilian palm-oil company to possess its sustainability certificate, for their involvement in fraudulent land titles. Perhaps Raimundo and the other indigenous and Quilombola community members will find a glimmer of satisfaction knowing that the injustice done to his family all those years ago is getting some payback, but what they really need is their land back. As long as unaccountable agricultural giants can ride roughshod over the law, backed up by powerful political friends and armed security, then the Amazon will continue to suffer extreme violence.

In May 2023, Gabriella swapped the bustle of São Paulo for the quiet of a redbrick Georgian mansion in the countryside north of London. Formerly the home of one of the UK's richest brewers and now a meeting centre, it was a curiously appropriate place to hold Global Witness's annual retreat. We have always been an organization that likes to party. However, it was there that she heard that Paratê Tembé's father – the *cacique* (leader) of the Tembé – had been shot dead by people with links to the drug trade.

'I feel that it's very naive for people to think that indigenous peoples are just going to live inside their territory and not try to leave to get their sustenance,' she told me. 'This [upheaval] attracts drug trafficking and other social issues that maybe wouldn't exist or maybe wouldn't be so harmful, if it wasn't for the control these large companies have on the territory. It's all a consequence.'

As the Amazon countries and the wider world become ever more aware of the vital need to preserve the Amazon, its best protectors continue to be criminalized and murdered.

On Sunday 6 August 2023, just days before President Lula hosted the Amazon Summit in Belém, Gabriella began receiving calls from an indigenous lawyer in Pará. BBF's security guards had opened fire on a demonstration by members of the Turé-Mariquita community in front of BBF's offices. Three people were injured, one seriously. At the time of writing, the National Council for Human Rights was on their way to investigate.

On 25 April 2012, a former colleague of mine, a Cambodian forest activist called Chut Wutty, was gunned down by the Military Police. He was the first person I knew personally who was murdered for the work they did. Sadly, he has not been the last. Since Wutty's killing, Global Witness has been documenting the murders of people who are defending their land, their culture and their way of life from the encroachment of loggers, agribusiness, oil and mining companies, large dams and other landgrabs.

Ten years after Chut Wutty's murder, we published our first 'Decade of Defiance', a record of the 1,733 killings of land and environmental defenders during that time. It worked out at just over three per week; and the most dangerous country in the world to be a land and environmental defender over that decade was Brazil.

In September 2023, Global Witness released 'Standing Firm', our 2022 annual report documenting the killings of land and environmental defenders over the year. Of the 177 people murdered, 34 were in Brazil, compared to 26 the previous year. Globally, indigenous peoples made up over 36 per cent of the total murders, with Afro-descendants – people like the Quilombolas – making up 7 per cent and small-scale farmers 22 per cent. Over 1 in 5 of the murders globally took place in the Amazon.

These are not just numbers: these are people whose names we know; we know what they were struggling for and how they died. There are countless more people whose deaths go unrecorded and whose names remain unknown to us.

If we are serious about defending the rights of our fellow humans and about preserving the natural world, then we must recognize that these land and environmental defenders are our best allies, that they are on the frontlines and that without them the battle is lost.

In September 2022, just over a month after our 'Amazon Palm' investigation, BBF won a court decision to repossess land from the local communities. The company's security guards began using violence to enforce this decision, in contravention of the legal requirement that government officials and Military Police be present.

The next day, the MPPA and the Tembé Indigenous People's Association (Associação Indígena Tembé do Vale do Acará), successfully appealed the court's decision and an interim decision prohibiting the land repossession was issued.

On 24 September, just nine days before the presidential elections, the Federal Public Ministry (MPF) of Pará announced they were investigating the shooting of three members of the Turiuara indigenous group between Acará and Tomé-Açu. The photo in the news report depicted a man slumped in the passenger seat of a white pickup truck, its windows shot out. Community members once again accused the security guards of a palm-oil company.

At the end of November and over the next few days, armed men suspected to be working for BBF attacked the local communities. Using a few tricks from their old playbook, they forced a number of community members, men and women, to lay face down on the ground and at gunpoint. More people were attacked, including a pregnant woman, and just in case the message wasn't clear enough, they threatened to shoot anyone who tried to protect their territory against BBF's reoccupation. Since then, the death threats against indigenous leaders have kept coming.

Global Witness contacted BBF, whose version of events was 'a series of simultaneous invasions of land owned by BBF', carried out by a group of indigenous and Quilombola individuals. The company denied that its security guards acted with violence and stated that the role of their private security team was to guarantee the physical integrity of the workers and the preservation of company property. They reinforced their commitment to maintain a constructive and open dialogue with the communities that live in the areas where the company operates.

'We bring to the world our products, respect towards people and the environment.'

—Agropalma website, 12 October 2023

'Our goal is to take care of the forest, creating jobs, generating income, and reducing the cost of electricity for the population, while respecting society and the environment.'

—Brasil BioFuels website, 12 October 2023

If you were looking to source genuinely sustainable palm oil and were concerned by the palm-oil industry's egregious reputation for committing human-rights abuses and deforesting tropical rainforests, you would doubtless be reassured by the websites of Brazilian palm-oil giants BBF and Agropalma. However, as with so many corporate assurances of companies' commitment to human rights and the environment, it pays to dig a little deeper.

Gabriella Bianchini is still in touch with the communities she met in 2022.

EPILOGUE

Global Witness was born when I volunteered for the Environmental Investigation Agency (EIA) in 1990 and met two people who became my best friends. Charmian Gooch was a young campaigner and Simon Taylor, like me, a volunteer fundraiser.

EIA was a tiny organization that used undercover investigations to expose issues like whaling and the wildlife trade, which was bringing elephants and rhinos to the verge of extinction. Inspired by their methodology, Charmian, Simon and I founded Global Witness, but our initial focus was the exploitation of natural resources like rainforest timber or diamonds to fund wars. Armed with an overload of naivety, an almost total lack of experience and no money, we carried out a series of undercover investigations to document and halt these criminal and murderous businesses. Rather oddly, we succeeded and accidentally gave birth to a pioneering concept: that corruption, environmental destruction, human-rights abuses and war were inextricably linked.

Through lack of capacity rather than lack of interest, Global Witness never worked on the wildlife trade, the issue that had first inspired us, but since those early days at the EIA it has been an issue that's held a place deep in my heart. So when Jake Lingwood, my publisher at Monoray, asked me to write a sequel to *Very Bad People*, he suggested that it comprise not just stories from Global Witness's archive, but also investigations by other organizations I knew. I leaped at the chance.

One of those organizations was the Wildlife Justice Commission, a niche Netherlands-based outfit that hires former cops and teams of other gumshoes to investigate and bring down wildlife-trafficking networks. Their successes are impressive and I wrote about their work in 'The Big Sleep' (see page 163), finally getting the chance, albeit vicariously, to investigate this disgusting business.

These and the other people I have written about in this book are my heroes and are truly inspirational. I have worked with some of them for years at Global Witness, while others I got to know only during the seven months it took to write the book; many others I have never met. But I stand in awe of all of them. What binds these amazing people is that against incredible odds they have achieved real change and have inspired others to do the same. Many of them have risked their freedom and their lives to make the sort of difference at global level that political leaders can only dream about. Or fear.

For years Nathalia Dukhan, her colleagues at The Sentry and a few courageous people in the Central African Republic have been doing more than most to lift the lid on the inner workings of the notorious Wagner Group and how it has become the covert and deniable arm of Russian colonial expansion in Africa. The Sentry sensed the danger posed by Wagner long before Vladimir Putin's megalomania manifested itself in his attempt to invade Ukraine, since when Wagner's brutality and ruthlessness has become common knowledge. I for one didn't mourn when Yevgeny Prigozhin's plane fell out of the sky.

When Slovakian investigative journalist Ján Kuciak and his fiancée Martina Kušnírová were murdered in the winter of 2018, Pavla Holcová and her fellow journalists, together with the backing of OCCRP, investigated the hell out of the case, exposing the corruption that went all the way to the top of the country's police, its judiciary and the government itself, which fell as a result. What the journalists achieved was to expose the rot of top-level corruption in one of the darling countries of the EU. What they found sickened them, but I marvel at their skill and power. Sadly, their job isn't over. In October 2023, Robert Fico, the corrupt populist prime minister they toppled, was returned to power. That's bad news for Slovakia, but at least the population have a clearer view of what they're dealing with – and Pavla and her colleagues are doubtlessly already on the case.

In Joseph Heller's classic anti-war book *Catch-22*, the ultimate capitalist Milo Minderbinder supplied bombs to the US Air Force and anti-aircraft ammunition to the Germans, ensuring that whatever the outcome of the war he would win either way. I laughed at the madness of it when I first read it in my teens, but then realized that this wasn't comedic irony but a finely observed reality. In 'Fuelling the Fire' (see page 7), Global Witness's data-investigation team didn't just expose the role of French oil giant TotalEnergies in supplying fuel to Russian airbases complicit in war crimes in Ukraine; they also cornered the company as it tried, unsuccessfully, to shirk its responsibility. It became a rather delicious scandal.

In *Very Bad People* I devoted a chapter to Global Witness's exposure of a corrupt billionaire Israeli mining tycoon called Beny Steinmetz, whose extraordinary business methods earned him billions in profits at the expense of the impoverished West African state of Guinea. 'The

Gatekeeper' (see page 199) enabled me to tell the story of how one of my workmates, Margot Mollat, together with two courageous Congolese whistleblowers and PPLAAF, the French group helping them, unravelled a corrupt network designed to enable another billionaire Israeli mining tycoon, Dan Gertler, to avoid US sanctions imposed because of his past corruption. It is the story of how one man obtained virtually total control of who gets access to the key strategic mining assets in one of the most resource-rich countries in the world, the Democratic Republic of Congo.

In a first for me as an investigator, *'Thunder'* (see page 79) metaphorically took me off dry land and into the longest pursuit of a pirate fishing vessel in history. It was one of the most exciting stories to write because it came down to a battle of wills between two captains and their crews, one of them being a mafia-style operation. Far away in France, the hard-bitten investigators of INTERPOL followed the chase, but protocol forbade them from communicating with the good guys. Starved of information and as far from help as it's possible to be, Peter Hammarstedt and his crew on the Sea Shepherd ship *Bob Barker* stuck it out on some of the wildest and remotest waters on Earth. Their courage in the face of those odds haunts me.

I hope that in 'Amazon Palm' (see page 277) I have managed to do justice to our intrepid investigative team – and the incredible courage of the indigenous peoples and traditional communities of the Brazilian Amazon, who, day in and day out, face off the might, corruption, political extremism and violence brought about by Big Agribusiness. What happens in Brazil and the Amazon in particular will determine whether humanity can get its act together to tackle climate change; and I hope the chapter illustrates how much we owe to some of the most vulnerable and tenacious people on Earth.

All of the amazing people I write about, together with countless more human-rights and environmental activists, journalists, political dissidents and others, are involved in an existential struggle for freedom and for the planet. They are facing crackdowns by autocratic governments while even 'leading democracies' like the UK are resorting to the repression of basic freedoms. A key tool of governments with something to hide is to spy on their own populations and I wrote 'The Spy Inside' (see page 239) to give a flavour of what this looks like, wanting to highlight the skill of those deep-dive data investigators at Citizen Lab who can detect if your phone has been infected with spyware and how close to home the problem is. It had certainly arrived on Global Witness's doorstep.

The Terrible Humans in this book, and the countless more terrible humans who could easily have a chapter devoted to them, are the antiheroes of eight seemingly separate stories. But, in fact, they are all linked – connected by what's at their root: the destructive and globally pervasive evils of political and corporate corruption, the rise in authoritarianism, organized crime, human-rights and environmental abuses and an insatiable thirst for and plunder of the world's natural resources, all governed by a lust for power and money.

It would be simple to lay these problems at the door of the world's most authoritarian states like Russia and China, but that would be too easy. The world's most powerful democracies are increasingly being split between left and right. People's democratic rights and the global environment are becoming acceptable costs of doing political and corporate business. Colonialism is alive and well as some of the world's most resource-rich but poverty-stricken countries in the world continue to be plundered of their wealth. It's only some of the methods or players that have changed.

What I hope I have shown in this book is that even when the odds seem insurmountable, ordinary people can move mountains. In *Very Bad People* I quoted Anita Roddick, the co-founder of the Body Shop, who said, 'If you think you're too small to have an impact, try going to bed with a mosquito in the room.' It was true then and it's true now. One particular example resonates with me because it is timeless.

Frustrated by the failure of years of campaigning and political appeals, a notorious group of protestors came together to create civic disorder. Everything else had failed and this was their last resort. They marched, they blocked roads, defaced pictures in art galleries and smashed windows. They disrupted church services, went on hunger strikes and destroyed public property. Governments and the forces of law and order treated them harshly, breaking up their demonstrations, criminalizing them, beating up some of the protestors, who were sometimes attacked by members of the public too. Many of these protestors were jailed for their actions. Sound familiar?

These were the Suffragettes. Their goal? The right of women to vote.

In the UK, just over a hundred years after these Suffragettes achieved their aims, Historic England recognized 41 sites of their sabotage by including them on the United Kingdom's Heritage List: official recognition of the importance and justice of their struggle. Similar stories could be told all over Europe, the US and elsewhere – and of course this cause is still being fought, as events in Iran, the Middle East, Afghanistan, India and elsewhere illustrate. Witnessing their courage, I don't doubt these women will eventually win; but the fight is murderously hard.

I wonder if it will take 100 years for the protestors of the youth climate movements – Extinction Rebellion, Just Stop Oil and other climate activists around the world – to achieve recognition similar to that of the Suffragettes. In 2124, will the leaders of the future look back aghast at the political failures and myopia of their predecessors a century before in tackling the root causes of corruption, war, climate change and environmental destruction and wonder how on earth these people could have been so dim, captured and criminally irresponsible?

Since I co-founded Global Witness just over 30 years ago, I have been privileged in having the best job I can imagine having. The people I've worked with are among the best people I can ever imagine working with, and many of them have been my best friends for decades. It helps that I get a nefarious pleasure in giving the Very Bad People of my first book and the Terrible Humans of this one a very hard time.

In November 2023, I stepped down from my role at Global Witness. The organization is in good and younger hands and is adapting itself for a very different world than the one that existed when Charmian, Simon and I started it in those pre-internet, pre-smartphone days. We three will remain on the board and will do all we can to help Global Witness achieve more and more. For me, campaigning and trouble-making is the oxygen of life.

Terrible Humans? Fuck 'em.

'Bad men need nothing more to compass their ends,
than that good men should look on and do nothing.'

John Stuart Mill (1806–73),
English philosopher and economist

RESOURCES

You can find out more about the work of the amazing individuals and organizations that are the heroes of this book here:

Chapter 1   Fuelling the Fire
Data Desk https://datadesk.eco

Chapter 2   Project Fat Cat
Aktuality www.aktuality.sk
Organized Crime and Corruption Reporting Project www.occrp.org

Chapter 3   *Thunder*
Interpol www.Interpol.int
Sea Shepherd https://seashepherd.org
Sea Shepherd Australia https://seashepherd.org.au

Chapter 4   Leave No Trace
The Sentry https://thesentry.org

Chapter 5   The Big Sleep

Wildlife Justice Commission https://wildlifejustice.org

Environmental Investigation Agency https://www.eia.org

Chapter 6   The Gatekeeper

Platform to Protect Whistleblowers in Africa https://pplaaf.org

Bloomberg News www.bloomberg.com

Chapter 7   The Spy Inside

Citizen Lab https://citizenlab.ca

Chapter 8   Amazon Palm

Repórter Brasil https://reporterbrasil.org.br

HOW TO HELP GLOBAL WITNESS'S INVESTIGATIONS

Global Witness is directly confronting the global economic systems – and the Terrible Humans behind them – that are profiting from and consequently perpetuating the climate crisis. Our goal is a more sustainable, just and equal planet. We want forests and biodiversity to thrive, fossil fuels to stay in the ground and corporations to prioritize the interests of people and the planet.

If you would like to support our work, you can do so at:
www.globalwitness.org/en/donate/

ACKNOWLEDGEMENTS

Without Charmian Gooch and Simon Taylor and our chats in the pubs of Farringdon over three decades ago, Global Witness would not have existed and many of the organization's successes wouldn't have happened. More than that, I would never have got to know or to talk to the fantastic people I've had the privilege of working alongside for most of my professional life and those who I met more recently while working on this book. To them all, thank you for making it all possible.

In particular, I want to thank Chloe Kormos, who gave up her valuable summer vacation to volunteer her time researching many of the chapters. Her work was brilliant and made the difference between meeting my punishing deadline or not.

When Paul Radu and Drew Sullivan founded the Organized Crime and Corruption Reporting Project (OCCRP) they probably little realized the amazing impact they would have. I hope I have succeeded in doing justice to their work, together with that of their fellow journalists who gave up their time to be interviewed for 'Project Fat Cat' (see page 41): Pavla Holcová, Eva Kubániová, Peter Bárdy and the many others who investigated the murder of one of their colleagues, Ján Kuciak, and his fiancée, Martina Kušnírová, in Slovakia. Thanks also go to Emma Prest, who gave me the idea for this chapter, and to Matt Sarnecki, whose documentary film *The Killing of a Journalist* was an invaluable source as well as being a powerful movie.

My current and former Global Witness colleagues Daniel Balint-Kurti, Alex Kopp, Margot Mollat, Nicola Namdjou, Alex Yearsley and the DRC guru, Bloomberg journalist Michael J. Kavanagh, all helped me piece together 'The Gatekeeper' (see page 199) and get a far better understanding of the DRC, the difficulties of investigating one of our most complex cases and dealing with the legal backlash. This story could not have been told without the information leaked by the courageous Congolese whistleblowers Gradi Koko and Navy Malela, and Gabriel Bourdon and Henri Thulliez of the French whistleblowing organization Platform to Protect Whistleblowers in Africa (PPLAAF), who helped them out of danger and enabled them to tell their stories.

My former Global Witness colleague Nathalia Durkan, now working for US organization The Sentry, is a mine of information on the Central African Republic. Her experiences and investigations and the risks she and her sources took to expose the operations of the infamous mercenary organization the Wagner Group are awe-inspiring. She also trusted me enough to introduce me to a key source, Abdoulaye Ibrahim, who was a fly on the wall of Wagner's operations there.

Thanks to Olivia Swaak-Goldman, Nathalie Veenman and Marianne El Hajj at the Wildlife Justice Commission for opening the doors to the secret world of their investigations into wildlife trafficking. Talking to a couple of the chief investigators, ex-cops Steve Carmody and Dave Andrews, about how they track down wildlife traffickers was a real education – added to which, despite the grim subject, their humour had me in stitches. Thanks also to Julian Newman at the Environmental Investigation Agency for taking time to give me his insights into the same brutal trade.

Gabriella Bianchini and Marco Mantovani from Global Witness's São Paulo office walked me through their brilliant investigation into the land-grabbing and violence suffered by indigenous peoples and traditional communities in Brazil's Pará state at the hands of agribusiness – in this case, industrial-scale palm-oil companies. Also to Ana Aranha and her organization Réporter Brasil, for their courageous investigations into the companies and political powerbrokers behind the destruction of the Amazon rainforest and especially for the sneak preview of their excellent film *Relatos de um correspondente da guerra na Amazônia*, which brings to life their brilliant work and the shocking violence taking place in the Amazon.

When Russia invaded Ukraine in February 2022, Global Witness immediately began to tackle one of Russia's biggest export earners, the fossil-fuel industry. My colleagues Louis Goddard, Ellie Nichol, Sam Leon, Jon Noronha-Gant, Mai Rosner, Lela Stanley and Louis Wilson all gave me invaluable insights into the madness of European funding of the instigator of the biggest war in Europe since the Second World War. More power to your elbows.

The interviews with the captain and various crew members of the Sea Shepherd ship *Bob Barker* made me want to drop everything and go to sea. Along with Siddharth Chakravarty, the captain of the *Bob Barker*'s sister ship, the *Sam Simon*, Peter Hammarstedt led the longest-ever pursuit of an illegal fishing vessel and as a swashbuckling adventure this one's hard to beat. Alistair Allan and Priya Holmes's memories of the dangers, the excitement and the day to day were invaluable. I also had the pleasure of reconnecting with an old friend, Alistair Graham, who from his lair in Tasmania has done more than most people to tackle the scourge of illegal fishing worldwide. He's also great fun. Thanks also to my former Global Witness colleague and ex-INTERPOL official Davyth Stewart for making the introductions to his former INTERPOL colleagues Alistair McDonnell and Mario Luís Alcaide, who in cooperation with Sea Shepherd ensured that international law enforcement tracked down one of their long-wanted quarries. Thanks also to my friend and fellow activist Beatrice Yannacopoulou for making the introduction to Peter Hammarstedt.

I owe a massive debt of gratitude to Ron Deibert, the founder of Citizen Lab at the Munk School of Global Affairs and Public Policy, University of Toronto, who opened my eyes to the terrifying use of spyware by authoritarian governments to take over the phones of journalists and pro-democracy and human-rights activists worldwide. The work of organizations like Citizen Lab is ever more critical in a world where democracy is being squeezed.

A special thanks to my agent, Eugenie Furniss at 42MP, and to all the team at Monoray: my publisher, Jake Lingwood, for asking me to write this book in the first place; to my editors at Octopus Books, Mala Sanghera-Warren, for her advice and . . . er . . . firm guidance, and Alex Stetter, and to Karen Baker, Hazel O'Brien and Elise Solberg for their unstinting support throughout.

I also owe a debt of gratitude to Julian Newman at the Environmental Investigation Agency for talking me though one of their amazing investigations which, through my own failings, didn't make the final cut, and to Rupert Quinlan and especially Anthony Esposito for their insights into the conflicts between Australian First Nations peoples and the Indian mining giant Adani. I dearly wanted to write a chapter about Adani's landgrabs in Australia but the Indian end of the research proved impossible in the timeframe I had.

Without the wisdom and support of Breda Daly, the love of my life, I could not have co-founded Global Witness in the first place. Her research on the Ruralistas in Brazil was invaluable to 'Amazon Palm' (see page 277) and her multiple read-throughs of various chapters were invaluable. More than that, without her love, support, brow wiping, patience and advice throughout the seven crammed months this book took to write, I simply couldn't have written it. Just so it's on record, I apologize here for the inescapable egocentricity that writing seems to demand.

INDEX